ÉLITISM, POPULISM, AND EUROPEAN POLITICS

D1477816

Élitism, Populism, and European Politics

Edited by

JACK HAYWARD

CLARENDON PRESS · OXFORD
1996

Oxford University Press, Walton Street, Oxford OX2 6DP
Oxford New York
Athens Auckland Bangkok Bombay
Calcutta Cape Town Dar es Salaam Delhi
Florence Hong Kong Istanbul Karachi
Kuala Lumpur Madras Madrid Melbourne
Mexico City Nairobi Paris Singapore
Taipei Tokyo Toronto
and associated companies in
Berlin Ibadan

Oxford is a trade mark of Oxford University Press

Published in the United States
by Oxford University Press Inc., New York

British Library Cataloguing in Publication Data
Data available

Library of Congress Cataloging in Publication Data
Élitism, populism, and European politics / edited by Jack Hayward.
Includes index.
1. Europe—Politics and government—1989–   2. Élite (Social
sciences)—Europe.   3. Populism—Europe.   I. Hayward, Jack Ernest
Shalom.
JN94.A91E44 1995   320.94′09′049—dc20   95–44775
ISBN 0–19–828035–1

1 3 5 7 9 10 8 6 4 2

Typeset by Graphicraft Typesetters Ltd, Hong Kong
Printed in Great Britain
on acid-free paper by
Biddles Ltd, Guildford and King's Lynn

PREFACE

On 17–19 September 1993 the Institute of European Studies of the University of Oxford organized the first of what have become a regular series of Europaeum Conferences. Under the impetus of the initial inspiration and continuing enthusiasm of Lord Weidenfeld and Sir Ronald Grierson, the Europaeum network of academic institutions hold an annual conference on a major theme, bringing together those directly involved in taking decisions, offering advice or assessing them. The theme selected for the inaugural conference was one which continues to preoccupy democrats conscious that popular support for the European integration promoted by their leaders was flagging. The title 'Are European Élites Losing Touch with their Peoples?' posed a rhetorical question which it was the task of those preparing the papers and their discussants to explore. The revised results of our deliberations are placed before you.

Several papers presented at the 1993 conference are not reproduced here, while others have been added subsequently. Particular thanks are due to those who acted as discussants or commentators: Vernon Bogdanor, Alain Camu, Lord Clinton-Davis, John Drew, John Flemming, Timothy Garton Ash, Jacques Gerstlé, David Goldey, Sir Ronald Grierson, Peter Gundelach, Peter Hartmann, Will Hutton, David Levy, Wolfgang Muller, William Paterson, Michel Vanden Abeele, Norbert Walter, Robert Worcester.

It is not possible to thank all those who unstintingly helped to make the conference a success. However, the Oxford Institute of European Studies gratefully acknowledges the generous financial support of ARCO and the Gruppo Marcucci, which allowed us to make the first Europaeum Conference a convivial as well as an intellectually stimulating occasion.

Jack Hayward

CONTENTS

LIST OF TABLES

LIST OF CONTRIBUTORS

Rudy Andeweg, Professor of Politics, University of Leiden

Vernon Bogdanor, Reader in Government, Fellow of Brasenose College

Nicholas Bosanquet, Professor of Social Policy, University of London

Jean Charlot, Professor of Politics, Institut d'Études Politiques, Paris

Ralf Dahrendorf, Warden, St Antony's College, Oxford

James Forder, Lecturer in the Economics of European Integration, St Peter's College, Oxford

Jack Hayward, Director of the Institute of European Studies, Professorial Fellow of St Antony's College, Oxford

David Hine, Official Student (Tutorial Fellow) in Politics, Christ Church, Oxford

Robert Lane, Emeritus Professor of Politics, Yale University

Michael Lessnoff, Reader in Politics, University of Glasgow

William Miller, Professor of Politics, University of Glasgow

Peter Oppenheimer, Official Student (Tutorial Fellow) in Economics, Christ Church, Oxford

Gianfranco Pasquino, Senator and Professor of Politics, Bologna Center of Johns Hopkins University

Jeremy Richardson, Professor of Government, University of Essex

Annis-May Timpson, Lecturer in English and American Studies, University of Brighton

William Wallace, Reader in International Relations, London School of Economics, and Professor of International Studies, Central European University

Introduction

Mediocre Élites Elected by Mediocre Peoples

RALF DAHRENDORF

While I was thinking about the theme of the First Europaeum Conference, I was struck by the remark of one of the Fellows of St Antony's
who had just come back from Venezuela. He told me that Caracas is
at this moment (September 1993) plastered with graffiti of a political
nature, of which one says: 'a mediocre president elected by a mediocre
people'. Reflecting on this phrase, I knew that it describes what I want
to talk about: mediocre élites elected by mediocre peoples in Europe.

The apparent gap between the electorate and its leaders in Europe
and elsewhere in the world has reminded me of my own entry into
politics, German politics at the time, in the late 1960s. Some of the
speeches I made had as their main subject something that was then
called a 'credibility gap' between the leaders and the electorate. Not
only was the credibility gap much discussed, but there were a great
many conferences in the early 1970s with subjects like 'Democracy in
Crisis', to quote the title of the book produced by the Trilateral Commission in 1973. One might be tempted to think of long cycles of the
disenchantment of the electorate with its leaders, cycles perhaps of
something like twenty years: the early 1990s, the early 1970s, the early
1950s, the early 1930s, the early 1910s, the early 1890s. But then I
have never been a great believer in these Kondratieff metaphysics, so
I discarded the idea at this point.

Returning to reality, it is striking that by the time the big academic
volumes about the disillusionment of the early 1970s were published,
mostly on the subject of governability, the countries of Europe, of
North America, and of some other parts of the world had actually found
a new stability. Indeed they had found not only a new stability, but

This is an edited version of the opening address to the Europaeum Conference on 17
September 1993.

a very unusual decade of stability. Whereas between 1979 and 1982 almost nobody in the major OECD countries found it easy, or even possible, to get himself re-elected, and therefore a whole lot of political leaders lost their positions, the subsequent period was one in which almost nobody found it possible not to get himself, or herself, re-elected. Perhaps we are now seeing the tail-end of this long period of astonishing stability. Twelve years of Reagan and Bush, and fourteen years of Thatcher and Major, twelve years of Mitterrand, eleven years of Kohl— clearly they are all now fairly close to the end of their effective political careers, if they have not reached it already. If one looks at a photograph of the twenty-five people who signed the Treaty of Maastricht in December 1991, fourteen are no longer in office a mere twenty months later. Now if you go back to the twenty months preceding Maastricht, you will find virtually no change, certainly no major change. One can even go back three years or four years before Maastricht and will not find any significant change, whereas one suspects that if we look forward another year or two, of the remaining eleven who are still in office today, five, six, seven will have joined all the other has-beens.

This is, in other words, a time of significant change. Is it just a time of one of these cycles in which a particular group of political leaders have reached the end of their useful public lives? Or is there something above and beyond the cyclical development? That is the question which I want to try and answer in my comments. Let me offer you essentially five ideas. I do so in a rather loose manner, which is perhaps appropriate for an address which is not intended to be a great contribution to scholarship, but is intended to be a contribution to discussion and reflection, and perhaps further work.

The first comment is quite clearly that the erosion of the 'class' basis of politics in the OECD countries has continued. This is not a very exciting statement—it has been said for a very long time—but it is nevertheless useful to reiterate and re-emphasize it. After all, even in the 1960s and perhaps the 1970s there was a general correlation between social position and political orientation. Today this is much harder to find. There have been significant changes in the underlying social structure of advanced countries. There has been what I sometimes call the emergence of a large majority class, the members of which may have very different real incomes, and even life-styles, but can, on the whole, hope to satisfy most of their aspirations without any fundamental change in the social and political conditions in which they are living.

This large majority class somehow removes part of the purpose from those parties to which advanced countries became accustomed in the years between the turn of the century and the late 1970s. Indeed, there have been curious reversals in the political support for traditional parties on the European continent, and notably in France and in Spain, but in some other countries as well. The observer notes with surprise the extent to which the socialists now rely on the rural and quite often the agricultural vote as well as the intensity with which socialist leaders seem to be concerned with agricultural interests. At the same time, traditional conservative parties have become parties of the cities and perhaps also of rising groups of 'yuppies'. But whatever may have happened here, the class basis of political affiliation has further been eroded, while there is no clear new structuration. There is no indication of the emergence of significant new social groups which will on the whole have a bias in favour of one or the other, or the third or the fourth, political party.

Thus, the predictive strength of social position for political behaviour is greatly reduced, a fact which is directly related to the volatility of the electorate, that is the readiness of voters to change their minds between elections, even between different levels of elections, local, regional, national, European. At the same time, there is a growing readiness of the electorate to think quite carefully about the effect of their own vote on the final outcome—tactical voting, as it is sometimes misleadingly called, for it should more appropriately be called rational voting. It is in any case not simply based on where one stands in the occupational or in the social structure. This clearly is one development which has removed a degree of predictability from our political systems, and may as a consequence have confused some of those in positions of responsibility, who are no longer so sure on whom they can rely and to whom they should address themselves in order to get support. This is not at all new, but it is useful to remember as part of a story.

My second point is more complicated, and it is not altogether easy to put it into clear language. In some ways it now emerges that the long period of the Cold War has created in all countries involved, and notably in the OECD countries, a fairly cosy political pact. Whatever the differences between the different parties and their representatives, when it came to fundamentals most, if not all of them, were on the same side. And since they were on the same side, they established a fundamental closeness which in different political contexts took different forms, but which created everywhere, as we now see, a rather close-knit political class. Sometimes the political class was so close-knit that it became possible to do things which, in the cold light of day, do not look as acceptable as they seemed when they were done.

The extreme cases are probably those of Italy and of Japan, in their different ways. Here are two countries which had virtually no change of government for over forty years. In both of them the political class somehow divided up patronage and, in important respects, public expenditure in ways which suited them. In both countries, the political classes could not imagine a world in which they were not in power, whatever power meant. In the process the two political classes became—and I think the word is not too strong—systematically corrupt. They used the opportunities afforded by office in order to cement their own positions of power. They also used the opportunities of office in order to satisfy the very worldly and material needs of their friends, their families, and their clients. Now, this process has suddenly come to an end. Shocking, and in some ways frightening, facts are revealed. The need for a change is evident, but the direction of change is not altogether easy to see.

I happen to admire the way in which Italians are trying to cope with this situation. I believe that none of us has any reason or right to decry the Italian developments, which on the contrary show extraordinary courage and readiness for change. One must hope that this attempt is successful. Initially, however, it reveals a degree of collusion among members of the political class, and also a degree of corruption, which is staggering. I heard the Italian Minister of Public Works saying that his budget had been cut by about 80 per cent, but he fully expected that so far as actual public works are concerned, he could achieve as much as all his predecessors with the remaining 20 per cent because the rest was used for other purposes.

These are fundamental and important changes, but they also tell a story about what went on before, and not a simple one. It is the story of corruption after a period of extreme stability, which was maintained not least by the existence of the Iron Curtain but of the Cold War.

Probably a slightly less extreme story, and yet also one of collusion, is that of the cosy corporatism of Germany, but also of Austria, of Sweden, and of a number of other countries. There probably was an element of corruption in that too. It is no accident that we had the recent incident of the Chairman of the Metal Workers' Union in West Germany who, in another capacity, as labour-nominated member of the supervisory board of a large company, may have been involved in a certain amount of insider dealing. He had to leave the board and resign the chairmanship of the union, although he remains on the supervisory board of another, very large company. This is only one example of many to show how this close corporatist world of intimate co-operation between business, trade unions, and different political parties has been maintained over quite a long period. Yet suddenly it is no longer working; suddenly it is no longer acceptable.

Somewhere in this area—and I regret the imprecision of this formulation—must lie the reason why it suddenly appears in quite a few countries that the normal democratic change of governing parties no longer does the trick of satisfying underlying changes in people's views and interests. It is no longer enough to have a new government. In some ways, the whole political class has to be exchanged. In some countries, like Italy and Japan, this is evident, in others it is not quite so evident but equally true. It would seem that the demand for a new start is widespread today. One must hope that this new start will not take violent forms. However, a more fundamental change of the ruling personnel will have to take place over time than is normal in the democratic process. This has many serious implications, including some for democratic theory. It actually means that the cosiness of a stable and long-serving political class prevents the democratic process itself from doing the trick of maintaining the legitimacy of governments. In order to bring about the necessary change, more drastic and fundamental adjustments are needed.

This leads me to a third reflection on the question of the relation between leaders and led in the OECD world. There is a sense in which it appears today that civil society is turning against government and those who govern. When I say this, I mean to imply that the normal relationship between the many associations and autonomous institutions of civil society and government is one of coexistence without any intimate or intense relationship with each other. The whole point about civil society in free countries is that people can live their lives without encountering government all the time. It is therefore not necessary for enterprises or for universities, for groupings of many kinds and at all levels, to worry about government every day or even every week. This coexistence is no longer the rule. There is a more intense relationship between the associations and institutions of civil society and government, and it is not a happy one. It is not a happy one from both sides, but this is above all true for civil society and its associations. Somehow or other, the associations of civil society feel that they can find their space only by attacking government and fighting the powers that be.

One of the important subjects of this conference is to analyse in greater detail the role of political parties in this connection. The impression is gaining ground that in the dichotomy between civil society and government, political parties—all traditional political parties—have become a part of the government side, rather than being mediators between civil society and government. When civil society turns against government, it turns, therefore, against the existing political parties as well. There is, as a result, a tendency for civil society to look for alternative expressions of interest, of aspirations, of goals, which are not compatible with the existing party system. In some cases, political parties are rejected as appropriate modes of expressing interests altogether. Instead, movements of many kinds are created. The term 'movement' is suspect for anyone who looks at the history of the century and is above all concerned with the future of liberty; but it is a term which has become quite widespread.

Let me add a fourth point. The old political class was national, with a preference for larger combinations on the international scale. It represented nation states, but was on the whole prepared to support developments which introduced these nation states into arrangements that called for the pursuit of international or intergovernmental arrangements which take some of the sovereignty of nation states away, or, more precisely perhaps, which lead to a certain amount of sharing of sovereignty. It is characteristic, in my view, of more recent developments that there is a strong local element in the preferences of many people—a strong local, and perhaps also regional, and even in a certain sense national, element in the ethnic sense of the term. Again, this is insufficiently represented and catered for by the political class.

There is thus the protest by civil society, but also that by smaller political units. One new major grouping which has tried to express this in Europe is the Northern League in Italy. It is already in a slightly complicated position now that it begins to realize that it might after all become one of the dominant political groupings in the country. But it certainly began by an appeal to many in certain parts of the north of Italy who do not want to finance either the corrupt Rome or the constituencies of the corrupt Romans in the south. On this basis the tendency gained ground for a while, and is still represented by some of the spokesmen who aim at splitting Italy or at least giving greater independence to those parts of the country which create its wealth.

In Britain this localism is quite likely to become a severe test for the Liberal Democrats, in the first instance. It has, of course, long been a test for the other two parties as well. There is in fact, as I recently learnt from an article by Vernon Bogdanor, nothing exceptional or new about the geographical division of the country, but it is nevertheless quite a drastic one, with the Tories virtually confined to the south and Labour to the north.[1] Much more serious developments, which have gone unnoticed elsewhere, have taken place in Belgium, where it is very doubtful whether the new King is actually the King of one country. Equally, in Spain it is doubtful whether the Catalans after the Olympic Games— it was bad enough during the Olympic Games—will regard themselves as rightly appearing under the Spanish flag. Then Canada; and we find similar, though perhaps not quite such serious, risks in a number of other countries. This localism, which seems endemic in post-communist Europe, leads to the risk of a break-up of traditional units of political organization watched by fairly helpless élites which do not know what to do about it.

Before I go on to my final point, let me add a cautionary footnote. This conference, like many others, makes generous use of the word 'Europe'. How could it not? It is a Europaeum Conference. But how European is Europe? What is one doing if one analyses politics and society in Europe? Is one talking about something which is more than a figment of statistics? What is the reality of the notion of a European society? And what is the reality of the notion of European politics? There can be little doubt that the Italian problems of today are almost entirely unlike those of the United Kingdom, which again are almost entirely unlike those of Germany. One has to go a long way out into space to gain the impression that diverse problems are in some ways similar. One has to look from a very great distance at countries of Europe to conclude that they form one society.

Nor is the unified cultural Europe any more real. A Fellow of St Antony's College pointed out to me that if one compares the best-seller lists of European countries one will find hardly any overlap between them; even the imported titles on these lists differ in different European countries. I recently met the editors of a newspaper in Freiburg in Germany who were talking all the time about the fact that Freiburg and Strasbourg and Basle had really become one region. When I asked them how many copies they sell in either Basle or Strasbourg, the embarrassed answer was zero. Nor do the people of Freiburg read the *Basler Zeitung*, or indeed the *Dernières Nouvelles d'Alsace*, and if you look at the papers themselves, they give you a very different picture of what is going on in the European monetary system, and at Brussels, as

8 *Ralf Dahrendorf*

well as in national politics. Thus I would just throw in a slight cautionary note as one generalizes about developments in Europe. I think we
are still a long way from legitimately talking about Europe as if it was
one social and political space.

Fortunately, on an academic occasion, one does not have to present
solutions. My fifth point is, therefore, more in the nature of prediction
than of solution. It is a question of what will happen. What would and
what should happen in the relationship between the powerful and the
powerless, between leaders and led? If you go to conferences where
there are politicians—and politicians who go to conferences are usually
ex-politicians or at any rate ex-ministers—they will all say that what
we need is leadership. What they mean is that they would like to be
back in power. If only they were back, all would be well. There is an
element of truth in this insistence on leadership. In confused periods,
the signals given by people who are widely recognized to have tried
and perhaps succeeded in making sense of issues and in pointing in
plausible directions are very important. The more confused the times
are, the more important are critical individuals. It is therefore a matter
of very great importance who follows the demise of the signatories of
Maastricht. We must hope that it will be a set of people who have a
clear sense of the future.

For the moment, confusion is the order of the day all over the OECD
world. French *cohabitation* is one illustration of such confusion not
made easier by the fact that the really problematic *cohabitation* from
the point of view of the Prime Minister is not that with his President,
but that with the Mayor of Paris. In Germany there is a fair chance that
after the elections of 1994 a grand coalition will have to be formed of
parties which once upon a time had about 90 per cent of the votes
between them, but which next year are not likely to have significantly
more than 70 per cent between them. It will therefore be a rather more
desperate coalition than the one of 1966. In Italy we have for the moment a non-political government of sorts. Most of its members know
that after April next year they will no longer be there. That depends on
when exactly the election takes place, and on a number of other things,
but it is certainly an unusual and confused situation.

In the United Kingdom one is almost tempted to say these days that
we already have a minority government, at any rate one in which the
Prime Minister finds it difficult to command a majority on any one
issue, though perhaps the ultimate issue is still one on which he can
get it.

What would happen if a new clarity emerged from such confusion? In the end, I suspect, nothing more drastic than, say, the election of President Clinton in the United States. I do not detect in the present condition, which I have described and tried to explain with a few hints and comments, a threat to democracy. I do detect a period in which there will be significant changes, including, in many countries, changes of institutions, and I only regret that so many of us have to live through the period of confusion, while the problems which have to be resolved are undeniably important. But in the OECD world at least, there is no need to worry about fundamental issues of survival in freedom. In that sense the experience of our days may after all indicate a phase in a recurring cycle.

NOTE

1. Vernon Bogdanor and William Field, 'Lessons of History: Core and Periphery in British Electoral Behaviour', *Electoral Studies*, 12/3 (1993), 203–24.

1

The Populist Challenge to Élitist Democracy in Europe

JACK HAYWARD

By the mid-1990s it has become fashionable to point to the emergence in Europe of populism, with or without a nationalist motive force. This usually takes the form of a passing reference, in the context of discussions of the loss of impetus in the movement towards closer integration in the post-Maastricht period. Whether it is attributed to primarily post-communist contextual reasons, as in most of Eastern Europe, or to the 'democratic deficit' afflicting the political-administrative institutions of the European Union, or the persistent economic recession and mass unemployment that has spread a profound sense of dissatisfaction with public decision-making, or the widespread discredit of public decision-makers in local and national politics and of prominent businessmen owing to the corruption exposed by investigative journalists and judges, there is a pervasive perception that the élites cannot be trusted to act in the public interest and have lost any claim they might have had to public deference. However, this populist phenomenon has seldom been subjected to close scrutiny. Consequently, it tends generally to be castigated, sometimes to be championed, but infrequently analysed. As it is not a wholly new phenomenon and has both in the past and at present assumed a variety of forms, it deserves a prior attempt at clarification and explanation, rather than a simplistic and expeditious judgement. Otherwise, one is liable to succumb to the tendency to stigmatize populism in the selfsame way that it itself frequently reduces complex reality to a demonological dichotomy.

1. Direct and Representative Democracy

Because populism lays claim not merely to being democratic but to embodying the most authentic version of democracy, it is necessary to place this claim in theoretical and historical perspective. Both the direct and representative forms of democratic government have a common derivation from public opinion, but this can be either mediated or unmediated. In the classical city state republics such as Athens, the citizens—who were only, it is true, a fraction of the inhabitants—played an active part in all the discussions that preceded the taking of decisions concerning the community. The implementation of those decisions was placed in the hands of officials, elected for short terms of office, subject to recall and severe punishment—including death—if judged by the citizen assembly to have failed in the performance of their duties. Thus full citizen participation and the continuous accountability of the officials to whom authority was provisionally delegated to act on behalf of the citizens was assured. This conception of democracy was revived in the seventeenth century, but its greatest exponent was Jean-Jacques Rousseau in *The Social Contract* (1762). Although his conception of popular sovereignty expressed through the general will, which could not be represented, was in principle confined to small states, with the qualification that only gods could rule democratically, it was subsequently 'applied' by Robespierre and the Jacobins to the whole of France by confiding all power to a representative assembly. Thus Rousseau's own self-proclaimed disciples quickly adopted 'government by assembly', despite the fact that the master had denied representation democratic legitimacy, parliaments being identified with the corrupt form it had assumed in eighteenth-century Britain.

Whereas both the Athenian and Rousseauian conceptions of direct democracy were in practice confined to the few, the late eighteenth century witnessed the explicit advocacy of the superiority of indirect democracy, in which the passive mass citizenry confided government affairs to an élite of active citizens. The leading exponent of this view, the abbé Sieyès, did not deny the legitimacy of direct democracy but regarded it as a crude, primitive, pre-modern version of representative democracy. Starting from Adam Smith's celebrated principle of increased productivity thanks to specialization through the division of labour, Sieyès argued that a representative system of government was not only applicable to large states but would allow the more capable and committed few to rule on behalf of the many, who lacked the leisure and knowledge to govern directly. Public affairs should be distinguished from private concerns and made the responsibility of a plurality of elected officials to avoid the alienation that would arise if all public powers were held in the hands of an individual or caste. This

separation of a professional political class—the constituted power—
from the rest of the citizens—the constituent power—would reconcile
the principle of democratic legitimacy from below with élite decision-
making effectiveness from above.[1]

The attempt to establish a representative democracy in France, based
upon an extended if not universal manhood suffrage, having quickly
degenerated into revolutionary and then Bonapartist dictatorship, let us
briefly consider the more successful experiment with representative
democratic government in the USA in the late eighteenth century. Instead
of purporting to transfer the sovereign power of the expelled monarch
to the people, as in France, the authors of *The Federalist Papers* sought
a liberal form of democracy in which those who governed should not
be granted unlimited power in the name of popular will. The role of the
electorate was to restrain the tendency of the elected to act in ways of
which the represented would not approve. Although the governing élites
should not be mandated delegates, they would be prudent in adopting
unpopular policies for fear of retribution at the next election. The
Montesquieu-inspired separation of powers would act as a further check
upon the inclination of popular majorities to be oppressive. However,
that critical if friendly analyst of *Democracy in America* Alexis de
Tocqueville warned that 'The absolute sovereignty of the will of the
majority is the essence of democratic government, for in democracies
there is nothing outside the majority capable of resisting it.'[2]

Despite the efforts of Tocqueville and J. S. Mill to liberalize this
democratic propensity, for example through decentralization and proportional representation, and the belief that an extended middle class on
the American pattern would ensure social if not political equality, they
remained suspicious of the dangers of a tyranny of the unenlightened
majority over the enlightened minorities with which they identified. As
Tocqueville confided in an introspective 1841 fragment: 'My mind is
attracted by democratic institutions but . . . I hate demagoguery, the
disordered action of the masses, their violent and unenlightened intervention in public affairs.'[3] Subsequent events in France were to lend
support to this fear of the degeneration of democracy into populism.

In the late nineteenth and early twentieth centuries, there was a
trenchant and withering onslaught by a group of élitist theorists upon
the representative democracy that was establishing itself as the only
legitimate basis of government in advanced industrial societies. Mosca's
claim that, whatever the form of government, the minority always ruled
either by manipulation or violence; Pareto's dismissal of the fiction of

popular representation in favour of rule by a 'demagogic plutocracy'; Michels's exposure of would-be democratic party politics as subject organizationally to the iron law of oligarchy: all of these élite theorists treated representative democracy as a myth.[4] Their delegitimization of democracy contributed to the rise of an ultra-populist fascism, to which Pareto and Michels but not Mosca were attracted. Pareto's theory of the circulation of élites offered the possibility that a dynamic conservatism would allow sufficient access by non-élites to political power through co-optation by a self-recruiting and self-perpetuating élite. This idea that it is the relative openness of the élite that allows it to keep its hold on power, which Tocqueville used to explain the enduring nature of the English aristocracy's standing by comparison with its French counterpart, was to become part of the theoretical basis of what has been called democratic élitism.

The anti-populist conception of democracy, which incorporated elements of the élitist critique, added to the need for open access to élite positions the crucial stipulation that the electorate should have the choice between competing élites, with no single élite becoming dominant. Joseph Schumpeter shifted the emphasis in democracy from the electorate to the leaders competing for their support, once it was conceded that the people could not themselves rule and must be represented.[5] This view was reinforced by the post-Second World War vogue for public opinion polling, which confirmed the political passivity of most citizens (*pace* Sieyès) and therefore confined the role of the people essentially to that of infrequent *voters* choosing between alternative political parties. Between elections, the pluralistic influence of political leaders was provided by pressure groups—prompting or restraining government action—but as these, like the political parties, were élite-dominated, the passivity of most citizens for almost all the time was regarded as acceptable within a liberal democracy.[6]

Élitist democracy has had a forthright protagonist in Giovanni Sartori, who defended the 'realism' of his Italian predecessors Mosca and Pareto but turned their analyses to liberal democratic purposes. In *Democratic Theory* (1962) and then in *The Theory of Democracy Revisited* (1987), Sartori stressed the quality of leadership of 'vertical democracy' over the quantitative mass participation of 'horizontal democracy'. He reminded his readers (following Thucydides) that Athenian democracy was at its height during Pericles' leadership and recalled James Bryce's remark that 'Perhaps no form of government needs great leaders as much as democracy does.'[7] Far from democratic experience encouraging voting, it has declined, so that the number of inert citizens has increasingly exceeded active citizens. Despite efforts to encourage participation by the ignorant, 'the democratic citizen in most instances does not know what the issues are, what solutions have been proposed, what consequences are likely to follow, and even what the candidates running for office (let alone the parties) stand for'.[8] However, the democratic ideal remains the direct involvement of equal citizens in government, so that representative democracy and the need for a representative leadership which exercises power as the meritocratic result of a *selective system of competing elected minorities*' is devalued.[9] 'A representative is not only responsible *to*, but also responsible *for*. This is the same as saying that representation intrinsically consists of two ingredients: responsiveness *and* independent responsibility.'[10] The latter was what professional political leadership was really about and should not be weakened in favour of the mass of passive citizens on pain of ineffective democratic government.

2. The Political Expression of Public Opinion

Following the Second World War victory over the aggressive populist totalitarianisms of Nazi Germany and Fascist Italy, in the context of the ongoing Cold War with the Soviet Union, élitist democrats emphasized the pluralist nature of liberal democracy. The American sociologist William Kornhauser bluntly wrote: 'A pluralist society supports a *liberal democracy*, whereas a mass society supports a *populist democracy* . . . In liberal democracy the mode of access [to power] tends to be controlled by institutional procedures and intermediate associations, whereas in populist democracy the mode of access tends to be more direct and unrestrained.'[11] Despite the crude over-simplifications involved in the concept of 'mass society', it had prior to Kornhauser been used in a more sophisticated way by a trenchant critic of the power élite which he argued had come to dominate modern political, economic, and military affairs.

Wright Mills drew a contrast between the classic notion of a 'community of publics' and the modern 'mass' which reflected the differences between a liberal and a populist style of politics. The community of publics was characterized by four features. First, the ratio of givers to receivers of opinion was roughly equal, whereas in a mass those who express opinions were a tiny fraction of those receiving them. Second, despite the existence of the media of mass communication, the possibility of quickly and effectively answering back an opinion, without suffering reprisals, was denied to most people. Third, the capacity of public opinion to influence important decisions was much greater than in a mass society, except during rare explosions of mass discontent. Fourth, 'the degree to which institutional authority, with its sanctions and controls, penetrates the public' is far greater in mass societies, so that public opinion is less shaped by free discussion than by mass manipulation.[12] This overdrawn dichotomy, of a passive and powerless mass at the mercy of a power élite, nevertheless helps us to distinguish between two variants of direct democracy, the plebiscite and the referendum, which have been used respectively to replace or assist the working of representative democracy.

It has been authoritatively asserted in a recent book on the resurgence of direct democracy that no one has produced a clear distinction between referendums and plebiscites.[13] I shall nevertheless venture to do so by arguing that a plebiscite is a populist device through which the people are treated by a government as a manipulable mass rather than a reasoning public. Two criteria allow us to identify which phenomenon we are facing. Who initiates the proposal on which the people vote and who phrases the question? What is the issue to be settled?

First, does the initiative come from above or from below? Where, as in Switzerland and Italy, the initiative comes from the citizens and not the government, we can speak of a referendum, although even there a special public or pressure group will often be the motivating force behind an initiative. France has a long experience of initiatives from above, with Napoleon and Louis-Napoleon's plebiscites demonstrating the use of mass support to legitimize the subversion of liberal democratic republics. De Gaulle placed the initiative in calling a referendum firmly in the hands of the President of the Republic, with the association of parliament, when the Fifth Republic was established. By contrast with this example of executive domination of the process, in Denmark one-third of the single-chamber Folketing can take the initiative in demanding a popular vote on most items of non-financial or treaty legislation.[14] The Danish case shows how direct democracy can be linked with representative democracy, a point to which we shall return.

Second, is the question on which the people vote intended to resolve a specific issue or is it primarily a pretext for securing blanket approval of the government? Are the voters being offered a decisive policy choice or are they invited to provide passive political support for a leader, to confirm the popular legitimacy of his authority. In the former case, we have a referendum, in the latter a plebiscite. Four main types of issue have been the subject of referendums.[15] First, the ratification of a constitution (or subsequent amendments to it) imparts democratic legitimacy to the institutional structures of government and to the guiding principles stipulated therein. Second, territorial issues, such as accession to the European Community, have sometimes been the subject of a referendum, although none of the original six members held one. Britain only did so to decide in 1975 whether to stay in the EC, while neither Greece, Portugal, nor Spain did when they joined. However, Austria, Finland, and Sweden did so in 1994 when they decided to join, while Norway's referendum led to rejection of EC membership. Third, controversial but cross-party issues, such as abortion and divorce, have been put to popular vote to avoid splitting parties, especially those in office. Italy, which is the only other European country that can even begin to vie with Switzerland (which had held 414 referendums by 1993, with a marked increase in the 1970s and 1980s, compared to twenty-eight in Italy since 1974), has been conspicuous in relation to such moral-cum-religious issues in the use of the referendum since the 1970s. Fourth, in these two countries, like several states of the USA, citizens can insist that certain issues be put to a referendum. When referendums are frequent, as in Switzerland, they are taken for granted, whereas when they are rare they dramatize issues, although, as we shall see later, in neither case does turn-out usually exceed that of general parliamentary elections. Swiss governments do not resign if their proposals are rejected, as in the 1992 referendum on membership of the European Economic Area, but in that case the narrow defeat (49.7 per cent voting in favour) was associated with a turn-out that rose sharply from a customary 40 per cent to 78 per cent.[16]

It is not always possible to separate the issue voted upon and the leader who has put the question. This was conspicuously the case with de Gaulle's 'referendums', which were also linked with an explicit vote of confidence in his leadership, so that when in 1969 the vote went against his proposals he resigned immediately.[17] The 1992 referendum on the Maastricht Treaty may have been on the specific issue in Denmark, but in France it was very much confused with a vote for or against Mitterrand. Nevertheless, it is possible in virtually all instances to assess fairly accurately whether the question is the real issue or simply a device for relegitimizing the leader, i.e. whether it is a directly democratic referendum or a pseudo-democratic, populist plebiscite. However, let us concentrate for the moment upon authentic exercises in direct democracy and seek to assess their advantages and disadvantages by comparison with representative democracy, although the advocates of the referendum as against the plebiscite regard it as an auxiliary rather than an alternative to the 'normal' electoral process.

Four principal virtues can be advanced briefly for the referendum. First, it disentangles issues that are confused in a 'take it or leave it' party electoral programme and so provides a more accurate popular verdict. Second, the referendum campaign helps educate at least some of the electorate about the issues over which citizens are invited to make up their minds, although in a plebiscite the issues are deliberately obfuscated. Third, casting their votes in a referendum gives citizens a sense of direct participation in decisions, and so they acquire a greater identification with public policies. Fourth, it strengthens the electorate against their representatives, who may—like all élites—misrepresent their views.

Four countervailing vices may be adduced to which referendums are prone. First, political problems are often interdependent and difficult to isolate, so attempts to deal with them piecemeal readily lead to divergent decisions and the inability to pursue consistent public policies. Second, referendums tend to highlight the inertia of public opinion, although Italy has recently provided a strong counter-example to habitual references to Swiss experience. Third, not merely are radical policies generally promoted by minorities, but the voters are not competent to decide complex issues and are susceptible to demagogic propaganda. Voters find it easier to judge the actions of their representatives retrospectively, by results. Fourth, recourse to direct democracy encourages the deferential politician who leads from behind. The cultivation of prevailing prejudices in pursuit of short-term popularity displaces courageous leadership that persuades the less well informed.

David Butler and Austin Ranney have conclusively shown that the claim that direct democracy maximizes voter participation is the reverse of the truth by comparing mean turn-out in parliamentary elections and in referendums. As Table 1.1 shows, with the exception of Belgium where voting is compulsory, turn-out in referendums has always been lower since 1945 in all twelve countries, often by a very large margin. Furthermore, both populism and liberal democracy share a reliance on voting which, as William Riker has shown, can be manipulated in ways that render their outcomes dubious, depending upon which voting procedure is adopted. Riker argues that the strength of liberal democracy

18 *Jack Hayward*

TABLE 1.1. *Mean turn-out in candidate and referendum elections in selected countries 1945–1993 (%)*

Nation	Candidate elections	Referendum elections	Difference
Australia[a]	95	90	−5
Austria	93	64	−29
Belgium[a]	92	92	0
Denmark	86	74	−12
France	77	72	−5
Ireland	73	58	−15
Italy	90	74	−16
New Zealand	90	60	−30
Norway	81	78	−3
Sweden	85	67	−18
Switzerland	61	45	−16
United Kingdom	77	65	−12

[a] Compulsory-voting laws.

Source: D. Butler and A. Ranney, *Referendums around the World* (Washington: AEI, 1994), 17.

is that its reliance on representatives makes only modest demands upon voting. It is sufficient that 'voting permits the rejection of candidates or officials who have offended so many voters that they cannot win an election'.[18] By contrast, 'Populism as a moral imperative depends on the existence of a popular will discovered by voting. But if voting does not discover or reveal a will then the moral imperative evaporates . . . We do not and cannot know what the people want. An election tells us at most which alternative wins; it does not tell us that the winner would have been chosen over another feasible alternative that might itself have a better claim to be the social choice.'[19] Riker concludes that because no popular will can be identified, still less that it is necessarily right, 'populism (is) unworkable' and 'the populist ideal is literally unattainable'.[20]

Unlike parliamentary elections and referendums, public opinion polls do not lead directly to decisions, but in the last half-century they have provided a way of testing the extent to which political élites accurately reflect mass views. As well as influencing the attitudes adopted by their representatives, who may adapt the timing and content of policies to conform with predominant public opinions, polls have offered a quantitative means of assessing those views directly, rather than relying on the qualitative judgements of politicians or journalists. The expertise of those traditional intermediaries having been challenged by the interposition of the pollsters to the point that much journalistic commentary is now implicitly or explicitly organized around their findings, it has become feasible to achieve some of the advantages we earlier attributed to the referendum. It is possible to disentangle the policy priorities that are packaged in a compendious electoral programme and discourage the misrepresentation of their views owing to élite ignorance or partisanship. However, it is likely to encourage the propensity to lead from behind, especially when the record and standing of leaders is subjected to frequent tests by the polls. Massive recourse to opinion polling, especially during election campaigns but with a tendency to be continuous, both reflects and exacerbates the anxiety of political élites on the score of their capacity to remain in touch with their potential voters. Popularity has become an obsessively more important criterion of fitness for public office and the ability to win elections bulks ever larger than the capability to govern.

3. Populism and Mass Subservience

Appeal to the whole people by populists simultaneously implies unity and duality and deliberately blurs the distinction. They seek to conjure up a mythical unity of nation, class, profession, and so forth, yet they also wish to pit the non-élite against the élite, to which a fictional unity is also attributed.

The great charm of 'the people' for a politician—and the fundamental source of exasperation for a political scientist—is that the term manages to be both empty of precise meaning and full of rhetorical resonance. When used to mean 'everyone', it is conveniently vague and *sounds* definite, conveying a sense of solidity and harmony. When used to mean a particular class or section of the population, it gains in definition but somehow manages to avoid losing its overtones of comprehensiveness and legitimacy.[21]

Going beyond this assessment of the subjective proclivities of the populist phenomenon, Margaret Canovan has affirmed: 'When the term is applied to devices of direct democracy like the referendum, to mobilization of mass passions, to idealizations of the man in the street, or to politicians' attempts to hold together shaky coalitions in the name of

"the people", what those who talk of "populism" have in mind is a
particular kind of political phenomenon where the tensions between the
elite and the grass roots loom large.'[22]

Populism confusingly has both a modernist, mass society aspect and
an anti-modernist, traditional aspect. Its emergence may correspond
particularly to the intermediate phase between the decline of established
élites and before the emergence of new institutionalized élites. Edward
Shils claimed that populism exists 'wherever there is an ideology of
popular resentment against the order imposed upon society of a long-
established, differentiated ruling class, which is believed to have a
monopoly of power, property, breeding and culture . . . It is impatient
of institutional procedures which impede the direct expression of the
popular will and the forceful personalities who assume the responsibility
of being vessels of the popular will,'[23] once they have ceased to appeal
to the populist imagination. All autonomous institutions are resented as
arrogant and secretive havens for the high and mighty, whose mutual
confidence all too readily takes the form of collusive activities that
should be exposed by a muck-raking popular press. The self-esteem of
the mass public is flattered by an 'inverted inegalitarianism' in which
'the people are not just the equal of their rulers; they are actually better
than their rulers'.[24]

Populism is not so much an ideology of its own as a feature of certain kinds of social and political movements—notably of the extreme
Right and Left—that flourish on the cultivation of conspiracy theories.
The more backward-looking variants of these movements, which are
allergic to being structured institutionally, are anti-urban, anti-capitalist,
and anti-Semitic. As Donald MacRae put it, 'The mobile townsman,
the unpredictable, untraditional, impermanent stranger—the Jew, the
European, the banker, the heretic: these provided the usurpers, the con-
spirators, the enemies,' leading to a sweeping zenophobia directed at
both 'the foreign poor and the foreign rich'.[25] Financiers—especially
foreign financiers—are a particular favourite of populist demonology,
but more recently it has become more fashionable to attack bureaucrats
and technocrats.[26]

In the search for a scapegoat for either the reality or the feeling
of popular relative deprivation, the early twentieth-century American
populist Huey Long generalized from his campaign against the Standard Oil Company: 'Corporations are the finest political enemies in the
world . . .'.[27] Ralph Nader was to repeat the operation in the late 1960s
and 1970s against General Motors, in his successful advocacy of the

consumer general interest in car safety.[28] Mrs Thatcher was able to develop a successful populist onslaught on a variety of established British institutions, including many associated with traditional conservatism, such as the Established Church, as well as those that were hostile, such as trade unions or Labour-controlled local authorities, or those who sought to be neutral, like the BBC and the universities, but were resented as harbouring a tolerant liberal cosmopolitanism. She often gave the populist impression that she was not in power even when she was Prime Minister, because she was seeking to break the stranglehold of interest groups, hostile institutions, and entrenched practices.

However, Thatcherism was unusual because it was an example of partial populism in a country where this phenomenon was exceptionally weak. She saw herself as an 'outsider' who, despite being leader of the Conservative Party, was being opposed by élitists inside and beyond her party. Her dictatorial style had closer affinities with populist leaders in the developing countries, and her appeal to the need to reverse national decline resembled the mass mobilization to overcome economic backwardness characteristic of such countries. However, in the British context, she was never able to become the embodiment of the nation in the way that leaders in single-party states that had only recently achieved independence could do, or seriously to pretend that all autonomous institutions could be subordinated to her will. She exercised her imperious authority only as long as she enjoyed a majority in the House of Commons to which she was accountable. The representative parliamentary élites, over whom she had ridden roughshod with such delectation, were finally able to remove her from power after eleven years in office.

4. Mediated and Unmediated Politics

As later chapters in this book (notably Chapters 6–8, by Hine, Andeweg, and Richardson) discuss in detail, the relations between the governmental élites and the mass public in liberal democracies are mediated by political parties and organized interests. The emergence of universal suffrage necessitated the development of mass parties, based mainly upon religion and class, augmented by urban–rural and centre–periphery tensions, which linked the party leaders, via their parliamentary parties and constituency activists, with their membership and voters. The decline of these parties in the second half of the twentieth century has varied between countries and type of party, with some parties or countries bucking the trend. Thus, whereas in Denmark, the Netherlands, and Britain party membership has fallen substantially, there have been modest increases in Germany and Belgium over the thirty years from the 1960s to 1980s (see Table 7.4 below). Again, whereas particularly large falls have occurred in the left-wing parties with the largest memberships— for example, the British Labour Party or the French Communist Party— there have also been significant falls in conservative and agrarian parties, with a more mixed but mainly negative record among Christian Democratic, Social Democratic, and liberal parties. The level of party activism has declined, so that the linkage between the leaders and the mass of voters has been weakened, although it is often the case that the leaders have more in common with the views of the electorate than with their partisans, as Tony Blair has shown in the rejuvenated Labour Party.

Political corruption (particularly through the links with party finance) as well as personal corruption, has become a systematic and endemic source of the discredit from which party élites and business élites suffer, both at the national and local levels. This has been connected in Europe, notably in Italy, France, and Spain, with prolonged periods in power of the same party or coalition, with the predictable tendency for absolute power to corrupt absolutely. Scandals have been associated with both the public sector and the private sector, as well as in the privatized sector, with domestic as well as foreign business. As parties have been able to rely less on the unpaid service of activists, their financial needs have grown. So the members of the legislative and executive élites have been inclined to resort to dubious sources of finance, exposing themselves to increasingly uninhibited judicial and journalis- tic censure, which in turn has undermined the shaky standing of the political class with public opinion. The cry 'Tous pourris' comes readily to the populist, and in the 1990s there has been plenty of ammunition to fire at those who have profited from or condoned such malpractices. Insufficient circulation of the élites has allowed too many politicians to rely upon the public relations resources of office as a substitute for remaining in touch with their erstwhile supporters. They have used public office for private or partisan benefit.

The decline in the ability of élite-directed organizations such as parties, trade unions, and churches to achieve mass mobilization has provided the political space for the emergence of élite-directing social movements that are disposed to use methods of political action other than voting for political representatives. Ronald Inglehart has stressed the increased 'likelihood that citizens will engage in a broad repertoire of elite-directing political actions, ranging from petitions to demonstrations to boycotts, unofficial strikes, occupying buildings, and blocking traffic, in order to articulate political grievances and put pressure on policy-makers to comply with their demands'.[29] In many liberal democracies, such unconventional events are an everyday reality. These phenomena show that such forms of direct protest, all of which were available—together with outright violence—before the era of universal suffrage and not expected to persist thereafter, have become recurrent symptoms of weaknesses in the working of representative democracy. Taken in conjunction with the increasing tendency to vote for non-governing parties (which reached 38 per cent in the first ballot of the 1995 French presidential election, with a further 21 per cent abstaining, and nearly 3 per cent—more than double the usual number—of spoiled votes), they result in élites frequently yielding to these various forms of public protest.

The discredit that has fallen upon conventional party politics has encouraged the development of what have been called 'new politics' and 'new populist' parties, as well as new social movements, but as not all of these are new, it is better to avoid this designation. Tom Mackie has proposed the term 'challenger' parties to cover those 'who are not serious contenders for government office, either because they are explicitly anti-system or because they are not regarded as suitable partners by existing government parties'.[30] From the late 1960s a variety of new social movements advocating environmentalism, opposing nuclear energy, and supporting feminism developed, but it was only the Green parties who sometimes gave this left-libertarian category of challenger parties electoral success from the late 1980s. In Belgium, Denmark, Germany, Norway, Sweden, and Switzerland, they had some success but seldom exceeded 10 per cent of the vote.

By the late 1980s neo-Fascist parties as well as 'new populist' parties were emerging as challengers on the extreme right, although it is not always easy to distinguish between them. Thus, whereas the Italian Social Movement was explicitly neo-Fascist, its transmutation into the National Alliance makes it more of a hybrid, while Bassi's Northern League and Berlusconi's Italian Force are explicitly populist, albeit of different types. In contrast to the left-libertarian parties, such as the Greens, that resist strong, personalized leadership, this is a feature of the neo-Fascist and new populist parties of the right. While appealing to the mass public against the élites who had reinforced the welfare state after the Second World War, concentrating their attack on establishment politicians and bureaucrats, as well as immigrants and welfare recipients, they are primarily but not simply protest parties.[31] They have been especially prominent in Austria (Haider's Freedom Party), France (Le Pen's National Front), and Italy. In Central and East Europe, presidential elections allowed right-wing anti-party politicians to win substantial but ephemeral votes (Tyminski in Poland 18 per cent, and Ganchev in Bulgaria 17 per cent),[32] while the threat from Zhirinovski encouraged Yeltsin to postpone presidential elections in Russia. The rapid revival of new-style communist parties demonstrated the capacity of the somewhat rejuvenated old élites to acquire popularity in an electorally competitive context.

The social movements that have come to the fore in recent years are informally organized to pursue specifically targeted protest activities. Like the party expression of the anti-élitist phenomenon, these movements are to be found at both the left and right extremes of the political spectrum, although campaigning for causes such as animal rights cannot be readily classified in this way. The left-libertarian movements are distinguished from mainstream left parties and interest groups by being concerned not with employment and income issues but with environmental pollution and feminist concerns. Herbert Kitschelt has argued that such movements tend to occur in countries which have comprehensive welfare states and are non-Catholic.[33] The propensity of mainstream élites to incorporate the demands of such movements varies, the contrast between the receptive Netherlands and unreceptive Britain being striking.

As in the case of the challenger parties, the authoritarian social movements of the right came later, partly as a reaction to the left-libertarians. The contrast in support is marked: the latter being strongest among the better-educated (especially students) and professions, while the former recruit especially among manual workers, farmers, and small businessmen. The authoritarian-right social movements are especially intolerant of ethnic minorities and homosexuals, but are also anti-feminist and anti-abortion. Kitschelt points out that 'the East European anti-communist transformation is characterised by an *absence of popular mobilisation*. It was instigated by the exhaustion of the incumbent elites and the action of counter-elites that were sporadically supported by a few mass demonstrations at critical historical junctures.'[34] Even early resistance by Poland's Solidarity union had weakened by the late 1980s and populist resort to anti-Market opposition to rising prices and un-employment, effectively exploited by recycled ex-communists, has proved effective in most post-communist countries.

To sum up, where representative institutions are firmly established, even when the élites can be said to have failed to satisfy the expectations of their electorates, populism has made few inroads. This would seem to be broadly the case in the United Kingdom, Scandinavia, and Germany. The existence of integrative institutions—political, economic, and social—has led to resistance to plebiscitarian leadership, although the sense of failure at the end of the 1970s in Britain led to the acceptance of a radical right-wing leader in the shape of Mrs Thatcher, who successfully mobilized sufficient public support against many irresolute Establishment institutions. Germany has shown that despite the potentially destabilizing effects of reunification, its integrative organizations have been strong enought to sustain the strains. In France, the Fifth Republic has provided the élites with institutions capable of containing a number of populist pressures, notably from the nationalist populism of Le Pen's National Front. However, the pressures have increased in the 1990s to an extent that has placed the mainstream parties on the defensive, as the anxieties and hardships of those who feared or experienced exclusion from the benefits of secure employment resulted in electoral vengeance upon those held responsible, leading to substantial votes for such shooting-star demagogues as Bernard Tapie in France. By contrast, in Italy and Greece, as well as in Russia and much of Eastern Europe, populism has been strong, reaching into government rather than protesting from outside. The relatively neglected Greek example is worthy of consideration.

Greece has witnessed the clash of two cultures: an introvert, pre-capitalist, authoritarian, clientelist 'underdog culture', steeped in an Ottoman, Orthodox Church, Balkan heritage and a cosmopolitan, pro-market, liberal democratic, and secular culture. The older culture fav-oured a 'populist discourse which belittled institutions and promoted the arbitrary exercise of power in the name of the people', exemplified by Greek Prime Minister Andreas Papandreou's remark: 'there are no institutions, only the People'.[35] As leader of the socialist-populist PASOK party, Papandreou provided the catch-all rhetoric that subsumed all the heterogeneous interests of the 'non-privileged' people against the élites, purporting to transcend social divisions but in practice sustaining the survival of the least competitive elements in Greek society. PASOK's domination in the early 1980s and return to power in the 1990s allowed it to reveal the populist nature of its ideology, organization, and policies. 'The plebiscitarian character and the paternalistic nature of PASOK's internal functioning stem from the fact that by reducing all differences to one major cleavage and oversimplifying the social and political space, populist logic does not allow the autonomous expression of different views. Instead it requires obedience to the leader who represents and incarnates the unity of the popular movement.'[36] Here we see the characteristic populist tendency to mobilize a legitimizing abstraction, the people, to bludgeon its plural components into acquiescence.

The application of party populism to organized interests was another feature of Papandreou's PASOK rule. The capture of peak organizations by compelling them to adopt election by proportional representation subjected their élites to 'drowning by numbers' and 'forced party divisions even when none existed or were relevant before, thereby destroying the cohesiveness of all associations, down to the smallest'.[37] Unlike most populist parties that are permanently excluded from government, once it achieves power, it seeks to partisanize all sectional interests, with the former underdogs becoming particularly oppressive masters. In Greece the partisan penetration of organized interests was applied to business as well as trade unions, in the former case by submerging the bigger businessmen by the PASOK's clientele of small shopkeepers and artisans. The mass membership had now to face a new élite. 'The *reductio ad absurdum* was provided by PASOK union presidents denouncing official strikes called by their own unions . . .'.[38] This example shows that when the impersonal élite institutions are not successfully playing their mediating role, the recourse to hyper-personalized populism, under the guise of challenging the élites, may result in an unsavoury brand of unmediated politics.

Legitimate public distrust of élites that have too often misused their positions for partisan and private profit has led to a virtual disappearance of the deference that previously allowed them the privilege of self-regulation. The combined attack of the judiciary and investigative journalism, in the name of the 'transparency' required for the enforcement of democratic accountability to the public, has exposed élites to a sustained suspicion of the rectitude of their motives which may amount to putting them permanently on trial.[39] In some respects, we may be returning to a softer version of Athenian direct democracy, when public denunciation and impeachment could lead to death or exile. Abuse and misuse of power, too long tolerated by élites that protected their own, have become the day-to-day target of journalists and judges, acting as tribunes of the people. Self-regulation having conspicuously failed, the old question of who shall stand guard over the guardians has re-emerged with a vengeance, reinforced by the publicity given to the accusations and the incriminating evidence by the mass media. Liberal democracy has perforce to rely upon élites of a free (but sensation-seeking) press and a relatively impartial judiciary to play their checking role upon governments and legislators within a pluralistic institutional system. The antidotes may share some of the ailments which they seek to contain if not to cure, but representative democracy has to live with the countervailing forces of élitism and populism. The mutual checks must also preserve a balance that avoids the tendency of leaders to forget how far they can go.

5. *National Populism and European Integration*

In the post-Maastricht period and in a context of economic recession and widespread political scandals (including fraud connected particularly with the working of the Common Agricultural Policy) the European Union generally and its Commission officials in particular have become a prime target of populist criticism. The 'closed politics' methods of decision-taking dictated by the need for intergovernmental bargaining, and the detailed regulatory directives and circulars required to implement decisions, have become the focus of much indiscriminate abuse. Particularly when decisions interfere with national practices and preferences, it is all too easy to mobilize mass resentment and to treat the European Union as a scapegoat for the unpopular consequences of what are often unavoidable compromises of a complexity which few grasp.

The Delors presidency of the Commission, which began so dynamically, ran into a reluctance of political leaders to press ahead with economic and monetary union, as well as ambitious schemes to combat unemployment. However much the former policy might be regarded as very much a matter for élite insiders, the latter was the sort of issue which would have allowed some retrieval of mass support that had drained away when integration ceased to be associated with prosperity. The two objectives are generally regarded as in conflict (see Chapter 2 below), but it is particularly dangerous if the former can be treated as the priority of the politico-economic élites and the latter is regarded as the prime concern of many in the mass public.

Like Monnet before him, but more obtrusively and in a context where 'there aren't enough Europeans to go around', Delors sought to coax and compel the official decision-makers down a road whose implications they only dimly perceived. This technique of *engrenage* endeavoured to pull the people along in the wake of the élites, thanks to the esoteric knowledge of Europe's ultimate destination which he and his small band of fellow insiders commanded.[40] Tim Garton Ash has cogently observed that 'from Messina to Maastricht, the *telos* was a substitute for the absent demos—with the hope of contributing to the creation of a new European demos from above'.[41] However, the failure of this new European people to emerge has meant that the populists have been able to exploit anti-élitist sentiments because, without the artefact of a European people, the necessary public support was lacking.

When the process of financial and currency integration was linked with the transfer of autonomous authority to those quintessentially élite institutions the central banks (all banks, as we have already mentioned, being a traditional bugbear of populists), the scope for a populist attack was substantially increased. This applied, in France for example, not merely to the extreme-right National Front[42] but also to Philippe de Villiers (both in the European and presidential elections) and to members of the Rassemblement pour la République such as Philippe Séguin, and from time to time Jacques Chirac. Yet France was officially committed both to the independence of its own Bank of France, as well as to the creation of a European Central Bank, if only to retain its privileged link with Germany. Ironically, given the populist allergy to the banking élite, Italy has frequently had recourse to its central bankers to head its governments when it has sought an apolitical corrective both to corrupt rule by the parties and to the incapacity of a populist coalition to establish an effective government.

It was significant that former EC Commissioners Jacques Delors and Raymond Barre, two potential candidates in the 1995 French presidential election who were amongst the best qualified and most pro-European integration, decided not to stand. In an atmosphere suffused with appeals to the underdog and coolness towards the pursuit of integration, they judged that they would not be able to carry through the policies they believed to be necessary. The victor, Jacques Chirac, deliberately and without inhibition (although not going as far as Le Pen and de Villiers) played the populist card, attacking the 'technostructure', the finance ministry, and the banking system in an orgy of anti-statist demagoguery against the 'experts' who had 'confiscated powers' from the people. He claimed in a Lorraine campaigning speech on 19 January

1995 that there were 'two possible attitudes. The first gives priority to statistics, the second to will',[43] and Chirac clearly subordinated rational calculation resulting in political resignation to an ambitious assertion of political will. In arousing expectations he would find difficult to satisfy, Chirac deliberately sacrificed the capacity to exercise power to the urge to win power. Encouraged by Philippe Séguin, an admirer of that unscrupulous but accomplished populist (and President of the Second Republic) Louis-Napoleon, he sought to placate those of his followers who disliked a single European currency by proposing that there should be a referendum before the decision was made. Himself a graduate of the École Nationale d'Administration, that sanctum of the French administrative–political–business interlocking directorate (like five others of the nine presidential candidates), the victor used to potent effect the anti-élitist populism that mobilized mass prejudices against technocracy but weakened democratic government in the process. For how can the suffrage-made élite manage without the meritocratic, school-made élite, derived from competitive examination rather than competitive election?

Strengthening the EU's capacity to take pivotal economic decisions requires increasing the legitimacy of its decision-makers, but there is an unwillingness among some member states to give it democratic legitimacy through a reform of the EU institutions. The reluctance of the British Government and a substantial section of public opinion to proceed with further integration and even the wish to backslide, and the rejection of EU membership in the Norwegian referendum, are reflections of a wider reluctance to engage in power-sharing in the name of national sovereignty. The élites may be divided over calculations of the relative merits of exercising a share of more effective power or having exclusive control over a less effective or wholly ineffective power. Members of the public, despite the tendency in certain countries (in Britain for tactical reasons, in France because of a hankering after direct democracy) to extend the use of referendums will not in any case usually have more than an indirect say in decisions. When they do, they will frequently form their judgements under the impact of simplistic slogans which ensure that the real choices are not properly posed in relation to their medium- and long-term causes and consequences. Attempts by élites to get in touch with their peoples are made difficult by the context of demagogic unreality with which much public debate is conducted, which is compounded by the loss of public trust in their capacity to act wisely (see notably Chapter 3). However, European politics will continue to remain primarily the responsibility of representative élites operating in an increasingly unpredictable environment, yet needing to be fully accountable to those that will have to live with the consequences of their decisions.

NOTES

1. See Murray Forsyth, *Reason and Revolution: The Political Thought of Abbé Sieyès* (Leicester: Leicester University Press, 1987), ch. 7 *passim* and pp. 56, 65. See also the comments on Rousseau and Sieyès in Jack Hayward, *After the French Revolution: Six Critics of Democracy and Nationalism* (Hemel Hempstead: Harvester Wheatsheaf, 1991), 11–14, 18–20.
2. A. de Tocqueville, *Democracy in America* (1835), ed. J. P. Mayer and M. Lerner (New York: Harper & Row, 1966), 227.
3. A. de Tocqueville, 'Mon instinct, mes opinions', MS (Nov. 1841), in Antoine Rédier, *Comme disait M. de Tocqueville* (Paris: Perrin, 1925), 48.
4. On Mosca, see John Meisel, *The Myth of the Ruling Class* (Ann Arbor, Mich.: University of Michigan Press, 1958). On Pareto, see S. E. Finer, *Vilfredo Pareto: Sociological Writings* (London: Pall Mall, 1966). See also Robert Michels, *Political Parties* (1911; Glencoe, Ill., Free Press, 1949). More generally, see Peter Bachrach, *The Theory of Democratic Élitism* (Boston: Little, Brown, 1967), 10–17.
5. Joseph A. Schumpeter, *Capitalism, Socialism and Democracy* (1942; 2nd edn. London: Allen & Unwin, 1947), chs. 21–2.
6. John Plamenatz, 'Electoral Studies and Democratic Theory', *Political Studies*, 6/1 (Feb. 1958), 1–9, discussed in Bachrach, *The Theory of Democratic Élitism*, 35–9.
7. Giovanni Sartori, *The Theory of Democracy Revisited* (Chatham, NJ: Chatham House, 1987), i. 163, quoting Lord Bryce, *The American Commonwealth* (1959), 432. For Sartori's comments on the élitists Mosca, Pareto, Michels, and Schumpeter, see ibid. i. 46–8, 148–54.
8. Sartori, *The Theory of Democracy Revisited*, 108; cf. Schumpeter, *Capitalism, Socialism and Democracy*, 261–2.
9. Sartori, *The Theory of Democracy Revisited*, 167; cf. 164–70.
10. Ibid. 170.
11. William Kornhauser, *The Politics of Mass Society* (London: Routledge & Kegan Paul, 1960), 131; cf. 60, 103–5, 122.
12. C. Wright Mills, *The Power Élite*, 1956, New York (Oxford: Oxford University Press, 1959), 303; cf. 302–4.
13. David Butler and Austin Ranney (eds.), *Referendums around the World: The Growing Use of Direct Democracy* (Washington: AEI, 1994), 1 n.

14. On the French, Italian, and Danish cases, see ibid., ch. 3, by Vernon Bogdanor. On Switzerland, see ibid., ch. 4, by Kris W. Kobach.
15. These categories are suggested ibid. 2–3.
16. See Kobach, ibid. 135.
17. Jack Hayward, 'Presidential Suicide by Plebiscite: De Gaulle's Exit', *Parliamentary Affairs*, 22/4 (Autumn 1969), 289–319.
18. William H. Riker, *Liberalism against Populism: A Confrontation between the Theory of Deomocracy and the Theory of Social Choice* (San Francisco: Freeman, 1982), 242; cf. 241–4.
19. Ibid. 238; cf. 236–7.
20. Ibid. 239, 241; cf. 10–14.
21. Margaret Canovan, *Populism* (London: Junction, 1981), 285–6; cf. 277.
22. Ibid. 9.
23. Edward A. Shils, *The Torment of Secrecy* (London: Heinemann, 1956), 100–1, 102.
24. Ibid. 101; cf. 99–100, 143–8, 155–8.
25. Donald MacRae, 'Populism as an Ideology', in Ghita Ionescu and Ernest Gellner (eds.), *Populism: Its Meaning and National Characteristics* (London: Macmillan, 1969), 157–8; cf. 156.
26. See Peter Wiles, 'A Syndrome not a Doctrine: Some Elementary Theses on Populism', in Ionescu and Gellner (eds.), *Populism*, 167–70.
27. Quoted by Canovan, *Populism*, 152, from T. Harry Williams, *Huey Long* (London: Thames & Hudson, 1969), 416.
28. Canovan, *Populism*, 218.
29. Ronald Inglehart, *Culture Shift in Advanced Industrial Society* (Princeton: Princeton University Press, 1990), 360; cf. 336 ff.
30. Tom Mackie, 'Parties and Elections', in Jack Hayward and Edward Page (eds.), *Governing the New Europe* (Oxford: Polity Press, 1995), 175. See also Thomas Poguntke, 'New Politics and Party Systems: The Emergence of a New Type of Party?' *West European Politics*, 10/1 (Jan. 1987), 76–88.
31. Mackie, 'Parties and Elections', 176–82 and tables on 189–91. See also Paul Taggart, 'New Populist Parties in Western Europe', *West European Politics*, 18/1 (Jan. 1995), 34–51.
32. Mackie, 'Parties and Elections', 186–7.
33. Herbert Kitschelt, 'A Silent Revolution in Europe?', in Hayward and Page (eds.), *Governing the New Europe*, 135.
34. Ibid. 149. See also Wlodzimierz Wesolowski, 'The Role of Political Élites in Transition from Communism to Democracy: The Case of Poland', *Sisyphus*, 2/8 (1992), 77–100: 94.
35. P. Niffiforos Diamandouros, 'Political Culture in Greece 1974–1991', in Richard Clogg (ed.), *Greece 1981–1989: The Populist Decade* (London: Macmillan, 1993), 18; cf. 3–6, 58.

36. Christos Lyrintzis, 'PASOK in Power: From "Change" to Disenchantment',
    in Clogg (ed.), *Greece*, 31; cf. George T. Mavrogordatos, 'Civil Society
    under Populism', ibid. 47–8, 54, 63 n.
37. Mavrogordatos, 'Civil Society under Populism', 54, 58.
38. Ibid. 59. On the role of the populist newspaper *Avriani*, see S. Pesmazo-
    goglou, 'The 1980s in the Looking-Glass: PASOK and the Media', in
    Clogg (ed.), 105–7, 111.
39. For a rather excessive statement of this view, see Alain Minc, *L'Ivresse
    démocratique* (Paris: Gallimard, 1995), chs. 4, 6, and esp. 8: 'La Menace
    populiste'.
40. For the technique of *engrenage*, see George Ross, *Jacques Delors and
    European Integration* (Oxford: Polity Press, 1995), 95, 254.
41. Tim Garton Ash, 'Catching the Wrong Bus? Europe's Future and the Great
    Gamble of Monetary Union', *Times Literary Supplement*, 5 May 1995, 3.
    On the theme of the absent European demos, see more generally J. H. H.
    Weiler, U. Haltern, and F. Mayer, 'European Democracy and its Critique',
    in Jack Hayward (ed.), *The Crisis of Representation in Europe* (London:
    Cass, 1995), 4–24.
42. On the populist nationalism of the Front National, see Nonna Meyer and
    Pascal Perrineau (eds.), *Le Front National à découvert* (Paris: Presses de
    la Fondation Nationale de Sciences Politiques, 1989) and Jack Hayward,
    'Ideological Change: The Exhaustion of the Revolutionary Impetus', in
    Peter A. Hall, J. Hayward, and H. Machin, *Developments in French Pol-
    itics*, rev. edn. (London: Macmillan, 1994), 25–7; cf. 263–5.
43. Quoted from a press report in *Le Monde*, 21 Jan. 1995 by Jean-Louis Saux,
    'Le Retour au peuple de Jacques Chirac'. See also, the articles by Bertrand
    Le Gendre, 'M. Chirac contre les "experts" ' and Ezra Suleiman, 'Les
    Élites et les exclus', *Le Monde*, 13 Jan. 1995. For earlier attacks on
    technocracy in France, see Jacques Ellul, *Le Système technicien* (Paris:
    Calmann-Lévy, 1977) and Yves Lenoir, *Technocratie Française* (Paris,
    Pauvert, 1977).

2

'Losing Touch' in a Democracy: Demands versus Needs

ROBERT E. LANE

Although it may be that journalistic, bureaucratic, and academic élites have 'lost touch with their publics', I will focus on elected élites. For what purpose would elected élites 'keep in touch' with their publics? To be re-elected, of course. But retaining office by elected élites has not, until very recently, been a problem in Europe, and even in the USA the current problem is only among executives and not the legislators of which we are speaking. This volume reveals a concern for something else: in the popular phrase, for the public's alienation, in academic language, for 'the confidence gap', between élites and their publics.[1] (Incidentally, if lack of confidence in parliaments is an indication of 'losing touch', we should observe that in the 1981–90 period there was no increase in 'losing touch' in the nine European countries studied by the European Values Study.[2]) In the final analysis, however, our concern is and should be with the effects of 'losing touch' on the public welfare. What social consequences flow from the alleged distance between elected élites and their publics?

The gravity of these consequences depends on what we mean by 'keeping in touch'. I treat this phrase here as dealing with political representation of two familiar kinds: the *delegate* theory, which emphasizes representatives' responsiveness to public demands, and the *trustee* theory, emphasizing responses to public needs. The distinction between demands and needs is crucial. It is the chopping-block for arguments about the purposes of representation, the fulcrum for theories of democracy, and the lever to pry open the meaning of 'losing

I am greatly indebted to my colleague Robert Dahl who saved me from many errors but could not prevent me from making many others. He is absolved from responsibility for the path I have chosen and thanked for showing me the minefields in the terrain I tread. I also wish to thank Rudolph Premfors, a visitor to Yale from the University of Stockholm, for his helpful advice on the saving values of communication and deliberation.

touch'. This chapter will examine the implications of that distinction, first by explicating the two theories of representation, then by examining the economic and cultural causes of the current support for the individualistic delegate theory. I turn next to the factual premises of the delegate theory, revealing the failure of that theory to comprehend public understandings and capacities. I will show that reliance on public demands for policy in many areas is more disruptive and less humane than reliance on needs. After briefly explaining why elected élites are more likely than their publics to harbour democratic sentiments, I return to the trustee theory, treating the risks in divorcing needs from wants and in licensing representatives to 'think for themselves', and redefining the idea of 'keeping in touch' with the public. I will close with a brief excursion into concepts of moral obligation among legislators. I entreat those readers who think that I am bringing Plato's *Republic* up to date to suspend their disbelief until the end.

1. *Elected Representatives and their Responses to their Publics*

By bringing together theories of representation with new research on public opinion and cognitive psychology, the chapter both strengthens the trustee theory of representation and reveals the political implications of public opinion and cognitive research.[3] The delegate theory of democracy is most familiar: legislators are to do what their constituents ask them to do, or, failing requests, what legislators believe their constituents would approve. The theory comes closest to describing the justification of the American political system, but also has application in European democracies. In so far as constituents think they know *how* public policy may satisfy their wants, the delegate follows instruction on specific policy measures, as well as on the ends to be pursued.

Trustees have fiduciary obligations to their constituents; they must promote the well-being of their constituents as best they, the trustees, know how. In enlisting the trustees' judgement, the distinction between demands and needs becomes important, for trustees are made responsible for the well-being of their constituents, and not just the satisfaction of their wants. To that end, they must keep in touch with these constituents' external circumstances (e.g. poverty) and internal dispositions (e.g. sense of insecurity, alienation), as well as their expressed wants, that is, their demands. In law, the concept of trusteeship, often for a minor or other ward, is well developed, featuring such concepts as

'prudence' and 'due care'. In contrast, although the idea of legislators
as trustees for the well-being of the nation is often accepted (e.g. the
US Constitution contains a 'general welfare' clause, the Federal government holds lands 'in trust' for the people), the concept and its
bounding constraints are not well developed. Legislators, therefore, will
have trouble discovering the appropriate energizing and restraining
injunctions governing their roles as trustees.

Political philosophers bridle at so expansive a term as 'needs', seeing
in it and the trustee theory an unlimited licence for authoritative and
authoritarian interpretation. These fears are understandable (after all,
modern political philosophers are guardians of the democratic process)
but exaggerated. I, at least, am reassured by the use of the concept by
contemporary philosophers and some political practices guided by the
trusteeship doctrine. Both Braybrooke and Griffin have defined human
needs in such a way as to make their wrongful appropriation less likely.[4]
Griffin, who finds 'desire' (or demand) without moral standing, limits
the concept to 'things that we aim at simply as normal human beings
rather than as the particular human beings we are, things that are both
necessary to and sufficient for a recognizably human existence'.[5] Martha
Nussbaum, adopting what she calls an 'Aristotelian essentialist' position, defines quality of life in terms of those 'things are so important
that we will not count a life as a human life without them', and couches
her list in terms of 'being able to . . .', for example, 'being able to live
to the end of a complete human life as far as it is possible . . . to form
a conception of the good and to engage in critical reflection about the
planning of one's own life . . . to live for and with others . . .'.[6] In his
reorientation of the United Nations Human Development Programme,
Amartya Sen has developed what he calls a 'capabilities approach'.
'The capabilities approach to a person's advantage', he says, 'is concerned with evaluating it in terms of his or her actual ability to achieve
various valuable functionings as a part of living. . . . The functionings
relevant for well-being vary from such elementary ones as escaping
morbidity and mortality, being adequately nourished, having mobil-
ity, etc., to complex ones such as being happy, achieving self-respect,
taking part in the life of the community', and so forth.[7] Incidentally,
the UN Human Development Programme is a case of trusteeship
relatively unhampered by the limiting considerations of the delegate
theory.

For whom is the legislative trustee a fiduciary representative: for his
constituents or for his nation as a whole?[8] In federal systems more than

in unitary systems, national legislators may tip the balance toward the nation, but all systems experience these conflicts. Under the rules governing delegates, these representatives would seem to be bound to give their constituencies priority over their nations, but there is a logic covering this familiar issue that drives them towards trusteeship for the nation. Since no nation could survive the parochialism of representatives acting wholly as delegates, and national survival is what most members of every constituency *implicitly* want and, when alerted, demand, we conclude that all representatives will to some degree consider themselves trustees for the nation.[9] To believe that the good of the nation is the sum of the goods of its several constituencies is to commit the fallacy of composition.

There are strong arguments against trusteeship which I will set forth later; in the meantime, let us examine some causes for the strength of the delegate model in contemporary times.

2. The Individualistic Assumptions of the Delegate Role

The delegate theory of representation is based on the belief that the public good is best protected when each person decides for himself about all matters connected to his own welfare. This belief, which I will call 'evaluative individualism', is assumed by market economics (where it serves more as an aid to theory than as a description of reality) together with its allied theories of rational choice in politics, by dominant utilitarian concepts of public welfare, individualistic theories of popular sovereignty, and Western philosophy and law.

The role of market economics in supporting the individualistic delegate theory of representation is substantial. Basically, the model of the (perfect) market stipulates that each individual acts alone in deciding what, on the basis of his own and his household's preferences, he should buy. Demand calls forth supply until demand is satisfied and declines; supply increases until rising marginal costs equal falling marginal demand. Competition regulates price. In the market model, the common good is promoted by a hidden hand aggregating individual decisions and then, somewhat circularly, the model claims that good to be defined by the outcome of these individual decisions. Economists then analogize governmental provision of goods and services to market provisions. For example, Musgrave states that 'the level [of public services] is correct if the social goods provided are such as would be bought and paid for voluntarily by consumers if availability could be made contingent on price payments'.[10]

Influenced by economists, some political theorists also analogize the market's individualistic paradigm to politics: voters call forth a supply of some desired good up to the point where some other good (including private goods) is more desirable to them; the government as supplier responds to these demands, and, as in the market, the common good is thereby achieved. But the analogy is more of a metaphor than a model and suffers from a variety of defects that impair its use to support the delegate theory where politicians, as suppliers, respond like firms to increasing demands. First, the beneficiaries of both public goods and entitlement programmes comprise a much larger group than those making the demands. Or, in reverse, the beneficiaries are often a much smaller group than the circle of those who pay the costs. Thus, the marginal utilities of the beneficiaries and of those who bear the costs are different. A second point is related: whereas the market permits the weighing of costs and benefits within the psyches of *individuals*, politics, as is well known, divorces benefits from costs, thus making the weighing of costs and benefits a *social* rather than an individual matter. Third, and crucial to my argument in favour of trustees, the effective 'demand' is often expressed by bureaucrats and politicians *prior to* the mobilization of demand by publics, as was the case with much New Deal legislation in the USA of the 1930s.

Fourth, members of the public often do not express their 'interests' in political life; indeed, as we shall see, self-interest is rather a rare motive for voting for a given candidate or party. Thus needs are different from demands in one important respect: they may be and often are assessed by people other than the individuals who possess or are said to possess a need. I may disagree with you about your needs, but not about your wants. It is partly for this reason that economists think of needs as 'vulgar',[11] for in the solipsistic code of economists it is impermissible to assess another's state of satisfaction (although it is all right to seek to awaken dissatisfaction). Compared to demands, needs are also inconvenient because their responses to price fluctuations are sluggish and because needs, again as compared to demands, do not register in the market.[12] But these are technical considerations. The facts are that individuals do not know best either the sources or the relative strength of their own well-being compared to that of others.[13] As is documented in the quality-of-life studies (and as we shall see further below), this faith in individuals' self-assessment is not well founded.[14] Although wrong, these assessments are resonant with our perceptions of ourselves. Who is likely to know better than I what my interests are and how they may be satisfied? We shall see.

Fifth, and partly for the above causes, decision-making processes in markets, where feedback is more informative, are quite different from those in politics, with the consequence that the individualistic assumptions of the market do not apply to politics. In short, the economistic assumption that individuals know what is best for them and can take effective action in politics parallel to their actions in the market is inappropriate.

Finally, the concept of the common good in politics is different from that of the market: it embraces market externalitics (such as pure air), ideals (such as equality), and the needs of those without money (that is, without effective market demand), considerations quite different from the forces making for market equilibrium.

The dominant utilitarian philosophy of our time assumes that the common welfare is the sum of individual welfares and that the summation process is more or less as Bentham said it was. This is misleading, for the interaction effect, such as is embodied in Hirsch's theory of 'positional goods', which diminish in their value to an individual when other individuals also have them, is, if not as large as Hirsch thought it was, still substantial.[15]

Fashionable, but I think transient, theories of rational choice make a similar set of assumptions: each person, whether politician, bureaucrat, or private citizen, pursues his self-interest without regard for externalities or communal interests. Only the delegate role is compatible with these individualistic assumptions—and then only if the processes of identification of a legislator with his publics such that he favours their welfare as well as his own is discounted. As for the underlying theory of rationality, the nearly total opposition of cognitive psychologists to this theory of cognitive processes seems to me to dispose of theories of rationality as working hypotheses: when rationalistic theories of decision-making are not tautological they are wrong.[16] Among other reasons for discarding the rationalism of publics are the following: as revealed in the studies of relative deprivation, people are more sensitive to group than to self-deprivation;[17] the 'logic of collective action' fails when 'free-riders' are informed of both their own and others' contributions to the collectivity and when rather simple devices for accountability are installed;[18] and a thorough and careful examination of the empirical evidence for rational choice finds that this evidence collapses when judged by the normal standards of science.[19]

Contemporary concepts of popular sovereignty reinforce these individualistic assumptions. Following the analogy of consumer sovereignty, popular sovereignty in politics becomes the collective expression of individual wants expressed to politicians individually or through the interest groups and parties that speak for individuals. In this version of popular sovereignty, two historical traditions are denied: Rousseau's idea of a general will containing the prescriptions that each person would want enacted if he knew what was best for the general public, and Burke's, de Maistre's, and Oakeshott's appeal to the inherited time-tested traditions of the society. Thus stripped, popular sovereignty has come to mean the unfiltered pronouncements of *vox populi*. To paraphrase Abraham Lincoln, it is government *by* the people, whether or not it is government *for* the people, which 'shall not perish from the earth'.

The political philosophy implicit in the idea of the legislator as delegate is majority rule, which, although we need such a decision rule for the trustees themselves, is nevertheless a philosophy that leaves critical questions unanswered. How shall we come to the point of 'taking rights seriously' if all legislators are delegates bound by constituents' wishes or demands?[20] What independent criteria of good and bad government may be considered by a legislature of delegates? Which of the many public demands shall be given priority, and by what criteria should a delegate choose among them? These and other questions cannot be answered without calling on legal and political philosophers, yet in the doctrine of evaluative individualism philosophy and ethics have no role in political debates other than to justify giving publics what they say they want. Moreover, trusteeship for a nation, which I said was implicit in the idea of informed desires or wants, implies substantive validity for that much abused concept the public interest; that is, it implies that there is a concept of what is best for society that does not entirely or even substantially hinge on the interests of the conceiver. But, a little like Thrasymachus, recent 'realists' have been at pains to point out that the public interest is only a phrase most frequently employed to rationalize group interests.[21] You have guessed the practical answer: delegates are all, to some extent, secret trustees exercising discretion according to their own concepts of their constituents' needs and of the the public interest, while concealing their trusteeship in a welter of claims that they are only doing what their constituents demand.

It is all too easy to caricature both the theory of popular mandates that supports a delegate theory of representation and the theory of fiduciary relations that supports the concept of elected élites as trustees. The delegate theory is congenial to the self-interest of legislators, for, in order to be re-elected, all elected élites and their party leaders must be concerned with appearing to be responsive to the demands of their publics. But also, because of the ambiguity of mandates and because of the requirements of their elected roles, all elected élites, individually or through their parties, must exercise some discretion in dealing with the unarticulated needs of their publics. In balancing these interpretations, I shall first present some evidence of constituents' incapacity to articulate their genuine interests and needs, and then discuss some substantive issues on which élites and their publics differ.

3. The Limited Competence of Individuals

The implicit assumptions regarding human capacities and behaviour underlying the theory of representation by delegates may be set forth as follows: (1) most people know their own best interests and rank them according to their priorities; (2) most people can explain and justify their own acts in terms of their conceived interests; (3) most people know how to advance their interests through public policies; or at least, (4) most people know how to choose candidates who will advance their interests; and (5) most people can monitor the performance of incumbents on matters related to the individual's own interests.[22] None of these assumptions survive current research on individual cognition and decision-making.

1. *Most people know their own best interests and rank them according to their priorities.* Of the many tests of this proposition, perhaps the test of transitivity (if x is preferred to y, and y to z, then x must be preferred to z) is the most telling. Economists *assume* transitivity as a necessary condition for rational choice. Experimental work with animals reveals a high level of transitivity, and some experiments with students also support the economists' assumptions. For example, when students are offered a series of choices of dating-partners they generally choose transitively.[23] But other studies show a systematic failure to choose transitively. One reason is that people are risk-averse with respect to gains and risk-accepting with respect to preventing losses,

even when the amount of money or lives or some other good is the same.[24] Another reason is that people cognitively compartmentalize their goods, sometimes violating the idea that money, as Schumpeter said, is simply the most saleable of all commodities. Thus, an experiment by Tversky and Kahneman shows that if subjects had purchased a ticket to the theatre for £10 and lost the ticket, they would not purchase another, but if they lost £10 they would. The authors report that their research illuminates 'decision problems in which people systematically violate the requirements of consistency and coherence',[25] that is, of transitivity in making choices.

Studies of subjective well-being or happiness support this doubt. Most people believe that they would be happy if only they had about 25 per cent more income, but these studies show conclusively that their beliefs are unfounded. These 'dreamers', we will say, are at level x. But those who enjoy income at a level 125 per cent of x are no happier than the dreamers at level x. Above the poverty level, there is virtually no relationship between level of income and level of subjective well-being or satisfaction with one's life. Elsewhere I have called this the *economistic fallacy* and explained its sources in both history and economics.[26] The consequence of this fallacy is that people slight the activities that genuinely do contribute to a sense of well-being: family life, friendship, and intrinsic enjoyment of work.[27] A review of studies of people's pursuit of happiness concludes: 'Simply put, they [most studies] suggest that people do not know what makes them happy and what makes them unhappy.'[28] The consequence is that the principal premiss of evaluative individualism, and therefore of the belief that people know their own best interests, is severely undermined and with it the delegate theory of representation.

2. *Most people can explain and justify their own acts in terms of their conceived interests.* There is a substantial body of evidence showing that people who seek to explain their acts cannot refer to internal cognitive or affective processes, which are no more available to their conscious minds than are the workings of their nervous systems. Rather, they borrow from their cultures available explanations of why, under similar circumstances, *anyone* might do what they did. Because the 'privileged information' derived from insight into the self is generally missing, people are often to themselves as outside observers.[29] Under these circumstances, it is the person, whether self or other, with the best theory of behaviour who can best predict and explain a person's course of action. If that 'other' is a legislator, we would hope

that he is a trustee, rather than a delegate who is bound to accept constituents' own interpretations of their behaviour.

Like explanations, justifications of behaviour rely on a set of misleading processes. For example, as people justify their choices—to themselves as well as to others—they manipulate their perceptions to ease the pain of believing they made a mistake. In a process called 'post-decision dissonance reduction', they exaggerate both the benefits of the chosen course of action and the defects of the courses of action not chosen.[30] When this process is added to a more general set of self-serving biases, we quickly understand why self-justification is rarely as persuasive as justification of a person's acts by outsiders.

3. *Most people know how to advance their interests through public policies.* Of course, farmers 'know' that higher support prices are in their interest, and employed workers 'know' that minimum-wage legislation will increase the wages of marginal workers. But élites also know that farm subsidies in, for example, the USA, encourage larger and more harmful farm subsidies in the European Community (whereas American farmers would probably be better off in a world with no subsidies) and that minimum-wage legislation may threaten unemployment for some of these same marginal workers because their work is no longer worth the higher costs to an employer. That is, legislative élites have available information on the *indirect* effects of public policies, effects which are sometimes over the perceptual horizon of most of the affected publics. Or, more likely, their lobbyists serve the short-term interests of their employers without regard to the whole class of persons they ostensibly represent. Legislators simply have more research available to them than do members of their publics.

4. *Most people know how to choose candidates who will advance their interests.* This is the place to bring forward evidence that members of the public seem not to act in a self-interested way in voting and opinion formation. Sears and Funk offer a thorough review of the (largely American) evidence that those with higher stakes in a policy outcome generally behave no differently from those with lower or no stakes in that outcome. These authors examined attitudes on a variety of issues, controlling for plausible demographic variables and underlying predispositions. They found: on issues dealing with the financing of schools, the attitudes and behaviour of people with children in school were little or no different from those of people without children in school; on issues involving the school busing of African-American children to

mostly white schools, the attitudes of people with affected children
were little different from those of people whose children were not
affected by the busing; on issues involving affirmative action, that is,
the promotion of employment of women in areas of predominantly
male employment or of African Americans in areas of predominantly
white employment, the attitudes of people whose jobs might be affected
by policies of affirmative action were minimally different from those of
people whose jobs were not affected; on issues of government support
for full employment, the attitudes of the unemployed were only trivially
different from those of people who held jobs (but on issues of job
security, people who felt their jobs were in jeopardy did have attitudes
different from those of people with secure jobs).[31]

In contrast, on the crucial issue of taxation, self-interested attitudes
and voting patterns were, indeed, evident. Reviewing many studies,
including one of the California constitutional amendment that strictly
limited the power of the State of California to raise taxes,[32] Sears and
Funk report: 'In almost all these cases . . . taxpayers' self-interest in
real ballot or legislative propositions have significantly influenced their
support for them.'[33] But they report a variety of other studies finding
'almost no evidence for self-interested attitudes on the part of taxpayers'
and 'no effects of home ownership on opposition to local property tax
increases for the schools'.[34]

Shifting from the explanation of tax-related self-interest to the ex-
hibition of self-interest by public employees where their jobs were at
stake, Sears and Funk found some evidence of self-interested attitudes
and voting behaviour, but when they came to recipients of public services
(including welfare services) and 'the generally economically discontented', they found 'very little evidence' of self-interest. On issues of
old-age pensions, public health insurance for the elderly, energy conser-
vation, inflation, and crime victimization, the affected publics revealed
no opinions different from those not affected.[35] Both US and European
studies find that people's perceptions of their own family financial situations have 'only a small effect' on voting behaviour. Businessmen
might be expected to be especially responsive to the appeals of self-
interest, and, indeed, they are when threatened by *impending* regulation. But, compared to businesses not regulated by the particular rules
in question, before the new rules were proposed and after they have
been established, the correlations between their political attitudes and
their imputed self-interest are 'generally non-significant'.[36]

After pursuing these inquiries into a variety of other matters, including fear of war, having been oneself or having a member of one's
family in active service in Vietnam, various allegations of 'pocket-
book' voting, and other matters, Sears and Funk 'conclude . . . that
personal self-interest generally has not been of major importance in
explaining the general public's social and political attitudes'.[37] But they
exempt certain tax issues and the behaviour of public employees from
this general conclusion.

What, then, organizes attitudes and guides political behaviour? By
and large, it is what Sears and his colleagues call *symbolic predispositions:* attitudes towards parties (still significant in the 1990s[38]), race,
nation and, to a lesser extent, general liberal conservative ideology.
These are learned early, crystallized in late adolescence, and tend to
persist, with a little erosion due to changed circumstances, throughout
a person's lifetime.[39] For example, it was attitudes towards race rather
than the exposure of a people's children to the effects of busing that
influenced attitudes towards busing. Moreover, Sears and Funk found
that where self-interested political behaviour was evident, e.g. among
taxpayers and public employees, self-interested responses failed to alter
these symbolic predispositions. Where they occurred, self-interested
responses turned out to be *ad hoc* and cognitively narrow.[40]

In the light of these findings, the proposition that 'most people know
how to choose candidates who will advance their interests' must refer
to a different set of 'interests'. The proposition now means choosing
candidates or parties that will reflect a person's general orientations
towards parties, race, nation, and ideology, a cognitively easier choice.
Yet even this choice is modified by the fact that in many countries it
is candidates for whom one votes, not just positions and policies and
parties, and there is substantial evidence that voters are influenced by
the inferred personalities of these candidates.[41] In parliamentary systems where one votes for party lists without knowing which of the
candidates on the list will actually serve, the personality of the party
leader has a similar if weaker 'distracting' influence. It is much harder
to know how to advance one's 'interests', or even one's symbolic predispositions, when these are filtered through candidate preferences.

The point is not that democratic processes fail to register relevant
preferences, but rather that the premises of a theory of representation
by delegates, or by cohesive parties whose legislative members think of
themselves as filling the role of delegates, have a weak empirical basis.

Legislative representatives and their party leaders must inevitably interpret for themselves what the voters *need* from a set of ambiguous demands. That is, to some extent all representatives must be trustees. 5. *Most people can monitor the performance of incumbents on matters related to the individual's own interests.* Setting aside the ambiguity surrounding both voters' knowledge of their own 'interests' and their pursuit of these 'interests' in electoral behaviour, this proposition calls for additional cognitive skills: voters must be able to follow legislative events so as to punish their enemies and reward their friends— the theory of retrospective voting. At the outset, this proposition confronts certain knowledge deficiencies among the electorate: only a little over half of the voters in both Britain and the USA know the names of their legislative representatives. Also, in the USA a large number of voters do not know which party controls the Senate or the House of Representatives, making retrospective voting extremely difficult. This problem is less urgent in parliamentary systems where a majority party controls the legislature, but it is still a problem where a diversified coalition is in control. Moreover, even if voters know which candidates or parties are responsible for the policies they wanted to advance or retard, voters' party loyalties and, to a lesser extent, beliefs about candidates' personalities, makes it difficult to reward and punish incumbents effectively. In short, the feedback system of democratic politics is, as Schumpeter said, less effective than the market's feedback system where personal experience with a product in a more transparent set of transactions provides better information on what to do next time.[42] One consequence of failed feedback is (or recently has been and no doubt will be again) increased tenure for legislative incumbents.

Almost thirty years ago V. O. Key, Jr. put forward what he called 'the perverse and unorthodox argument . . . that voters are not fools'. For example, Key found that voting decisions closely corresponded to policy preferences, people who switched parties revealing more policy differences from their former parties than the party loyalists.[43] They are not 'fools' in that sense. More recently Benjamin Page and Robert Shapiro wrote in a similar vein of the 'rational public', basing this judgement on fifty years of public opinion surveys. In order to support their 'commitment to democracy', these authors argued that policy preferences are 'rational in the sense that they are *real*' (not meaningless or random), 'generally *stable*' (i.e. rarely fluctuating back and forth), '*coherent* and mutually consistent . . . [with patterns that] *make sense*

in terms of underlying values', '*understandable*', '*predictable*' (in their
response to events), and 'constitute *sensible* adjustments to the new conditions'.[44] Although the work uses survey data to support inferences
that are quite inaccessible to surveys,[45] it is persuasive in showing that
opinions are often responsive to news reports, that voting decisions
are often consistent with policy preferences, that demographic groups
tend to support politicians who, in turn, favour these groups, and that
occupational changes can be shown to account for many changes in
public opinion. By focusing on majorities, the authors are able to avoid
accounting for often large minorities that do not show these 'rational'
tendencies. Where there are defects, Page and Shapiro tend to blame
the media, failure of education, manipulation by politicians, and other
matters external to the public.

What Key, Page and Shapiro, and others writing in this vein do not
show is that people know their own best interests and can rank them,
can explain and justify their own acts on the basis of their *own* interests rather than those of conventional others, can assess the indirect
consequences of policies they prefer, and choose candidates who will
advance their material interests (as contrasted to their party preferences and symbolic interests). To some extent they can monitor the
performance of incumbents, switching to another party when dissatisfied with a current state of affairs, but even such negative retrospective
voting risks supporting a party even less favourable to their perceived
values. Of course, the analysis of these processes does not touch the
issue raised in the next section, namely, the less humane, less democratic, and less tolerant views of the less educated compared to the
more educated. And the rationality of non-voting is only the 'rationality' of public choice: voting is more trouble for the individual than it
is worth.

To find that one's 'commitment to democracy' is satisfied by the
quite sensible findings of Key and of Page and Shapiro is strange. In
an era of homelessness, rising crime-rates, poor schools, deteriorating
infrastructure (roads, bridges, and sewers), growing inequality, drug
abuse, a television wasteland of violence and titillation, and, above all,
chronic unemployment, one may say that the public behaves 'rationally'
in a logical sense but one would have to add that this kind of 'rationality'
is not enough and that it is not reasonable to wait for a public 'mandate'—except in a spirit of indifference to the needs of the public. The
analysis is the triumph of a concern for process over outcomes—and
for polling over the more basic research on cognition.

4. *Where Opinions of Élites and Publics Differ*

Delegates are uniquely reliant on the opinions of mass publics; trustees are more reliant on their own inferences from multiple sources of evidence—including, of course, what the public says it wants. From the large literature on the way opinions of less educated publics and more educated élites differ,[46] I will select eight themes for brief exploration. These are not, of course, new discoveries of the characteristics of mass opinion; the purpose of illustrating them here is to shed light on the meaning of 'keeping in touch with the public' and therefore on the problem of political representation. For this purpose I will rely upon two chapters in this volume (3, by Miller, Timpson, and Lessnoff; and 10, by Bosanquet) and two compendious sources of public opinion research: the Center for Election Studies (CES) of the University of Michigan and the European Values Studies (EVS) of 1981 (and 1990).[47] Although the prevalence of the attitudes and behaviour reported differ by country, the direction of the educational effects seems to be similar in most of the Western countries studied (see Table 2.1). Compared to political élites, mass publics are:

1. *Less interested in politics and less likely to discuss politics*. A special compilation of data from the EVS on Italy and Germany gives Table 2.1. The same source shows that education has similar effects on a variety of other measures of political involvement in these and other countries.[48]

2. *Less supportive of open discussion of conflicting opinion and more willing to forbid discussion of policy issues considered to be 'sensitive'*. In this volume Miller, Timpson, and Lessnoff reveal several substantive areas where mass publics are more willing to ban discussion than are university graduates and politicians: defence plans, health plans, and to some extent, economic plans.[49] Support for restricting the press was also greater among mass publics than among politicians in treatments of 'dramatic crimes' and 'crimes among blacks' (but not 'racial–religious incitement').

3. *Less tolerant and more punitive towards disliked groups*. Ever since the 1950s it has been known that the less well educated are more intolerant of outgroups. Recently the CES report revealed how this is expressed in current American politics: (*a*) support for 'civil rights leaders' (mostly African Americans) in pressing for greater rights increases markedly with level of education (Miller, Timpson, and Lessnoff report that British university graduates were *more* willing to ban 'racial

Robert E. Lane

TABLE 2.1. *Interest in and discussion of politics by level of education in Italy and Germany 1988 (%)*

	Age at which education completed			
	12 or younger	13–15	16–19	20 or older
Not at all interested in politics:				
Italy	68	50	31	19
Germany	29	14	11	5
Never discuss politics with friends:				
Italy	65	51	34	15
Germany	39	25	16	9

Source: Italy and Germany: A Dual Portrait with the Tools of Social Research, special collection of EVS data comp. for Seminar at Villa Vignoni, 20–3 Nov. 1988, 70–1. Courtesy of Juan Linz, Yale University.

incitement' than mass publics—a reversal of their relative positions on media licence on other issues. These authors note that support for censorship has strong ideological or consequentialist components); (*b*) support for 'desegregation' (as contrasted to 'segregation') of African Americans increases markedly with level of education—but note that neither support for racial integration in schools nor support for busing children in order to integrate schools is related to level of education.

4. *Less likely to support legal due process for people accused of crimes.* In a society alarmed by high or rising crime-rates, the protection of the rights of the accused seem to the less well educated to be 'coddling criminals' and to release criminals back into the streets where they may commit further crimes. The CES report shows that the United States is just such a society: support for legal protection of the rights of the accused (as contrasted to 'stopping crime') increases somewhat with level of education.

5. *Morally more rigid and conventional, moralistic, and more ready to make categorical moral judgements.* The increased levels of education attained by the publics of the USA and Western Europe since the Second World War have confounded age and education. A French report on the EVS disentangles these influences and shows that in France, although age is the stronger force, more education tends to increase support for 'permissiveness' (as contrasted to stricter discipline) in

socialization and to increase feelings of uncertainty (dependence on circumstances) in defining good and bad conduct.[50] In the USA the CES report reveals the effect of education on another facet of conventional morality: (*a*) support for policies designed to equalize the roles of women and men increases markedly with level of education; (*b*) support for legislation restricting women's rights to abortion decreases dramatically with level of education.

6. *More nationalistic and less international in outlook.* The EVS asked respondents the degree of pride they felt in being nationals of their respective countries. The answer 'very proud' declines generally with level of education and 'not at all proud' rises sharply with more advanced (university) education. In the CES report: (*a*) support for US involvement in foreign affairs (as contrasted with the view that 'US should not concern itself with foreign affairs') increases dramatically with level of education; (*b*) support for foreign aid increases markedly with level of education.

Towards the end of the Cold War (1986), support for 'co-operation' (as contrasted to 'getting tougher') with the Soviet Union increased somewhat with level of education.

In Europe, the greater nationalism of mass publics compared to elected élites is seen in the greater support for the Maastricht Treaty by parliaments than by publics in referendums in Denmark and France.

7. *Less able to weigh the costs of policies supported.* A variant between publics and political élites is suggested by the problems posed in Bosanquet's chapter in this volume. Bosanquet's argument and evidence show that the public fails to balance the cost of one public policy against the cost of another; it also fails to balance costs against resources and does not understand the effect of the implied tax or deficit on the social allocation of resources and the productivity of the system. But, as revealed in a different study, even in those instances where costs are given (in opinion surveys and special studies), the public seems insensitive to these costs, revealing a much lower 'price elasticity' for public goods than for private goods.[51]

8. *The instability and inconsistency of mass opinion in the face of counter-arguments.* Using a split sample technique, Miller, Timpson, and Lessnoff were able to assess the effects on support for constraints on a free press of appeals to 'the national interest'. Results show that these appeals were substantially more effective in increasing the support of the mass public, as contrasted to support by politicians, for banning publication of defence plans and health plans, presumably

because élites were already familiar with the arguments in each case. And again, compared to politicians, mass publics were more influenced by arguments claiming that dramatic crime-reporting may 'increase crime' and may interfere with 'fair trials'.[52] With respect to both censorship of government plans and to crime-reporting, the public's greater vulnerability to arguments suggests a less stable, and therefore probably less well considered, set of opinions than those held by political élites.

Other studies show that when people who take a policy position contrary to their basic values are exposed to counter-arguments, these counter-arguments tend to be *more* effective in changing the opinions of the educated than the uneducated because the educated are more able to see the relevance of the principles involved.[53] Thus, it is *consistency* rather more than stability that characterizes the opinions of better-educated publics.

In sum, delegates, bound to follow the demands rather than the needs of their publics, will be less supportive of free speech, less tolerant of unpopular groups, less supportive of legal due process, morally more rigid, more nationalistic, less prudent in finances, and less consistent in their policy preferences and expenditure patterns than political élites now are.

5. Why Élites and Publics Disagree

Demographic 'explanations' have been said to be 'explaining by giving social addresses'; that is, locating a differential incidence of something demographically does not, in fact, explain why people with different social addresses respond differently. To move from social addresses to causal explanations, let us look at the way education, income, and holding public office influence attitudes and cognitions.

Education

Education is confounded in the CES and most EVS reports with level of income, but even with income controlled, we know that racial prejudice, opposition to abortion rights for women, opposition to civil liberties and the rights of the accused, opposition to equal rights for women, and American isolationism in foreign policy including opposition to foreign aid are all greatly reduced by education beyond high-school level.[54] So is the general personality syndrome of authoritarianism which informs many of these attitudes.[55] In the chapter by Miller, Timpson, and Lessnoff, which contrasts the opinions of mass publics with the opinions of university graduates and politicians, two other variables might be confounded, level of education and role in public life; both were effective in increasing support for open government and in reducing the effect of appeals to 'the national interest', but, because graduates and politicians tended to agree, the evidence suggests that the role of education was more important than the role of public office.[56]

Education achieves these effects in a variety of ways, a few of which we may briefly mention here. It reduces reliance on the immediate and the perceptual, thus permitting consideration of things distant in time and place,[57] e.g. the longer-term future and the experience of other countries. It permits holding preferences in suspension while analysing the actual problems at hand.[58] One way of doing this is to make it possible to accept disliked features in liked objects and liked features in disliked objects, that is, learning to tolerate the pain of cognitive dissonance.[59] Education facilitates both analysis of problems into its component parts and also reintegrating the parts into complex wholes.[60] And formal education is only the beginning. Hyman, Wright, and Reed comment: 'If we accept the argument that formal schooling before adulthood is preparation of a lifetime of learning, then our data present strong evidence for the conclusion that our schools are achieving this goal to an observed degree.'[61]

Social democrats (American liberals) are torn between two honourable values: equality and education. In their desire for equality they like to think of mass publics as having qualities these publics do not have. Hence, they can support the delegate theory of representation as a way of serving the *demands* of the public without facing its consequences. On the other hand, these same social democrats fear the élitist implications of acknowledging the political merits of their other value, education. The trustee model is more candid. Acknowledging the limitations of the less well educated, that model restores the value of education, attends to the *needs* of the public, perhaps thereby risking, but for the reasons given, more likely further promoting, the goal of greater equality, or, as I prefer, the relief of poverty.

Higher Income and Greater Economic Security

The insecurity created by lower income is reflected in the following CES data: in 1986 (a year of relative prosperity) the proportion of people anticipating that next year would be better declines with each decline in level of education. Measured by an index representing those anticipating that their financial situations would be better next year minus the proportion believing that their situations would be worse, the picture goes from optimism to increasing pessimism: college (university) +9; high school −6; grade school −11.[62] Feelings of insecurity lead people to retrench, to move more cautiously, to limit imagination and exploration.[63] Although the poor do not worry more than the better-off, their worries are usually less tractable and soluble; they are more anxious. 'Since anxiety reduces the range of cues attended to . . . anxious people find that their precious attentional resources are even more limited than usual, precisely when they can ill afford to be worrying instead of working.'[64] Poverty and economic insecurity are stressful and 'people under stress are more susceptible to illness, depression, anxiety, low self-confidence, and dissatisfaction than are people not experiencing stress'.[65] Low income is associated with lower sense of efficacy and lower levels of self-attribution (belief that one is the cause of one's own fate). Low self-attribution, in turn, is associated with lower than average political participation, belief (for African Americans) in the impossibility of peaceful social change, low interpersonal trust, general expectation of failure, low achievement (in cross-cultural tests), heightened reactions to stress, pessimism, and lower self-esteem.[66]

Consider the fact that fear of the power of the federal government decreases markedly with level of education (CES). Given that tax and transfer policies are the government's way of helping the unemployed and the 'working poor', the greater fear of the power of the federal government by the less well educated seems to confirm my earlier discussion of the failure of self-interest to guide political opinions. But the larger point is not that the less well educated fear the government more than the better-educated but that they fear the power of *all* agencies (except, marginally, unions) more than do the better-educated. They fear what they do not understand (low political information), what they cannot control (external attribution), what threatens to disturb their adaptation to their current situations. And the dominant response to fear is avoidance, in this case avoidance of involvement with government at any level.[67]

The answer to the deleterious consequences of poverty and insecurity, with their attendant stress and external attribution, is not government by the rich and secure but relief of the insecurity of the poor, or better still, the relief of poverty itself. Nevertheless, political élites, who rarely suffer from financial insecurity, although their jobs are periodically up for auction, are in a position where they can interpret the needs of their poorer publics and, under favourable circumstances, take steps to relieve the consequences of poverty in ways that the poor and insecure cannot themselves anticipate or comprehend, let alone demand.

Holding Public Office

The characteristics of political élites derive from (1) self-selection, including motivation, (2) public acceptance and support, and (3) the role requirements of office. Although there is a considerable literature on the motivation of those who enter politics, much of it reflecting the 'compensatory hypothesis', that is, the desire for office to compensate for low self-esteem, this hypothesis seems to have earned a well-deserved burial. In fact, those political leaders in the USA who have been examined have a slightly higher self-esteem than others—about the same as equivalent business leaders.[68] Nor is it the case that they are more power-orientated than others; by projective tests of the 'need for power' it appears that students planning to go into politics have a lower power-orientation than have those planning to enter teaching.[69] In another study of power motivation and achievement motivation, state and local political figures scored about the same as a sample of businessmen, with some indication that in both groups those who succeeded were somewhat higher in power and achievement motivations than those who remained at relatively low levels.[70] The authoritarian personality has a special relation to power: contemptuous of the powerless and servile to the powerful. A small study of South Carolina legislators found that these public figures were less authoritarian than the general public.[71] From this brief and inadequate review, one may infer that wherever they have been assessed, the motivation and training in office of political élites does not seem to reflect the pathologies sometimes attributed to them.

I know of relatively few studies comparing legislators with matched publics, but some time ago (1965), Hadley Cantril queried legislators and educated publics in six countries about their interests and concerns. He found (especially for the less developed countries) that legislators 'showed somewhat more concern with their country's position [in the world] and were more concerned [about] assurance of its independence'. As Bosanquet's data also suggest, 'parliamentarians on the whole exhibit a greater sensitivity to the problems of achieving and ensuring an efficient, balanced, and stable government'. Parliamentarians in less developed countries were 'more aware of the need to lift the nation up economically through greater technological advancement'. On the other hand, they 'showed a somewhat narrower range of concerns than did the most educated citizens [because], being elected from local districts . . . they must utilize their positions to get attention to and benefits for the problems facing their local constituents'.[72] That is, in this respect they were delegates.

I have found no studies of the educational effects of the role requirements of legislative office. To fill that vacuum (and risking the charge that I am comparing idealized legislators with actual laymen), let me quote from Graham Wallas's impression of how British parliamentarians must change from particularistic to universalistic cognitive patterns: 'Now the first virtue required in government is the habit . . . of looking . . . through a list of candidates for an appointment and weighting the qualifications of the man whom one has never met by the same standards as those of the man whom one has met, and like or pitied, the day before.'[73] John Stuart Mill argues against short-term self-interest in politics in much the same way. We do not know the degree to which such standards of fairness prevail in the face of pressures to reward followers and to build up party support, but at least it is the case in the USA that 'affirmative action' to increase the proportions of minorities and women holding jobs is more evident in the federal bureaucracy than in private firms and that this policy is fully supported by Congress. When Harry Truman, from a border state then marked by strong prejudice against African Americans, became President, he took dramatic steps to desegregate the armed services. As he explained, 'I am president of *all* the people.'

In this set of scattered examples of the personality attributes of legislators and executives and of their ways of responding to the requirements of office in the face of opposing or indifferent publics, one other point is relevant to the public intolerance and failure to support legal due process mentioned above. 'Political elites are more favorable than the public at large to civil liberties in concrete situations.' Moreover, the political élites tend to pass on these tolerant views to their children,[74] suggesting that the support of civil liberties is not merely learned in office but is something these élites bring to their offices.

6. The Trustee Role Revisited

The trustee model is vulnerable to many kinds of criticism, each with only a partial rebuttal. Contemporary history has not encouraged trusteeship. Given the major corruption revealed in Italian and Japanese politics in the mid-1990s, the indulgent yielding to current demands for low taxes insufficient to meet expenditures in US and British politics, the vulnerability of French and US legislators to pressure from special interests, and, above all, the failure of OECD politicians to take responsibility for the full employment of their publics—given these deficiencies, it is easy to ridicule the idea of legislators as trustees at this time. Moreover, in these days of a large 'confidence gap' revealed in attitudes towards politicians (and others, too),[75] the trustee is not likely to receive the one thing indispensable to the role, public trust. Accepting for the moment the premiss of many chapters in this volume, we might say that having lost touch with their publics, legislative élites cannot now expect their publics to have much confidence in the élite's judgements. Alienation, if that is the proper term, feeds on itself, preventing its own solution.

These considerations lead to a fundamental point: political prescriptions must vary according to the culture and social requirements of the times; they are not, like the *Republic*, eternal statements based on readings of an eternal human nature. In Europe in the nineteenth century and in Latin America today, one might modify the prescribed balance between responsiveness to public demands and responsiveness to some combination of conscience and the findings of social research. Both values and facts are important. (I deal with values and conscience below.) Where there is a tradition of the rule of law and where social science is institutionalized and protected, the hoary arguments for 'government by the people' must be modified. Prior to social research, opinions were more or less equal in that anybody's 'facts' were as good as anybody else's. The social and policy research available to, if not always used by, legislators, changes that.[76] I cannot believe those critics who hold that the investment in policy research has all been in vain. In any event, all policies are experiments moderated by experience: if 'supply-side economics' turns out to be deficit-financing in periods of prosperity, thrusting additional burdens on publics coming only a few years later, over time the results are noted. And if state ownership of the means of production leads to swollen bureaucracies, that too is noted.

Is it the case that my arguments against the delegate theory of representation leads inevitably to the discard of elections themselves? It is not. Elections legitimize regimes; they indicate levels and sources of discontent (without specifying remedies); they validate the idea that it is the welfare of the public and not the welfare of the legislators that is at stake; they give to participants a sense of control over what happens to them (as psychological research shows, even the 'illusion of control', as in selecting a lottery ticket, is rewarding);[77] they reinforce and sometimes alter impressions on which party stands for what; and they are occasions for informing some portions of the public on the contested issues and proposed solutions, even if this information is heard and noted only by the educated élite. None of this is jeopardized by the trustee theory of representation.

What I am arguing for is the development of a culture of, and role specifications for, parliaments whose members think of themselves as trustees for the welfare of their constituents and nations, responsible for what happens to them whether or not their publics know precisely why 'the shoe pinches'.

Consider the following arguments against trusteeship.

1. *Trusteeship opens the door to abuses of power.* Released from moral obligation to accept public demands as binding guides to policy advocacy, trustees are free to employ their power to advance their own partisan, perhaps self-serving, interests. In rebuttal, one may say that because of its fiduciary ethos, trusteeship also restrains the kind of abuse of power common among delegates whose interpretation of their roles often leads to a kind of inauthenticity, the characteristic abuse of power which mimics but does not serve the authentic delegate model. Knowing that voters are usually poorly informed about legislators' voting records, legislative élites often offer only symbolic rewards to their less organized constituents or seek to satisfy their publics by 'taking positions' without actually promoting the desired policies.[78]

Because élites are richer and more educated than their publics, the trustee system loads the dice in favour of the rich and more educated; that is, it leads to inegalitarian outcomes. But it is the Left, rarely cited for superior wealth, that espouses a needs approach to politics and fosters a welfare state owing much, at least historically, to the intervention of bureaucratic and political élites.[79]

2. *The trustee model robs publics of their sense of control over their own lives.* To be in control of one's life is not so much a matter of

controlling the policy preferences of politicians as it is to be free from the exigencies of economic want and economic insecurity discussed above.[80] The divorce of what is called 'internal political efficacy', the belief that one is effective in politics, and 'external political efficacy', the belief that politicians care about what the public thinks and are responsive to public needs,[81] is modest testimony to the difference between a sense of personal control and a sense of political control.

3. *The trustee model deprives publics of incentives to participate in politics, breeding apathy.* The literature on turn-out does not reveal any significant influence of perceptions that political élites are more concerned with inarticulate needs than with articulated demands.[82] If anything, perception that politicians care about the well-being of their publics, even to the extent of seeming to jeopardize their chances of re-election, stimulates political interest.

4. *The trustee model loads responsibilities on élites that they cannot handle.* The fact is that expert élites themselves often do not know how to translate problems into policies. Or, if they have a rough idea, they find it hard to predict the side-effects or externalities of the policies recommended or adopted. Recently, when Britain was forced out of the European Exchange Rate Mechanism many economists predicted inflation, but a year later the apparent result was not inflation but modestly accelerated economic growth. When President Bush ordered US troops into Somalia, he declared that this was a short-term intervention designed only to promote the distribution of aid to a starving people. A year later the troops had been expanded and were engaged in suppressing militant obstruction by the same warlords who had prevented distribution in the first place. In claiming that élites sometimes have a better grasp than do their publics on the indirect effects of a policy but sometimes cannot themselves anticipate outcomes, I offer only weak support for the trusteeship model, but no support at all for the delegate model of representation.

5. *Élites elected because of their party or regional or ethnic identifications are not recruited in such a way as to be properly vested with the powers of trustees for their publics.* The point is not well taken, for if élites were elected by their constituents because of these constituents' parochial or ethnocentric views, we would be better off if these élites were to see their roles to be those of trustees and not those of delegates. In violating the prejudiced demands of their constituents, would a trustee be electorally punished? There is some evidence to suggest that legislators have considerable room for discretion: even in the American

system, which most closely resembles the delegate model of representation, there is a substantial area wherein a legislator can depart from
constituents' demands without incurring electoral punishment.[83]

6. *Compared to* ad hoc *opinions, the superiority of opinions reflecting deliberation can be best assured by encouraging public deliberation.* I have tried to avoid utopianism and piety in my account and
to credit my opponents with a similar effort. Parliaments are deliberat-
ive bodies; publics are not. At least in the USA, of all the activities
members of the public engage in, public affairs is the one they like
least.[84]

7. *All of the defects of cognition which are found among the general
public also infect the all-too-human élites.* But, because of their greater
education, their greater access to research, their frequent discussion of
issues, and their responsibilities for dealing directly with policy problems, these defects are reduced. As Bryce once said of democracy, its
chief virtue is not that it is an ideal form of government but that there
is nothing better. So is it with the model of trusteeship in representative
democracy.

7. Moral Obligations of Legislative Roles

How can we justify the behaviour of a legislator who keeps in touch
with relevant publics in the delegate's sense of responding to their
demands but who fails to keep in touch with these publics in the sense
of responding to their needs? What is an acceptable justification for
addressing demands but not needs?

A justification for failing to accept responsibility for the general
welfare of one's constituents has many possible expressions. In spite of
the clarifications of Griffin, Nussbaum, and Sen mentioned earlier, there
remain deep ambiguities in the very concept of need, ambiguities that
reach into concepts of personality, society, well-being, and justice. But
assuming that one can identify needs in the broad sense of security
from hunger, lack of shelter, illness, ignorance, loneliness, there are the
further dilemmas of priority: which needs come first? whose needs
come first? There are the dilemmas of what Boulding calls 'traps':[85]
does serving a short-term need lead to longer-term dependency—the
'poverty trap', but also the 'infant-industries trap'. Recently Hardin has
argued that for any act of altruism there must be an equally moral
concern for the effect of that act upon the character of the recipient:[86]

does a government provision corrupt the person provided for (asked only of the poor)? The earlier discussion of evaluative individualism gives other dilemmas: should we not rely upon the 'needy' individuals themselves to claim their needs? And, of paternalism: it is paternalistic and an act of supererogation for governments to advise people what they need. There are also plausible theories of general welfare that inhibit serving constituents' needs in particular cases: perhaps Bosanquet's arguments regarding the effects of welfare on productivity would qualify. A variety of more or less legitimate justifications are easily found—and some illegitimate ones as well. Utilitarians fear the 'utility monster' who claims that he has an infinite variety of needs demanding to be served—but we have here entered into the delegate's realm of demands. Another false plea is based on the ignorance of the legislator. The theory of democracy relying on public mandates does not require a legislator to *know* the public's needs, but other versions of democratic theory would say that a legislator is negligent if he does not at least know the circumstances of his constituents: he *should* have known.[87]

The point I wish to make is that pleading a delegate theory of the legislative role in the face of public exigency is not morally persuasive. It would not be an acceptable defence to say, in effect, 'I am not responsible for the welfare of my constituents except as they press me for action'; that is, 'I am a delegate and not a trustee'. Acknowledging all the ambiguity of the legislative role, I do not believe this distinction has sufficient moral weight to serve as a defence. One reason is that, unlike the satisfaction of needs, the satisfaction of either one's own or one's constituents' wants or demands has no necessary moral standing except as it bears on the fulfilment of a contract or promise. But that defence is invalid in the sense that one cannot promise to ignore needs without at the same time promising to violate a more general obligation to help others when one can. In the broader moral theory of responsibility, to know of some impending harm to another and to fail to take remedial action when one might do so is considered more culpable than mere negligence. I would argue that a member of the legislative élite is morally culpable when he fails to seek to remedy the plight of his constituents.

Unhappily, the specification of the role requirements of a legislator are vague, vaguer than the role requirements of a civil servant or even a journalist. It is time to clarify, and if necessary to extend, the role obligations of elected élites.

NOTES

1. Seymour Martin Lipset and William Schneider, *The Confidence Gap: Business, Labor and Government in the Public Mind* (New York: Free Press, 1983).
2. Sheena Ashford and Noel Timms, *What Europe Thinks: A Study of European Values* (Aldershot: Dartmouth, 1992), 92.
3. For theories of representation, see e.g. Hannah Pitkin, *The Concept of Representation* (Berkeley: University of California Press, 1967); Robert A. Dahl, *Democracy and its Critics* (New Haven: Yale University Press, 1989); Bruce Cain, John Ferejohn, and Morris Fiorina, *The Personal Vote: Constituency Service and Electoral Independence* (Cambridge, Mass.: Harvard University Press, 1987); J. Roland Pennock and John W. Chapman (eds.), *Representation*, NOMOS, 10 (New York: Atherton, 1968).
4. David Braybrooke, *Meeting Needs* (Princeton: Princeton University Press, 1987). James Griffin, *Well-Being: Its Meaning, Measurement, and Moral Importance* (Oxford: Clarendon Press, 1986).
5. Griffin, *Well-Being*, 53.
6. Martha C. Nussbaum, 'Human Functioning and Social Justice: In Defense of Aristotelian Essentialism', *Political Theory*, 20 (1992), 202–46: 208, 222.
7. Amartya Sen, 'Capability and Well-Being', in Martha Nussbaum and Amartya Sen (eds.), *The Quality of Life* (Oxford: Clarendon Press, 1993), 30, 36–7.
8. Hereafter, unless the referent is to a specific person, 'his' means 'his or her', 'he' means 'he or she', and 'himself' means 'himself or herself'.
9. The case of members of the European Parliament follows this same logic, but is not yet parallel because of the uncertain degree of public support for a binding European community of nations; we cannot, therefore, base the argument on implicit wants and would have to take the step of speaking of latent needs for such a community of nations.
10. Richard A. Musgrave, 'When is the Public Sector too Large?', in Charles L. Taylor (ed.), *Why Governments Grow: Measuring Public Sector Size* (Beverly Hills, Calif.: Sage, 1983), 51.
11. Harvey Liebenstein, *Beyond Economic Man: A New Foundation for Microeconomics* (Cambridge, Mass.: Harvard University Press, 1976), 180.
12. David Levine, *Needs, Rights, and the Market* (Boulder, Colo.: Rienner, 1988).
13. Andrews and Withey asked their respondents to assess the well-being of their neighbours and then these authors compared these answers to the respondents' assessment of their own, the respondents', well-being. Comparing the answers, these authors report that 'The inference is strong that *we as a people do not really know how each other feels*,' and hence the comparative well-being of ourselves. Frank M. Andrews and Stephen

B. Withey, *Social Indicators of Well-Being: Americans' Perceptions of Life Quality* (New York: Plenum, 1976), 191.

14. Robert E. Lane, *The Market Experience* (New York and Cambridge: Cambridge University Press, 1991), ch. 27.
15. Fred Hirsch, *Social Limits to Growth* (Cambridge, Mass.: Harvard University Press, 1976).
16. Richard J. Herrnstein, 'Behavior, Reinforcement, and Utility', in Michael Hechter, Lynn Nadel, and Richard E. Michod (eds.), *The Origin of Values* (New York: Aldine de Gruyter, 1993); Stephen E. G. Lea, Roger M. Tarpy, and Paul Webley, *The Individual in the Economy* (Cambridge: Cambridge University Press, 1987).
17. Faye J. Crosby, *Relative Deprivation and Working Women* (New York: Oxford University Press, 1982); W. G. Runciman, *Relative Deprivation and Social Justice* (Berkeley: University of California Press, 1966).
18. Robert E. Lane, 'Failure of the Logic of Collective Action: "Rational" Work Avoidance and Social Loafing', in Harry Redner (ed.), *An Heretical Heir of the Enlightenment: Politics, Policy and Science in the Work of Charles E. Lindblom* (Boulder, Colo.: Westview, 1993).
19. Donald P. Green and Ian Shapiro, *Pathologies of Rational Choice Theory: A Critique of Applications in Political Science* (New Haven: Yale University Press, 1994).
20. Ronald Dworkin, *Taking Rights Seriously* (Cambridge, Mass.: Harvard University Press, 1977).
21. See e.g. Glendon A. Schubert, *The Public Interest: A Critique of the Theory of a Political Concept* (New York: Free Press, 1961).
22. In referring to 'most people' I am acknowledging the distinction between the relatively rare pattern of 'sophisticated voting' and the voting pattern of all others. The original formulation of an electorate composed of both an uninformed public, whose pattern of voting resembled the processes of random choice, and a sophisticated and informed public, was in Philip E. Converse, 'The Nature of Belief Systems in Mass Publics', in David Apter (ed.), *Ideology and Discontent* (New York: Free Press, 1964). For later work, see e.g. Paul R. Abramson, John H. Aldrich, Phil Paolino, and David Rohde, ' "Sophisticated" Voting in the 1988 Presidential Primaries', *American Political Science Review*, 86 (1992), 55–69.
23. Lea *et al.*, *The Individual in the Economy*, 113–15. Summarizing their review of research on transitivity, these authors find that with respect to the generality of this canon of choice, 'the answer still is not clear' (p. 115).
24. Daniel Kahneman, P. Slovic, and A. Tversky, *Judgment under Uncertainty: Heuristics and Biases* (Cambridge, Mass.: Cambridge University Press, 1982).
25. Amos Tversky and Daniel Kahneman, 'The Framing of Decisions and the Psychology of Choice', *Science*, 211 (30 Jan. 1981), 453–8: 453. See also

Amos Tversky, 'Intransitivity of Preferences', *Psychological Review*, 76 (1969), 31–48.

26. Lane, *The Market Experience*; 'Work as "Disutility" and Money as "Happiness"': Cultural Origins of a Basic Market Error', *Journal of Socioeconomics*, 21 (1992), 43–64.

27. 'Work as "Disutility" and Money as "Happiness" '; Andrews and Withey, *Social Indicators of Well-Being*.

28. Richard Nisbett and Lee Ross, *Human Inference: Strategies and Shortcomings of Social Judgment* (Englewood Cliffs, NJ: Prentice-Hall, 1980), 221.

29. Daryl J. Bem, 'Self-Perception Theory', in Leonard Berkowitz (ed.), *Advances in Experimental Social Psychology*, vi (New York: Academic Press, 1972); Nisbett and Ross, *Human Inference*, 196–226.

30. Leon Festinger, *A Theory of Cognitive Dissonance* (Stanford, Calif.: Stanford University Press, 1957).

31. David O. Sears and Carolyn L. Funk, 'The Role of Self-Interest in Social and Political Movements', *Advances in Experimental Social Psychology*, xxiv (New York: Academic Press, 1991); Richard A. Brody and Paul M. Sniderman, 'From Life Space to Polling Place: The Relevance of Personal Concerns for Voting Behavior', *British Journal of Political Science*, 7 (1977), 337–60.

32. David O. Sears and Jack Citrin, *Tax Revolt: Something for Nothing in California* (Cambridge, Mass.: Harvard University Press, 1982).

33. Sears and Funk, 'The Role of Self-Interest in Social and Political Movements', 37.

34. Ibid. 37, 38.

35. Ibid. 38–9, 40–5. For example: 'The personal impact of inflation quite consistently has had no influence on voters' choices.'

36. Ibid. 51.

37. Ibid. 47.

38. On page 121 of Chapter 6 of this volume, David Hine says: 'Electoral accountability is the *sine qua non* of representative democracy, and in most of Europe is still organized along more or less "party" lines.'

39. David O. Sears, 'The Persistence of Early Political Predispositions', in Ladd Wheeler and Philip Shaver (eds.), *Review of Personality and Social Psychology*, iv (Beverly Hills, Calif.: Sage, 1983).

40. Sears and Funk, 'The Role of Self-Interest in Social and Political Movements', 56. On the endurance of socio-political attitudes through life, see Duane F. Alwin and Jon A. Krosnick, 'Aging, Cohorts, and the Stability of Socio-political Orientations over the Life-Span', *American Journal of Sociology*, 97 (1991), 169–95.

41. Donald R. Kinder, M. D. Peters, Robert P. Abelson, and Susan T. Fiske, 'Presidential Prototypes', *Political Behavior*, 2 (1980), 315–38; Robert

Abelson, Donald Kinder, Mark Peters, and Susan Fiske, 'Affective and Semantic Components in Political Person Perception', *Journal of Personality and Social Psychology*, 42 (1982), 619–30; Eric Anderson and Donald Granberg, 'Types of Affective Evaluators in Recent US Presidential Elections', *Polity*, 14 (1989), 147–55.

42. Joseph A. Schumpeter, *Capitalism, Socialism, and Democracy*, 3rd edn. (London: Allen & Unwin, 1950), 259–62.

43. V. O. Key, Jr., *The Responsible Electorate: Rationality in Presidential Voting* (Cambridge, Mass.: Harvard University Press, 1966).

44. Benjamin Page and Robert Y. Shapiro, *The Rational Public: Fifty Years of Public Opinion Surveys* (Chicago: University of Chicago Press, 1992), p. xi. In many ways, this work is a delayed attack on Converse's idea of public opinion as including many 'non-attitudes', that is, casually expressed, easily changed *ad hoc* opinions on public matters (Philip E. Converse, 'The Nature of Belief Systems in Mass Publics', in David Apter (ed.), *Ideology and Discontent* (New York: Free Press, 1964)). In my opinion, after three decades of criticism the idea of non-attitudes in its original form does not survive.

45. For example, processes that can only be ascertained by laboratory techniques (like reasoning) are analysed on the basis of public opinion polls; things that can only be discovered by *individual* data (such as stability of opinion) are analysed on the basis of group data.

46. See e.g. Abramson *et al.*, ' "Sophisticated" Voting in the 1988 Presidential Primaries'; Paul M. Sniderman, Richard A. Brody, and Philip Tetlock, *Reasoning and Choice: Explorations in Political Psychology* (Cambridge: Cambridge University Press, 1991).

47. For the CES, the source is Warren E. Miller and Santa Traugott, *American National Election Studies Data Sourcebook 1952–1986* (Cambridge, Mass.: Harvard University Press, 1989), 155–256. In the citations from this work, only those items are included where there is a marked and consistent change as one goes from grade school to high school to college (university) educational level. Unless otherwise noted, the figures are for 1984 or 1986. What is known as the European Values Study was initiated by the European Value Systems Study Group in 1978 and conducted by Gallup International in 1981. Through the courtesy of Juan Linz, an early participant in the study group, I have consulted printouts of the raw data by Gallup and many of the derivative works cited here in the appropriate footnotes. Some of these works were loaned to me by Linz, to whom I express my gratitude.

48. On reading daily newspapers, see *Italy and Germany: A Dual Portrait with the Tools of Social Research*, special collection of EVS data compiled for Seminar at Villa Vignoni, 20–3 Nov. 1988, 72. For similar patterns in the United States, see Miller and Traugott, *American National Election Studies Data Sourcebook*, ch. 5.

49. Ch. 3 in this volume.
50. Jean Stoetzel, *Les Valeurs du temps présent: Une enquetête européenne* (Paris: Presses Universitaires de France, 1983), 209.
51. Donald Philip Green, 'The Price Elasticity of Mass Preferences', *American Political Science Review*, 86 (1992), 128–48.
52. Miller and Traugott, *American National Election Studies Data Sourcebook*, ch. 5.
53. Sniderman *et al.*, *Reasoning and Choice*, ch. 12.
54. Herbert H. Hyman, Charles R. Wright, and John Shelton Reed, *The Enduring Effects of Education* (Chicago: University of Chicago Press, 1975).
55. Paul M. Sniderman, *Personality and Democratic Politics* (Berkeley, Calif.: University of California Press, 1975).
56. Ch. 3 in this volume. There is another consideration, however, which further confounds the results of this study: the introduction of a symbolically appealing phrase like 'national interest' introduces a distracting theme that only the more educated voters can sort out from the main policy issue. See Lance Bennett, *The Political Mind and the Political Environment* (Lexington, Mass.: Lexington-Heath, 1975).
57. Jerome Bruner, 'The Course of Cognitive Growth', *American Psychologist*, 19 (1964), pp; repr. as Warner Module No. 400 (Andover, Mass.: Warner Modular Publications, 1973).
58. James Bieri, A. L. Atkins, S. Briar, R. Lobeck, H. Miller, and T. Tripodi, *Clinical and Social Judgment* (New York: Wiley, 1966).
59. Festinger, *A Theory of Cognitive Dissonance*.
60. Herman A. Witkin, R. B. Dyk, H. F. Faterson, D. R. Goodenough, and S. A. Karp, *Psychological Differentiation* (New York: Wiley-Erlbaum, 1974).
61. Hyman *et al.*, *The Enduring Effects of Education*, 92.
62. Ibid. 233.
63. J. Aronoff, *Psychological Needs and Cultural Systems* (Princeton: Van Nostrand, 1967).
64. Susan T. Fiske and Shelley E. Taylor, *Social Cognition* (New York: Random House, 1984), 209.
65. Antonia Abbey and Frank M. Andrews, 'Modeling the Psychological Determinants of Life Quality', in Frank M. Andrews (ed.), *Research on the Quality of Life* (Ann Arbor, Mich.: Institute for Social Research, 1986), 88–9. These authors are here relying on research reported in R. D. Caplan, A. Abbey, D. J. Abramis, F. M. Andrews, T. L. Conway, and R. P. French, *Tranquilizer Use and Abuse* (Ann Arbor, Mich.: Institute for Social Research, 1984).
66. Bonnie R. Strickland, 'Internal–External Control Expectancies: From Contingency to Creativity', *American Psychologist*, 44 (1989), 1–12.
67. The classic study of response to fear is Irving L. Janis and Seymour Feshbach, 'Effects of Fear-Arousing Communications', *Journal of Abnormal*

'Losing Touch' in a Democracy

and Social Psychology, 48 (1953), 78–92. Later studies have shown th fear appeals can, under certain limited circumstances, lead to increased efforts to cope with a frightening situation. See (1984) research by Krober-Riel, reported in Karl-Erik Wärneryd, 'Economic Psychology as a Field of Study', in W. Fred van Raaij, Gery M. van Veldhoven, and Karl-Erik Wärneryd (eds.), Handbook of Economic Psychology (Dordrecht: Kluwer, 1988), 32.

68. Sniderman reviews compensatory theories, especially those of Harold Lasswell, and finds ample grounds to reject them. See his Personality and Democratic Politics, 262–301.
69. David G. Winter, The Power Motive (New York: Free Press, 1973), 106.
70. Rufus P. Browning and Herbert Jacob, 'Power Motivation and the Political Personality', Public Opinion Quarterly, 28 (1964), 75–90.
71. J. B. McConaughy, 'Certain Personality Factors of State Legislators in South Carolina', American Political Science Review, 44 (1950), 879–903.
72. Hadley Cantril, The Pattern of Human Concerns (New Brunswick, NJ: Rutgers University Press, 1965), 294–7.
73. Graham Wallas, Human Nature in Politics (Boston: Houghton Mifflin, 1909), 237.
74. Gail L. Zellman and David O. Sears, 'Childhood Origins of Tolerance for Dissent', Journal of Social Issues, 27 (1971), 109–36: 131. The reference to 'concrete situations' is necessary because an endorsement of abstract statements supporting 'free speech' does not predict attitudes in concrete situations.
75. Lipset and Schneider, The Confidence Gap.
76. See Robert E. Lane, 'The Decline of Politics and Ideology in a Knowledgeable Society', American Sociological Review, 31/5 (1966), 649–62.
77. Ellen J. Langer, The Psychology of Control (Beverly Hills, Calif.: Sage, 1983).
78. For symbolic rewards, see Murray Edelman, The Symbolic Uses of Politics (Urbana, Ill.: University of Illinois Press, 1964). For 'taking positions', see David Mayhew, Congress: The Electoral Connection (New Haven: Yale University Press, 1974). In passing, note that publics are not guiltless in this respect, favouring ends (e.g. integrated schools) but opposing the means (e.g. busing African-American children to white schools).
79. See e.g. Hugh Heclo, Modern Social Politics in Britain and Sweden (New Haven: Yale University Press, 1974). Social élites make equally significant contributions; see e.g. William Beveridge, Full Employment in a Free Society (London: Allen & Unwin, 1944).
80. Herbert M. Lefcourt, Locus of Control: Current Trends in Theory and Research (Hillsdale, NJ: Erlbaum-Wiley, 1976); Strickland, 'Internal–External Control Expectancies'.

81. M. Margaret Conway, *Political Participation in the United States*, 2nd edn. (Washington: Congressional Quarterly Press, 1991), 45.
82. Ibid.; Ada W. Finifter, 'Dimensions of Political Alienation', *American Political Science Review*, 64 (1970), 390–1; Raymond E. Wolfinger and Steven J. Rosenstone, *Who Votes?* (New Haven: Yale University Press, 1980).
83. See e.g. Raymond A. Bauer, Ithiel de Sola Pool, and Lewis Anthony Dexter, *American Business and Public Policy: The Politics of Foreign Trade* (New York: Atherton, 1963).
84. John P. Robinson and Philip E. Converse, 'Social Change Reflected in the Use of Time', in Angus Campbell and Philip E. Converse (eds.), *The Human Meaning of Social Change* (New York: Russell Sage, 1972).
85. Kenneth E. Boulding, *The Meaning of the Twentieth Century* (London: Allen & Unwin, 1965).
86. Hardin, *Morality within Limits of Reason*.
87. See e.g. Cass R. Sunstein, 'Preferences and Politics', *Philosophy and Public Affairs*, 20 (1991), 3–34.

3

Freedom from the Press

WILLIAM MILLER, ANNIS-MAY TIMPSON, AND MICHAEL LESSNOFF

1. Press Freedom

A free press has a central role in theories of liberal democracy. The First Amendment to the US Constitution linked individual citizens' freedom of speech with freedom for the press. Mill denounced the 'peculiar evil of silencing the expression of opinion'. In a liberal democracy a free press is necessary to inform the public, to open minds to new viewpoints, and to hold the powerful in check by exposing their sins and criticizing their policies.

But the relationship between press freedom, individual liberty, and democracy has always been somewhat ambiguous. Our vision of a free press threatened by government is easily replaced by that of an ordinary individual threatened or misled by powerful press interests. The range of published information and views may be limited by owners, advertisers, or governments applying formal or informal censorship, by threats of legal action from powerful interests exposed to scandal, and, not least, by the apathy and prejudice of the mass of readers and viewers. It may be distorted by the pursuit of commercial profits and journalistic reputations, or by pressure from lobbyists and 'spin-doctors'. Obviously the particular mix of corrupting influences is likely to vary a great deal between print and broadcasting, and between state and private enterprises, but constraint and distortion are endemic.

2. Three Concerns

This has led to three main concerns about the press: bias, censorship, and the abuse of press freedom.

The research was supported by the ESRC under grant number R232637.

Bias is alleged in both the selection and the treatment of political issues. For example, at the 1992 general election taxation came a poor fifth in the list of issues named as most important by the voters but second on the list of broadcasting priorities, second on the list of newspaper front-page leads and top of the list of newspaper editorials.[1] The circulation of national dailies supporting the Conservative government was over two and a half times the circulation of those supporting the Labour opposition. The partisan bias, particularly in the tabloid press, was crude, aggressive, and unrepresentative of its readers. Broadcasting is required by law to be impartial, but the government always generates more news and gets more coverage than the opposition parties—especially outside election periods, but also within them.[2]

Recent governments have used direct censorship (for example, the ministerial order banning television and radio interviews with supporters of Irish terrorists) as well as intimidating tactics (for example, the prosecution and imprisonment of civil servants and journalists, or the seizure of the BBC Television series *Secret Society*) and a general culture of secrecy to suppress information about security and other matters.[3]

Legislation forbids publication of statements likely to incite racial hatred, and the press has been heavily criticized for sensational crime-reporting and intrusions into the private lives of politicians and ordinary people. However, such reporting is often seen more as an abuse than an expression of press freedom.[4]

3. Four Élites

Explicitly or implicitly we focus on four different kinds of élite—and on some of the subdivisions, particularly ideological subdivisions, within them. First there are those who are directly responsible for the content of the press—owners, editors, journalists; and those who are directly responsible for the legal framework in which it operates—the government. Any discussion of press bias, censorship, or abuse implicitly reflects upon the actions of these élites.

But we shall also consider the views of wider, less immediately responsible élites who help to define the broader political culture—in particular, what might loosely be called the 'chattering classes' and the 'political class'. For this we shall draw upon our British Rights Survey (November 1991–November 1992), which comprised in-depth forty-two-minute interviews with 2,060 members of the general public and

1,244 senior local government politicians. Because we over-sampled university and polytechnic graduates in the general public sample we can extract 414 interviews with graduates from that sample. (In analyses of the public as a whole these graduates are, of course, downweighted to their correct population proportion.) We take this sample of graduate opinion as a measure of the views of the educated élite. The senior local government politicians—mainly leaders of party groups on councils throughout Britain—are not directly involved in controlling the press, but they are deeply involved in party politics and they have more experience of executive government than most members of parliament. At the same time they are not tainted by high office in central government; so they are more able to articulate personal opinions rather than mounting a formal defence of current ministerial decisions. We take them to represent the views of the broad political élite.

4. Bias

We might expect people to detect, and possibly deplore, the extreme partisan bias of the print press. Overwhelmingly people quote broad-casting, especially television, as their main source of national and international news.[5] Rightly or wrongly, the public rate television as the most complete, most accurate, fairest, quickest, and clearest source of national and international news.[6] (The print press scores somewhat better on regional news and much better on local news.) By a majority of about three to one they judge television to be politically unbiased.[7] By contrast the minority who fail to perceive political bias in the paper they read is as small as the minority who do detect bias on television.[8] (The minority of viewers who do perceive bias on television tend to be divided over whether ITV favours Labour or the Conservatives, though by a growing margin that has now reached around three to one they see BBC1 as biased towards the Conservatives rather than Labour.[9])

Does this mean that the print press is out of touch with its readers while broadcasting is in touch with its viewers? Not quite. While people say the print press is biased and that it is not their main source of news, they still continue to buy and read it in very large numbers. True, sales have declined by 8 per cent and readership by 19 per cent over the last decade.[10] None the less, sales are still enormous: the print press must be doing something right.

The question about people's 'main source of national and international news' is valid enough but limited in its scope. That is not the only or even the prime function of the press. One obvious alternative is entertainment. Yet even within the strictly political arena people look to the press for more than news and information: they also seek advice, interpretation, guidance, or support. While bias must be judged negatively from an information perspective it may be judged more positively from a guidance perspective. Indeed people may even find the bias in their newspapers helpful.

When asked to rate the usefulness of television and their newspapers for 'keeping them informed on the issues' 56 per cent rated television more useful against only 22 per cent who rated their paper more useful—a majority of 34 per cent for television. But when asked to rate the usefulness of these media for 'helping them decide how to vote' only 36 per cent rated television more useful, 24 per cent their paper, and fully 40 per cent rated television and their paper equally—a majority of only 12 per cent for television. So a large majority preferred television for information, but there was a fairly even division of preferences for guidance. Amongst regular readers of the down-market tabloids the *Sun* and *Star*, the contrast was even more striking: amongst their readers, a majority of 55 per cent preferred television for information but only a majority of 10 per cent preferred television for guidance.[11]

Other evidence suggests that people react against the relative impartiality of television, accusing it of bias towards their opponents while reacting favourably towards their paper, which they see as slightly more favourable to their own political viewpoint than do other readers (with different political viewpoints) of the same paper.[12] One explanation is that people feel, rightly or wrongly, that they can choose their paper but not their television. There are more newspapers, and more obvious differentiation between them, than there are television channels. People who find the *Sun*'s political line offensive can keep it out of the house, but those who find BBC news politically offensive find it more difficult to avoid—even in an age of four 'terrestrial' and many 'satellite' or 'cable' channels. Another explanation may be that people have come to expect broadcasting to give them information and the print press to give them comment, advice, and opinion. Overt political bias on the BBC or studious neutrality on the front page of the *Sun* may seem as incongruous as a pint in the kirk or a sermon in the pub.

That does not mean that the print press is necessarily in close touch with its readers—simply that it is less out of touch than at first appears.

It remains true that readers of every newspaper except the *Guardian* rated television more useful than their paper for providing issue information.[13] Even for providing political guidance a (smaller) majority of *Mirror*, *Sun*, and *Star* readers preferred television; *Express*, *Mail*, and *Telegraph* readers were evenly divided; and only amongst *Guardian* readers once again did a clear majority rate their paper above television. Politically therefore, the *Guardian* is very much in touch with its readers, the *Telegraph* and the up-market tabloids less so, and the down-market tabloids—especially the *Sun* and *Star*—moderately out of touch, though the *Sun* and *Star* may be more in touch with their readers in other, non-political, ways. We should certainly not assume that the gross discrepancy between the political partisanship of the tabloids and the party votes of their readers is the true measure of how far they are 'out of touch'.

5. Censorship

As part of their attempt to strengthen the authority of central government, recent governments have taken a series of actions to tighten their control of information and ensure that government remains confidential—at least until the government itself decides to be open. Our British Rights Survey provides information on both public and élite attitudes to publication of confidential government documents.

All our interviews were carried out using our own very flexible version of the CATI (computer-assisted telephone interviewing) technique. One feature was that many questions appeared in several variant forms. For some questions there were only two variants, for others as many as a dozen. When the computer controlling the interview reached a particular question it used a random-number generator to decide, randomly, which one of the several versions of that question it would display on the screen. The interviewer read out the question as it appeared and the computer recorded on its disk which variant of the question was used on that occasion along with the answer given by the interviewee. As part of a battery of Agree/Disagree questions we asked:

Newspapers which get hold of confidential government documents about [defence/economic/health service] plans should *not* be allowed to publish them [(*null*)/because publication might damage our national interests].

Agree/Disagree? Strongly or Not?

This question came in six different versions depending upon whether the question asked was about defence, economic, or health plans; and upon whether it did or did not add the argument that publication 'might damage our national interests'. Since these six variants were randomly assigned to particular interviews then, with all the usual caveats about sampling errors, we can attribute differences in the answers to differences in question-wording. And since no one person was exposed to more than one variant of the question, no one was under any pressure— logical or psychological—towards spurious consistency. So we have a good measure of how far support for censorship depends upon the topic (defence, economic, or health plans); how much it depends upon an explicit reference to the 'national interest'; and how much it depends upon the interaction between the two, i.e. how much influence references to the 'national interest' have within different topic areas.

We can also collapse the results of all six versions of the question together to get an overview of public attitudes to the publication of confidential government documents without distinguishing topic area or whether or not appeals were made to the national interest. Obviously the wording had an influence on the answers, but, taking all the interviews together, 58 per cent of the public, yet only 44 per cent of graduates and 45 per cent of politicians, would ban publication of government secrets.

Both public and élites were strongly influenced by the policy area involved: roughly 30 per cent more would ban publication of defence plans than of health service plans. Overt appeals to the national interest also had an effect, though a much smaller one.

The interaction of policy areas and appeals to the national interest is revealing. Amongst the public, overt appeals to the national interest increased support for a ban on publishing economic plans by 18 per cent and for a ban on publishing defence or health plans by half that amount. The relevance of the national interest to health plans is difficult to establish, while its relevance to defence plans is difficult to overlook. Hence the greater effectiveness of appeals to the national interest in the 'grey area' of economic plans. Amongst politicians overt appeals to the national interest really only worked at all with economic plans and were even slightly counter-productive when advanced as a reason for banning publication of health plans. Graduates' reactions were somewhere between those of the public and politicians.

As might be expected, those who place themselves on the left are much less willing to ban publication of government secrets than those

TABLE 3.1. *Effect of policy areas and overt appeals to national interests on willingness to ban publication of confidential government documents* (%)

	Public	Graduates	Politicians
In all interviews	58	44	45
Without appeal to national interests	53	40	41
With appeal to national interests	64	47	48
Effect of appeal	+11	+7	+7
Defence plans	75	61	61
Economic plans	51	39	43
Health plans	47	29	30
Difference between defence and health	+28	+32	+31

TABLE 3.2. *Effect of appeals to national interests on willingness to ban publication of secret plans in different policy areas* (%)

	Public	Graduates	Politicians
Defence plans			
Without appeal to national interests	72	59	60
With appeal to national interests	80	64	63
Effect of appeal	+8	+5	+3
Economic plans			
Without appeal to national interests	42	30	34
With appeal to national interests	60	47	51
Effect of appeal	+18	+17	+17
Health plans			
Without appeal to national interests	42	27	31
With appeal to national interests	51	30	28
Effect of appeal	+9	+3	−3

on the right. Amongst the public, the difference between left and right is 35 per cent, amongst graduates 54 per cent, and amongst politicians 55 per cent. These left–right differences remain almost constant across policy areas, from defence through economic plans to health plans. The left is traditionally suspicious of secret government and doubly so when the government in office is right-wing. As we shall see later however, the left is not so libertarian on other aspects of press freedom. On the right and in the centre, élites have views which closely reflect the views

TABLE 3.3. *Willingness to ban publication of government secrets,
by where respondents place themselves ideologically* (%)

	Public	Graduates	Politicians
On the left	40	18	18
In the centre	57	52	52
On the right	75	72	73
Difference between right and left	+35	+54	+55

of ordinary centre or right-wing people; but on the left, élites and public part company—left-wing élites are less than half as favourable to censorship as left-wing members of the public.

Educated and political élites are more committed than the public to free speech and press freedom both in principle and in practice. Their decisions about press censorship are linked more closely to their principles.[14] And, unlike the public, politicians react against spurious appeals to the 'national interest' in situations were the national interest is unlikely to be at risk. In short, the élite, especially the political élite, is a lot more sophisticated and a little more liberal than the public on publication of government secrets. However, most of the discrepancy between élite and public occurs on the left where the élite have a very much more liberal attitude than their people. In so far as broadly defined élites are out of touch with their people on this, it is left-wing élites that are out of touch.

Governments are another matter. If we stand back from the differences between public, graduates, and politicians and look at the actual degree of public support for a ban on publication of confidential documents, there is clearly no mandate for a blanket ban. Overwhelmingly, the public is willing to ban publication of defence documents and it is willing to take account of the elusive 'national interest', but there is clearly no majority for a ban on publishing government secrets just because the government wishes to keep them secret. Where government can be open without endangering the defence of the realm, the public clearly does not regard government documents as legitimate secrets. And that does imply a revolutionary change in British government's 'standard operating procedures'. As we shall see later, a Freedom of Information Act is enormously popular with the same people who are willing to give serious consideration to the preservation of defence secrets. On secrecy, British governments are seriously out of

touch with the people, and even more out of touch with the political
class outside government itself.

Of course, governments do make some exceptions in regard to secrets. 'Leaks' of confidential government papers seem to be acceptable
provided the government itself—or even an inner circle around the Prime
Minister—does the leaking. That was Heseltine's complaint in the
Westland Affair at the end of 1986, and Air Chief Marshal Sir Michael
Graydon's apparent complaint (later denied, of course) at the end of
1993.[15] But in reality government by orchestrated leaks is closer in
concept to censorship than to freedom for the press. It is just another
form of government control and manipulation.

6. Abuse of Press Freedom

The third area of concern involves the abuse of press freedom: an
irresponsible press publishing material that is not so much secret as
offensive—offensive either to intellectual norms or to the targets of its
abuse. Censorship, and more especially public support for censorship,
applies to much else besides government secrecy. Often it involves the
principle of free expression more than freedom of information.[16] So, in
this section, our focus changes from consumers to producers, from
readers and viewers to journalists and programme-makers, and from the
government's desire to censor publication of its secrets to the public's
desire to censor what it finds irresponsible or disagreeable.

We might caricature the difference between this section and the
previous one by suggesting that we turn now from the question of
censoring the qualities to the question of censoring the tabloids, but that
would be unfair to both. In the midst of our survey field-work it was,
after all, the unimpeachable *Scotsman*—not the tabloids—which first
printed details of Paddy Ashdown's private life. That raises another
problem: reaction to scandals may be intense but short-lived. To avoid
misleading findings we spread our interviews evenly over a ten-month
period, interviewing an approximately random subsample each week.
So our results are affected by neither the peaks nor the troughs of
scandal-mongering, but reflect both.

Mallory Wober has explored the limits to public acceptance of violence, sexuality, and coverage of the Royal Family on British television.[17] Our prime concern here is with less cultural and more political
topics but our objective is fundamentally the same: to map at least a

sector of the boundaries of public acceptability. We began with a battery of five questions, first asking:

Some people think there should be no restrictions on what can be published in
books and newspapers or screened on television, but others disagree. For each
of the following please say whether you think it should be [*allowed* on television without any restrictions, or *restricted* for example to late night view-
ing, or *banned* from television altogether/*allowed* in newspapers without any
restrictions, or *restricted* for example to books, or *banned* from publication
altogether.]

A randomly selected half of the interviews asked about television and
the other half about newspapers. This introduction was followed by a
list of five items that might be allowed, restricted, or banned. Three
used randomly varied wording. The list was:

1. Pictures of extreme violence.
2. Abusive attacks on [the Christian religion/minority religions such as the
   Muslim or Hindu religion].
3. Interviews with supporters [of IRA terrorists/Protestant terrorists in
   Northern Ireland].
4. Stories that intrude into [ordinary people's/leading politicians'] private
   lives.
5. Lies and distortions of the truth.

On average neither public nor politicians made much distinction between
television and the print press. Support for censorship varied sharply
with news-*topic* but not with news-*medium*. So we shall combine answers to questions about television and newspapers and refer to them,
generically, as questions about 'the press'.

Most people opted for some degree of restriction on such publications.
We shall focus on those who took the most extreme view and called for
an outright ban. John Stuart Mill put the view that we should tolerate
even the publication of what we take to be 'lies and distortions of the
truth' because we may be wrong; that the best defence against the
publication of lies is uncensored publication of truth, not censorship of
lies; and that, in the end, truth will drive out lies. In any case, who has
the authority to define a 'distortion of the truth'? This is not a question
that troubles either public or élites, however: three-quarters support an
outright ban on publication of lies and distortions of the truth. In this
respect, at least, Britain is not a nation of John Stuart Mills!

People are only a little more tolerant of intrusions into the private
lives of ordinary people (though here Mill might also be intolerant): 64

per cent of the public and 55 per cent of élites would ban them. But they were very much more tolerant of intrusions into even the *private* lives of leading politicians: only 43 per cent of the public, 34 per cent of politicians, and 30 per cent of graduates would ban them. In the majority view, public figures do not have private lives.

In October 1988 the then Home Secretary, Douglas Hurd, issued an order to the BBC and IBA under the 1981 Broadcasting Act banning both networks from broadcasting any words spoken by a person 'representing or purporting to represent' organizations which included the illegal IRA and UVF and the (then) legal Sinn Féin and UDA, except where those words were spoken in parliament or during an election campaign.[18] Only half the public, one-third of politicians, and a quarter of graduates—a minority in each case—support that ban. Neither public nor élites drew any distinction between IRA and Protestant terrorists.

The public and more especially élites draw a sharp distinction between abuse of Christianity and abuse of minority religions 'such as Muslim or Hindu religions'. Amongst the public 32 per cent would ban abusive attacks on Christianity but 44 per cent would ban attacks on minority religions. Politicians were even more willing than the public to tolerate abuse of Christianity (only 21 per cent would ban it) but even less willing to tolerate abuse of minority religions (49 per cent would ban it). Graduates were the most willing to tolerate abuse of all kinds of religion but they too made a sharp distinction between Christianity and minority religions. Racial and religious discrimination can favour minorities. It is important to note that no one in our survey was asked about both Christianity and minority religions; no one was under pressure to make an explicit distinction between them; no one was even aware that we intended to compare attitudes to the abuse of different religions.

Finally, just a third would ban pictures of extreme violence. While we did not distinguish between news and entertainment, the context of the interview probably focused respondents' imaginations towards violent news rather than violent films.

We put three further questions about censorship of offensive items: sensational crime stories, and stories that might intentionally or unintentionally incite racial or religious hatred. First, we asked whether 'heavy television and press coverage of dramatic crimes like murders or terrorist incidents should be banned'. In one-third of the interviews, randomly chosen, we added the phrase 'because it may encourage others to commit more crimes'; in another third we added 'because, later on,

TABLE 3.4. *Support for a ban on publication of five offensive items* (%)

	Public	Graduates	Politicians
Lies and distortions	77	74	75
Intrusions into the private lives:			
Of ordinary people	64	55	55
Of leading politicians	43	30	34
Difference	+21	+25	+21
Interviews with supporters of:			
IRA terrorists	50	25	36
Protestant terrorists	45	26	35
Difference	+5	−1	+1
Abusive attacks upon:			
The Christian religion	32	21	21
Minority religions	44	38	49
Difference	+12	+17	+28
Pictures of extreme violence	32	27	33

it may prevent an accused person getting a fair trial'; in the remaining third we added no justification for a ban. Élites were significantly less willing to ban heavy crime coverage and also less easily influenced by arguments for a ban. Without a justification for censorship, 31 per cent of the public supported a ban, rising to 47 per cent and 53 per cent when we put the 'encourage more crime' and 'fair trial' arguments respectively. Élites were almost uninfluenced by the fear of 'encouraging more crime' and only influenced by a desire for a 'fair trial'.

Secondly, we asked whether newspapers 'should be banned from publishing research showing very high rates of crime among blacks'. In half the interviews we added 'because this may encourage prejudice against them'. Support for a ban was twice as high amongst the general public as amongst élites. Once again argument had an influence, though a modest one.

Thirdly, we asked: 'Do you think it should be against the law to write or speak in a way that promotes [racial/religious] hatred?' In half the interviews (randomly chosen) we used the word 'racial', in the other half 'religious'. The offence of racial incitement was introduced in 1965 and extended in the 1986 Public Order Act. It is now an offence to publish or broadcast, except on BBC and IBA (Independent Broadcasting Authority) programmes, anything likely to stir up race hatred *whether or not that is intended*; and it is an offence *even to possess*

TABLE 3.5. *Effect of arguments in favour of censorship of crime coverage and racial or religious incitement* (%)

	Public	Graduates	Politicians
Heavy coverage of dramatic crimes:			
Without argument	31	19	24
With 'more crime' argument	47	26	26
With 'fair trial' argument	53	40	43
Effect of 'more crime' argument	+16	+7	+2
Effect of 'fair trial' argument	+22	+21	+19
Publication of crime-rates amongst blacks:			
Without argument	35	3	18
With 'prejudice' argument	46	24	25
Effect of argument	+11	+11	+7
Racial or religious incitement:			
Racial incitement	70	75	81
Religious incitement	58	63	69
Difference	+12	+12	+12

such material unless ignorant of its contents—though prosecutions have been rare.[19] Large majorities of both public and élites supported a ban on racial incitement, and smaller majorities supported a ban on religious incitement. Of all our questions about censorship these were the only ones where graduates were *more* favourable to censorship than the public, and the only ones apart from the question about 'abusive attacks on minority religions' where politicians were more favourable to censorship than the public.

We saw earlier that people who place themselves on the left are far less willing to ban publication of government secrets than those on the right. The left are also much less willing to ban interviews with apologists for terrorism. But left–right differences on censorship of sensational crime stories, press intrusions into private lives, or publication of lies and distortions are small. Indeed, amongst politicians, it is those who place themselves in the *centre* of the political spectrum who are most willing to ban such publications—not those on the right. And it is the *left* who are most keen to ban racial incitement. So each part of the political spectrum has its own 'hit-list' for censorship.

None the less, the only issues which *sharply* divide left and right put right-wingers in favour of censorship and left-wingers against. So, overlaid on top of each ideological camp's tendency to draw up a

TABLE 3.6. *Willingness to ban publication, by where respondents place themselves ideologically*

% who would ban publication of:	Public			Graduates			Politicians		
	Left	Centre	Right	Left	Centre	Right	Left	Centre	Right
Confidential government documents	40	57	75[a]	18	52	72	18	52	73
Interviews with terrorist supporters	35	48	55	13	31	34	17	40	57
Sensational crime coverage	35	45	48	23	30	31	21	38	35
Intrusions into private lives	51	53	55	37	48	39	37	50	47
Lies and distortions	77	75	80	69	74	82	70	78	76
Incitement to racial hatred	75	71	62	79	71	74	87	80	73

[a] Highest percentage italic.

private hit-list there is evidence that the left are generally less comfortable with censorship. Apart from the issues of government secrets and interviews with terrorists, ideological differences are small and élites represent their people equally well across the ideological spectrum.

How far do élites represent the public on censorship of offensive items? There is no difference between public and élites on censorship of lies and distortions, or pictures of extreme violence. Élites have less tolerance than the public for racial or religious incitement or abuse of minority (and only minority) religions. Élites have more tolerance than the public for all other kinds of offensive item, including items that might encourage racial prejudice without intending to do so. With two exceptions, differences between public and élites are not usually large, however. The two exceptions involve publication of sensational crime reports or racial-crime statistics. In both cases, élites are much more tolerant than the public.

Amongst the public there is an overwhelming majority only for bans on lies, distortions of the truth, and intentional racial incitement. There is a smaller majority for a ban on intentional religious incitement (but not for abuse of minority religions, still less of Christianity) and intrusions into the private lives of ordinary people. Racial incitement is already banned. But there is no majority for a ban on intrusions into the private lives of senior politicians. Indeed there is a large majority against such a ban. And there really is no majority for a ban on interviews with terrorists, even though that is also banned already.

In short, the general public, and intellectual or political élites still more, would be as much in favour of loosening controls on the press as tightening them. What offends them most of all is lies and distortions of the truth—where government is at least as guilty as the press. The public simply do not accept the culture of excessive secrecy and routine lying, the spate of denials followed by grudging and unrepentant admissions that seems to characterize so much of government behaviour.

Indeed the public combine a low opinion of some sections of the press with a low opinion of government and parliament. To say that publication of certain things 'should be banned' is not to say who should do the banning. It may be more of a moral than a legal demand. And the government may be the chief culprit: the accused, not the judge.

We asked people to use marks out of ten to indicate how important various institutions, existing or proposed, were for 'protecting citizens' rights and liberties'. In a battery of nineteen possible protectors of

TABLE 3.7. *Average marks out of ten for protecting citizens'*
rights and liberties

	Public	Graduates	Politicians
Freedom of Information Act	7.8	8.0	8.3
Quality papers like the *Guardian*	6.4	6.7	7.0
Television	6.3	6.3	6.5
Quality papers like the *Telegraph*	6.2	5.9	6.3
Back-bench MPs in parliament	5.7	6.1	6.6
Tabloid papers like the *Mirror*	4.4	3.3	4.3
Tabloid papers like the *Sun*	3.3	2.3	2.8

liberty we included various sections of the press, a proposed Freedom of Information Act, and back-bench MPs. Although we did not include the government as such, it seems reasonable to suppose that it would score even less than back-bench MPs.

A Freedom of Information Act topped the whole list with a score of about 8 out of 10. Television and quality papers such as the *Guardian* and the *Telegraph* scored over 6 out of 10, and the tabloid press around 3 or 4 out of 10. Public opinion certainly did not rate the tabloid press well. But they rated television and the quality press well ahead of members of parliament, and a Freedom of Information Act far above both. Élites, especially the political élite, were a little kinder to parliament but still put it no higher than television and the quality press, though they took a particularly dim view of the tabloids.

We also asked directly whether '[television and the press should be more independent of government control/there should be more government control of television and the press]'. As usual, a randomly selected half of our interviews used each form of words. Irrespective of which way round we put the question the division of opinion was very clear: three-quarters of both public and élites agree the press should be more independent; while three-quarters of the public and an even larger majority of the élites oppose more government control.

Public support for censorship did not translate into public support for tighter government control of the press.[20] Of course, those who were more willing to censor the press were usually less opposed to government control, but, on balance, they still opposed it. If we take willingness to ban: (1) interviews with terrorists; (2) intrusions into private

TABLE 3.8. *Opposition to government control of the media (%)*

	Public	Graduates	Politicians
Agree media should be more independent of government control	76	78	74
Disagree that there should be more government control of media	74	88	85

lives; (3) heavy coverage of crime; (4) publication of confidential government documents on economic or health (but not defence) plans; and then count the number of items out of these four which people are willing to ban, we can construct an index of hard-line censorship attitudes.

Amongst the public, 88 per cent of those who would ban none of these four oppose government control of the media, compared to only 52 per cent of those who would ban all four—a difference of 36 per cent. Clearly there is a marked relationship between support for censorship and support for government control. But even in the most extreme category—those who wish to ban all four items—the balance of support is still tipped towards more media independence rather than more government control. Even in that extreme category less than half the public and only a third of graduates or politicians tilt towards more government control. And it is a very extreme category that contains very few people—less than 14 per cent of the public, 10 per cent of politicians, and even fewer graduates.

Moreover, this four-item index was carefully chosen to best predict support for government control. On other items, such as a ban on lies and distortions, a ban on racial incitement, or a ban on abuse of minority religions, those who favoured censorship actually opposed government control of the press slightly *more* than those who did not. While many people dislike particular things that appear in the press and would willingly ban them, they do not trust government to do it.

7. In Touch: Vice or Virtue?

Does it matter whether the opinions of élites accurately represent the opinions of their people? A populist might argue that élites should faithfully reflect the views of their people. A critic of populist democracy would distinguish people's emotional prejudices and gut, 'knee-jerk' reactions from their informed and considered opinions. Indeed the critic might accuse populists of not merely pandering to ignorance, intolerance, and xenophobia but actually encouraging them for narrow political or commercial advantage. A disciple of John Stuart Mill might argue that everyone has a duty to form the best-considered views they can on the issues, and that education and political participation (not least in local government) are important means of acquiring both the necessary information and the skills needed to handle it. Now if education and participation improve the individual's capacity to act as a citizen, then those who already are educated and involved might be expected to provide valuable guidance and leadership on the issues— unless, of course, they develop a self-serving class interest. In themselves, education and participation should help to make the educated and political élites representative of the views that the people themselves would have if they thought about the issues at greater length. Unless there is reason to believe that their views have been corrupted by self-interest, it is reasonable to give the views of the educated and involved more weight than those of the uneducated and politically inexperienced. That is, after all, one of the powerful arguments for representative rather than plebiscitary democracy.

And it is an argument that seems to run through much of the discussion in other chapters about the divergence of mass and élite opinion towards the European Community and its institutions. It is alleged that Europe's problems with primitive, negative, destructive, and often ill-informed nationalism flow from national governments and politicians being too close to their peoples rather than too distant from them, too willing to pander to negative populist sentiment, too fearful of articulating a rational positive vision for the future.

Whether or not that is true on Europe, a frequent criticism of the tabloid press is not that it fails to represent its readers but that it represents their prejudices all too well, that it is too much in touch with their fears, that it does too little to challenge their ignorance and too much to encourage their intolerance and xenophobia. Our evidence that so many of its readers rely upon it for political guidance is proof that it is to a degree 'in touch' with them and will probably be a comfort to convinced populists but not necessarily to others.

On the issues of censorship and government control of the press and television there are clear differences between the public and the educated or politically involved élites. Despite the antics of the tabloids, public support for censorship is limited; yet it is even more limited amongst graduates or local politicians. The differences are perhaps not large enough to justify fully a claim that these élites are out of touch with the people. But in so far as the claim is justified, in so far as there are differences, in so far as there is a problem, some might argue that the fault lies with the people, not the élites. These élites are less favourable to secrecy, more sensitive to spurious claims that the 'national interest' is in danger,[21] and more willing to bear the costs of an open society (such as press intrusions into private lives); they are more intolerant than the public only towards intentional racial or religious incitement. Since it is not obvious that these élite views reflect the corruption of self-interest, it is likely that they reflect the effects of education and political experience.

Central government, however, constitutes a very different élite. Authoritarianism is the occupational disease of governments, however long and successfully they try to resist it. The broad political élite of politicians outside Westminster are more willing than the general public to let the press publish confidential government documents. The government itself may hesitate to prosecute, but can hardly be expected to approve that much openness in government. It backed the notorious *Secret Society*; 'Zircon' raid on BBC Scotland (which, ironically, revealed no use of confidential documents in the end). Ministers such as Mr Peter Lilley clearly regard publication of confidential govenment documents even on such innocuous matters as social welfare as a form of theft which relieves them of any obligation to comment upon their contents, while colleagues such as John Patten happily discuss the content of 'press leaks' (his words, not ours) of non-governmental documents.[22] It is specifically government confidentiality, not confidentiality in general, that concerns government. Similarly, the broad political élite of politicians outside Westminster are more willing than the general public to allow interviews with terrorists or their apologists, while ministers have issued orders banning them and threaten to tighten restrictions on reporting terrorists' views even further. Again, the broad political élite of politicians outside Westminster are more willing than the general public to permit press intrusions into private lives—and are massively in favour of allowing press intrusions into the private lives of senior politicians. And politicians outside Westminster are even more massively opposed than the public towards government control of press and television. But central government, encouraged by MPs on both sides of the House including Gerald Kaufman, has repeatedly threatened new privacy legislation if the press does not voluntarily accept more restraint.

All of this hints at a paradox, though an easily understood paradox: politicians outside Westminster are more tolerant of press freedom than the general public, while central government is less tolerant than the general public. So élites outside and inside government both fail to reflect the opinion of the general public with complete accuracy, but in opposite ways. Populists and liberals might agree on this fact but disagree on whether it is a problem and, still more, on how it might be resolved.

NOTES

1. David Butler and Dennis Kavanagh, *The British General Election of 1992* (London: Macmillan, 1992), 268, 163, 201, 199.
2. W. L. Miller, *Media and Voters* (Oxford: Oxford University Press, 1991), 69.
3. K. D. Ewing and C. A. Gearty, *Freedom under Thatcher* (Oxford: Oxford University Press, 1990).
4. Malcolm Hurwitt and Peter Thornton, *Civil Liberty: The Liberty–NCCL Guide* (London: Penguin, 1989), ch. 2.
5. Barrie Gunter and Paul Winstone, *Television: The Public's View 1992* (London: Libbey, 1993), 43.
6. Ibid. 45.
7. Ibid. 48.
8. Miller, *Media and Voters*, 109.
9. Gunter and Winstone, *Television*, 56.
10. Calculated from David Butler and Dennis Kavanagh, *The British General Election of 1983* (London: Macmillan, 1984), 178–9; and Butler and Kavanagh, *The British General Election of 1992*, 181–2.
11. Miller, *Media and Voters*, 123.
12. Ibid. 177.
13. The analysis compared regular and persistent *Guardian* readers with regular and persistent *Sun* or *Star* readers (taken together), *Mirror* readers, *Express* or *Mail* readers (taken together), *Telegraph*, *Times*, or *Financial Times* readers (taken together), and those who did not read any particular paper regularly and persistently. See ibid. 123.
14. The relationship between principles and practice is explored in W. L. Miller (ed.), *Alternatives to Freedom: Arguments and Opinions* (London: Longman, 1995). See also W. L. Miller, A. M. Timpson, and M. Lessnoff, *Principles and Practice: The Political Culture of People and Politicians in Contemporary Britain* (Oxford: Oxford University Press, 1996).

15. See the report by David Fairhall, Defence Correspondent, 'Air Chief Claims Portillo Aiming to Discredit RAF', *Guardian*, 9 Nov. 1993, 22, in which Fairhall writes, 'He did not name Portillo but said the Air Force knew who had instigated the "disreputable" campaign to discredit the RAF by alleging it was far less efficient than the Israeli Air Force. . . . Air Chief Marshall Sir Michael Graydon was delivering the 1993 Andrew Humphrey Memorial Lecture in London.'

16. The influence of these two principles on public opinion is disentangled in Miller (ed.), *Alternatives to Freedom*.

17. See Mallory Wober, *Lines and Liberties: Attitudes to Religion, Ethics and Innovation on Television* (London: IBA, 1989); *The Role of Television in the Wake of the 'Satanic Verses'* (London: IBA, 1990); *Rules and Regulations: Attitudes to 'Drawing the Line' on Television* (London: ITC, 1991); *No Menace to Monarchism: Stable Attitudes after Discussion of a Widely Publicised Book* (London: ITC, 1992).

18. Ewing and Gearty, *Freedom under Thatcher*, 243. The UDA was legally banned later.

19. Hurwitt and Thornton, *Civil Liberty*, 40–1.

20. For brevity we use the phrase 'support government control of the press' as a shorthand for 'support more government control of press and television or oppose the idea that they should be more independent from government'.

21. See our finding about the effect of appeals to the 'national interest' as a reason for suppressing publication of confidential government documents on health plans.

22. On the BBC's *World this Weekend*, 14 Nov. 1993, for example.

4

From Representative to Responsive Government?

JEAN CHARLOT

The received wisdom is that representative democracy in Europe and elsewhere is in crisis and that this is shown by a rise in abstentionism, a drop in party identification, and a growing independence of the voter with regard to all political parties; together with an increase in the number of floating voters and a growing lack of trust in the political élite. However, these factors vary considerably from one country to the next, from one type of election to another, and according to the candidates and the issues. The 'new electors', estranged from parties and even from politics, may on occasion sway the result; they none the less remain a minority group within the electorate and, except in Italy and in Belgium, the regime remains legitimate.

Far from losing contact with their electors the European political élites seem to have found new ways of keeping in touch with what they want. It must be stressed from the outset, however, that these new links between peoples and governments and oppositions are tenuous, fragile, and difficult to interpret.

1. Elections Make a Difference

'Do parties matter?' Does the swing from left to right in two-party systems or in systems where two major coalitions of parties seek power make a difference? Do the policies followed differ?

Richard Rose tried to answer this question with regard to Great Britain in the 1960s and 1970s.[1] His conclusions, which are both solid and qualified, remain valid and may be applied to other countries. They shed new light on the diagnosis of the present crisis of representative government in Europe. Rose showed that in Britain the two major parties, Conservative and Labour, offer the electors a complete, specific programme of government at each general election. This programme or manifesto includes 100 or so concrete proposals which can easily be translated into bills and laws even if there are too many to be dealt with in a single term of office.

Moreover, an examination of the facts showed that election promises were, for the most part, kept by those who had made them. The promises that were not put into effect were in a minority and U-turns were very rare. A careful analysis of the election manifestos of parties that have won elections in the various European countries and the extent to which they have carried out their programmes shows Richard Rose's conclusions to be valid everywhere. This goes against the cynicism of those who claim that election promises are only made to be broken. It contradicts the received wisdom that these days candidates and parties appeal through 'vague images in which the personality of the leaders figures more prominently than specific policy measures'.[2] An examination of France bears out Rose's conclusions. Of the 110 proposals put forward by François Mitterrand in the 1981 presidential campaign, 90 per cent were put into effect within the socialists' first year of government 1981–2: substantial increases in the minimum wage and in social benefits; retirement at age 60 instead of 65; a fifth week of paid holidays; extension of workers' rights in industry; nationalization of thirty-nine banks and nine industrial groups; tax on wealth; decentralization to the regions, departments, and communes; abolition of the death penalty. Some promises such as the return to proportional representation for the election of members of Parliament were put into effect totally later on, and a few, such as the reduction of the working week, partially.

Few commitments were totally abandoned, and when they were the reason was obvious: the integration of private schools into the state system because of mass demonstrations in 1984; the giving of the right to vote in local elections to immigrants who had not acquired French nationality because of the hostile pressure of public opinion. The new Rassemblement pour la République–Union pour la Démocratie Française parliamentary majority and the Chirac government in 1986–8 were just as respectful of their contract. They had promised their electors and carried into effect: the return to a majority system of voting; the suppression of the wealth tax, deregulation of prices, exchange-rates, credit, and employment; the privatization of some twenty firms and banks before the October 1987 share crash. The right, too, had had its problems. It also had to give up its Education Bill, under pressure from the street

90 *Jean Charlot*

and its reform of the Nationality Code. It was to establish the latter six years later, in 1993. In the interim, the left, in power from 1988 to 1993, once again put into effect most of its electoral promises.

In his study Richard Rose showed, however, that the latitude of parties whether of left or right was limited by external constraints. It is relatively simple for a government with a disciplined party majority to make new laws and put its promises into effect; it is much more difficult for it to manage the economy given the impact of the European Community and of the wider world outside. A national government's capacity to act is restricted by financial speculation on the international exchange market, the regulations of the International Monetary Fund and the European Monetary System, commercial agreements within and without the European Community, and by the General Agreement on Tariffs and Trade. This is even truer in times of crisis when public money becomes rare and needs, in particular social needs, increase. In this wide economic and financial field, the similarities between left and right policies owe more to constraints than to any ideological consensus. It is because of these constraints that complete U-turns are not rare. In France in 1982–3, for instance, the socialists, converted to the defence of the franc, followed a policy of budgetary restraint and of modernization of industry, even though this meant an increase in unemployment. The RPR–UDF right in 1993, in a period of zero growth, faced with an increasing budget deficit, increased social contributions and taxes instead of reducing them, as it had promised. External constraints were once again in evidence when in 1993 international speculation forced the Balladur Government to agree to a *de facto* devaluation of the franc.

Until the summer of 1991 and the wide political debate surrounding the referendum on the Maastricht Treaty the French did not realize the extent to which French policy had been Europeanized. Today they are wary of the transfer of sovereignty to Europe. Even though they believe that European Union is a necessity, they are unwilling to accept the constraints it imposes and the rapidity with which it is, in their opinion, being implemented. Resistance is even stronger to international constraints, especially those coming from the USA.

The crisis of representative government in Europe can be better understood within this framework. It does not on the whole concern the legitimacy of the various regimes (with the exception of Italy and Belgium), although it may concern electoral law. It focuses on the inefficiency of financial and economic policies at a time when the social and human effects of the crisis are considered unacceptable by public opinion: massive unemployment, growth of poverty, growing insecurity, fear for the future of children, etc.

National political élites are contested and considered responsible for the economic and social crisis, whereas in fact their capacity to act is strictly limited by the Europeanization of national policies and by the importance of an international monetary system of which the peoples of Europe are only just beginning to be conscious. Governments in Europe are paying the price of a lack of open government and democratic debate on their European policies. With the exception of Britain, governments and administrations of the member states, spurred on by the Commission in Brussels, have acted alone, taking for granted the commitment to Europe of their peoples. It is surprising that this crisis of confidence should have occurred at a time when the political élites in the advanced industrial democracies had never before been so well informed of the political expectations and reactions of their peoples.

2. *Opinion Polls and the Link between Élites and their Peoples*

In 1945 in Britain Gallup, the only institute of public opinion in the country, in the only survey that it had published before this first post-war election, announced the defeat of Churchill and a Labour victory with a considerable majority. The editor of the *News Chronicle* hid the prediction on an inner page in small print. He had had no faith in the verdict. In 1987 in Britain seven institutes of public opinion published fifty-five polls. Their messages were often reproduced as headlines in some fifteen different newspapers or television channels. This does not take into account constituency polling, or the polling of a specific category of voters (women, new electors, electors from ethnic minority, etc.), nor the exit polls.[3]

In France in 1965, when the first President of the Fifth Republic was elected by universal suffrage, two opinion polls—IFOP (founded in 1938) and SOFRES (founded in 1962)—carried out a dozen pre-election surveys. In 1981, when the presidential elections brought the left back to power after twenty-three years, twelve institutes of public opinion published 160 polls before the election. This does not take into account the private polling done for candidates. The *Sondoscope*—the French review of polls—has recorded in the eleven years of its existence 6,595 political opinion polls published in France, roughly 600 a year—500 in

1981, 721 precisely in 1991—on average two a day.[4] The figures
may vary from one democracy to the next but the dramatic increase
in the number of institutes and of surveys means that opinion polls
today are an institution that modifies the functioning of representative
government.

Political élites—governments, in particular—have realized more or
less rapidly in each country the help opinion polls can be when it comes
to decision-making. The pioneering role played in this field by F. D.
Roosevelt on the advice of Hadley Cantril is well known. Today in the
USA the federal government is the biggest client of the polls and in
1970 three-quarters of the members of congress already commissioned
their own private polls. For the same reasons, in France in 1945 de
Gaulle, on the recommendation of André Malraux, was the first to
commission opinion polls. 'Opinion polls are like medicine,' Malraux
had said, 'less precise than the pollsters claim, but more precise than
anything else.' Today a special division linked directly to the Prime
Minister, the Service d'Information et de Diffusion (SID), analyses the
polls published each week in the media and pulls out all the information
which can be of use to the government. Each month the SID commissions
a survey on the government's action, policies, popularity, etc. Whenever it is felt necessary, the SID also commissions *ad hoc* polls on
sensitive issues (such as the Gulf War or the nurses' strike) or on some
initiative the government is planning. In this way £300,000 are spent by
the government on private polls. This does not take into account surveys financed by ministries—Defence, for instance, where the polling
budget is ten times greater than that of the SID, or Education, Economy
and Finance, Agriculture, etc. Regular polls, polls in times of crisis,
polls accompanying specific government decisions, the special analysis
of published polls for ministers, all show the importance given by the
French government to public opinion.

The impact of this continuous, organized, and institutionalized analysis
of public opinion is considerable. I have studied the memoirs of some
thirty different political leaders in different democracies and noted
systematically all the references that are made to public opinion—how
it is defined, the need felt to study it, how this is done, what account
it takes of it, and how important the writers thought public opinion
was.[5] Most of the authors recognized the nature of what can be called
the 'opinion cycle': an initial 'honeymoon period', followed by a drop in
popularity and then improvement towards the end of the mandate. They
also commented on the ephemeral effects of rallying round the flag and

the leader when there was a serious international crisis. They also noted variations of public opinion in times of domestic crisis or when elections are drawing near—in other words at times when electors are able to wield power.

May 1968 is a good example: Michel Jobert, who was at the time in Georges Pompidou's kitchen cabinet at Matignon, expressed surprise that on 12 May neither major politicians nor the Communist Party had realized the weakness of 'the State . . . deprived of the support of public opinion . . . vulnerable, unsure of itself and of what it represented'.[6] Georges Pompidou, the Prime Minister of the day, believed that public opinion wanted violence to be controlled. 'Avoid tragedy as far as the students are concerned (France does not accept the possibility of its young being killed, nor could I stand the idea) and all political intrigues would soon be submerged in ridicule.'[7] De Gaulle, who was then President of the Republic, found the situation difficult to manage and did not act until he had events once again in hand. Pompidou remembered that, according to what de Gaulle himself had said earlier, 'only a direct appeal to the people can help one dominate a crisis'.[8] He therefore sought to gain time while waiting for the inevitable wind of change in public opinion: 'Riots in the streets, the unbelievable scenes at the Sorbonne and the Odéon, the economic paralysis would sooner or later enable the tables to be turned. Already in the provinces a weariness and irritation were growing.'[9]

Watergate's effect on Richard Nixon is another striking illustration of the weight of public opinion in times of domestic crisis. Nixon went from despair to hope and back again. The American President knew that his fate was in the hands of public opinion, as indicated by the opinion polls, to a much greater extent than in those of his enemies in Congress. He believed that the real risk of being impeached came from public opinion and that he was in circumstances similar to those of an election campaign when each side tries to win over public support.[10] He followed, with a growing disquiet, the rise in his unpopularity until in the polls those in favour of his impeachment became the most numerous[11] and he was forced to resign in order to escape being tried by the Supreme Court. It had become obvious that he no longer had the support necessary to lead a government to the best advantage of the country.

Opinion polls also played their part in the downfall of Mrs Thatcher. The vote of the Conservative parliamentary group, which forced her out of office, would of course have been impossible without the intervention of a handful of party leaders—Howe, Heseltine, etc. But would

Jean Charlot

they have spoken out and would they have been followed had not opinion polls first shown the drop in Conservative voting intentions and later, during the leadership crisis, the potential scores Conservatives would have were Heseltine or Major to be leader?

During such dramatic events public opinion shows its sovereignty. But in fact the power of the people is also present in the day-to-day record the opinion polls give of what people want, how they judge, and whom they prefer. One of Michel Rocard's advisers explained to us that during Rocard's prime ministership a series of opinion polls had been commissioned allowing him to follow the evolution of the morale of French public employees, the expectations and fears concerning immigration, and the single European market. During the crucial period of German reunification both French and German opinion had been closely followed. Opinion with regard to major governmental projects such as the Contribution Sociale Généralisée, a new solidarity tax, were measured three times: first before the subject was broached by the government, so that the government knew what aspects of the system of social protection could not in the eyes of the French people be tampered with; then a second time before the arbitration of the Prime Minister and President to test the popularity of the different, sometimes contradictory, reforms proposed by the ministers concerned; lastly, to see how best to present the government's measures. These measurements of public opinion can in fact modify things. The Rocard Government stressed, for instance, in its Bill on the Minimum Subsistence Benefit that it would be accompanied, as the public wanted, by serious efforts to reintegrate beneficiaries in society. To give another example, the low morale of public servants caused him to revise their salary grid and give general pay increases. The attachment of the French to the notion of inheritance caused the Government to give up the socialist temptation to increase death duties; and the hostility of the public to the measure caused the Government to drop any idea of giving immigrants the vote in local elections, even though this was an old socialist promise.

Michel Rocard went even further; he defended a new theory of the links between political élites and the people. In his speech at Joué-les-Tours, on 20 September 1990, speaking of the unpopularity of the Socialist governments of Pierre Mauroy and Laurent Fabius, which had preceded his own, he said: 'Governments today must, however difficult it is, seek the support of public opinion.' And he went on to say that 'in a modern democracy such as ours, parties have not the legitimacy, are not founded to do anything except what the French people want'.

This conception was, he claimed, contrary to the Leninist conception of a political party as 'a conscious organized avant-garde of the people, purporting to know better than they where their interests lay'. Rocard is convinced that the people, collectively, is more intelligent than any single individual, that it knows what it wants and above all what it does not want, and he underlined that 'harsh measures and unpopular measures' were not synonymous. 'When sacrifices are asked of the French, they always consent if they are convinced of their necessity and if they consider them just.' The reforms that political élites want to implement must, if they are to be 'of some duration and depth', be set in train 'at a rhythm acceptable to the public, never slower, never faster'. Rocard's theory has in a sense been proven a posteriori in France. The popularity of Edouard Balladur in 1993, despite his harsh policy of recovery and reform, shows that the French can accept sacrifices. The crisis of support for European Union caused by the Maastricht Treaty shows that the people cannot be pushed faster or further than they want to go. This Rocardian version of democracy is not shared by all Socialist leaders. Pierre Mauroy, for instance, condemns 'this new form of direct and permanent democracy through the opinion polls' in the name of representative democracy and his conception of the state; Laurent Fabius rejects the idea, as he puts it, of the Socialist Party as a 'barometer-party' and sees it rather as a 'party of social change'.

3. An Opinion-Led Democracy?

The controversies concerning the polls and their role are not limited to political élites. In France, at least, passionate ideological debate—which may surprise by the violence of the terms and arguments used—has developed among specialists in the social sciences since Pierre Bourdieu in 1973 declared that 'There is no such thing as public opinion.' He claimed that opinion polls were without any scientific worth and were conducted by pollsters for commercial and manipulative aims.[12] Seventeen years later Bourdieu's disciple Patrick Champagne, while remaining more than ever convinced that polling was a false, manipulative science, corrected his master on one point: public opinion must exist since political scientists and pollsters have managed in the space of twenty years to make people believe in its existence.[13] Pollsters are, according to these neo-Marxists, unscientific and incapable of understanding the problems of the data collection and analysis of public opinion. Their criticism refuses to take into account the increasing sophistication of polling. It rests, moreover, on the assumption that the masses, since they do not know everything about politics, are incapable of taking part in political debates and would in any case have no influence on the issues put on the agenda.[14] Political scientists and poll experts for their part say that such neo-Marxist criticisms as Bourdieu's stem in fact from a rejection of universal suffrage and of individual beliefs in the name of a collectivist, avant-gardist logic and a certain disregard of the citizen and his capacities for political knowledge, judgement, expression, and choice.[15]

Political élites in democratic systems sought to know what the people thought long before opinion polls were invented. Émile Combes, the Radical Third Republic Prime Minister who brought about the separation of church and state in France, gives in his memoirs the recipe for feeling the pulse of public opinion at the beginning of the century:

My department [Lower Charentes] was considered to be of middling opinion, equidistant from the extremes of left and right. I was therefore able when I wanted to test the ideological beliefs of the French . . . to apply the scientific method par excellence, the experimental method which goes from the known to the unknown. Following this I was authorized to believe that France as a whole would welcome the separation of the church and state as my own department did.[16]

More generally, letters received, opinions solicited or volunteered, walkabouts, demonstrations, and press commentaries were used and continue to be used as indicators of public opinion by politicians. Opinion polls have not changed politicians' recognition of the importance of public opinion for their election or re-election—but they have changed the method of apprehending it.

The public opinion gauged by the old indicators is the opinion of the active, of whom there are very few between elections. Nor are they very representative of the opinions of the electorate as a whole, with whom they are often confused. Politicians today know the difference and it is through opinion polls based on representative samples of the electorate that they try to predict their electoral future and that of their party, and if necessary take action to improve their chances.

Irving Crespi, Vice-President of the Gallup Group, speaks of the popularity surveys of American presidents as continuing elections that transform a former intermittent electoral process into a continuing process of which the actual elections represent periodical climaxes.[17]

The substitute for the electorate, between elections, is henceforth public opinion as opinion polls reveal it, as the media present it, and as the politicians analyse it. This has without doubt been the major effect of opinion polls. The evaluation and control of the political élites by the people no longer depend on the intermittent rhythm of the elections, but are registered continuously by opinion polls. This evaluation of politicians by the public is not only global and general, but also detailed, precise, clear, and concrete, thanks to the questions put. The voice of the people can be heard by those who want to hear it at all times. The opinion poll has become a new means of political participation: informal, neither regular nor routine, individual, freely given or refused. Its political influence is far from negligible. The spreading of opinion polls has reinforced the importance of public opinion—that is, of the electors— in politics and has led to an increased level of direct democracy in democratic representative systems. 'The rapid toing and froing between electors and the elected through elections and opinion polls has changed the very nature of representation if only on account of the speeding up of the process of adjustment.'[18]

Does this mean that we are in the process, in the industrial democracies like those of the European Community, of becoming a 'democracy of public opinion' instead of a 'democracy of political parties', just as at the end of the nineteenth century parliamentary democracy gave way to party democracy? Bernard Manin thinks that this metamorphosis of political representation is at the root of the crisis of representation in Western democracies. The public-opinion democracy is in his opinion a new type of democracy characterized by the personalization of political choice, the attention given to the 'images' of individual and collective political actors, the floating vote of well-informed, politicized voters, and the constant presence of the people's voice.[19] This model, even if stimulating, seems to us an exaggeration of the facts.

The ideal type of public-opinion democracy does not have the same explanatory capacity as that of party democracy or, before that, of parliamentary democracy. Even in a political system as personalized as that of the Fifth Republic in France, the political groups—the parties in particular—still play a crucial role in the selecting of candidates and in their chances of success, beginning with candidates for the presidency; in the formulation of presidential or legislative party programmes, which should not be thought of as simple regroupings of symbols and of political images; in party discipline in Parliament; in setting the agenda for political debate in the country, the media, and the Assemblies. In

other words, both what is on offer and the regulation of personal ambi-
tions remain firmly in the hands of the parties.

Moreover, the voice of the people, even if it is more clearly heard
than it used to be, thanks to opinion polls, is more or less listened to,
according to the institutions, the political subcultures, and the circumstances. Dictatorships and authoritarian regimes ignore the opinions
of their peoples. In presidential regimes like that of the Fifth Republic
political élites are more inclined to heed public opinion than they are
in parliamentary regimes, like that of the French Fourth Republic. Under
the Fifth Republic, as in the USA, political élites have used popularity
figures as a precious political resource. Under the Fourth Republic
popularity was viewed with suspicion. The politician who was anxious
about his popularity, as were Antoine Pinay and Pierre Mendès-France,
were quickly accused by the political class of using the street against
Parliament. 'If Pinay was toppled—Vincent Auriol, the President of the
Republic noted in December 1952—it was because he was popular and
if that was the case it was because he had brought prices down.'[20] In
the same way it can be said that parties of government are more sensitive
to the expectations and reactions of public opinion than are permanent
opposition parties. And that among the parties of government, voter-
directed parties—that is, parties considering their voters rather than
their activists or leading figures as the basis of their legitimacy[21]—pay
more attention to public opinion than do activist parties. In this respect,
the debate opposing Michel Rocard to Pierre Mauroy and Laurent
Fabius on the role of public opinion in the parties and in the action of
the government can be analysed as an internal debate on the nature of
the Socialist Party. Is it a voter-directed party or an activist-directed
party?

Circumstances also play a part in the attention paid to opinion polls
and public opinion. When they are in power, politicians cannot always
in fact follow public opinion, nor can they ignore it indefinitely.
Demagogues who follow public opinion slavishly and those who refuse
to listen to the voice of the people at all have little chance of remaining
in power. Ministerial élites must take into account not only the judgements of public opinion, but also the actions of activists, their own
limited resources, and of course external constraints. In other words,
public-opinion democracy—to a much greater extent than party democracy or parliamentary democracy—maintains within itself its own
limitations. Opinion-poll democracy is largely mythical. The only new
aspect—and it is one of importance—is that the people can be better

heard today than in the past and that the confidence of the people in the political élites is not automatic nor necessarily durable and must be continuously renewed. The political élites and the parties have not lost their power over the political output, although the political input has become much more demanding and autonomous than it used to be. The power of public opinion has grown and it puts pressure on governments, but the decisions remain in the hands of the political élites, who ignore voters' expectations at their peril.

NOTES

1. Richard Rose, *Do Parties Make a Difference?* (London: Macmillan, 1980).

2. Bernard Manin, 'Métamorphoses du gouvernement représentatif', in Danielle Pecaut and Bernardo Sorj, *Les Métamorphoses de la représentation politique au Brésil et en Europe* (Paris, Édition du CNRS, 1991), 31.

3. Ivor Crewe, 'Matters of Opinion', *Social Studies Review*, 6 (Nov. 1990), 47–52.

4. *Sondoscope* (Feb. 1992).

5. Jean Charlot, 'La Popularité comme ressource politique entre les élections', report to the Colloque de l'Association Française de Science Politique sur la popularité politique, Paris, mimeo, 1991.

6. Michel Jobert, *Mémoires d'avenir* (Paris: Grasset, 1974).

7. Georges Pompidou, *Pour rétablir une vérité* (Paris: Flammarion, 1982).

8. Ibid. 71.

9. Ibid. 182.

10. Richard Nixon, *Mémoires* (Paris: Flammarion, 1978).

11. Ibid. 677, 689, 700, 722.

12. Pierre Bourdieu, 'L'Opinion publique n'existe pas', *Les Temps Modernes*, 318 (Jan. 1973), 1292–1307 and 'Remarques à propos de la valeur scientifique et des effets politiques des enquêtes d'opinion', *Pouvoirs*, 33 (Apr. 1985), 131–9.

13. Patrick Champagne, *Faire l'opinion* (Paris: Éditions de Minuit, 1990).

14. For a more realistic view of the political competence of citizens, see Russell J. Dalton, *Citizen Politics in Western Democracies* (Chatham, NJ, Chatham House, 1988), 13–76.

15. Alain Lancelot, 'Sondages et démocratie', *SOFRES: Opinion publique* (Paris: Gallimard, 1984), 257–66 and Gérard Grunberg, 'Les Ennemis de l'opinion', *Débat*, 66 (1991), 44–54.

16. Émile Combes, *Mon Ministère: Mémoires 1902–1905* (Paris: Plon, 1956), 195.

17. Irving Crespi and Harold Mendelsohn, *Polls, Television and the New Politics* (San Francisco: Chandler, 1970).
18. Gérard Grunberg, 'Sondages d'opinion, participation et représentation', in CEVIPOF, *L'Engagement politique: Déclin ou mutation*, ii (Paris: Presses de la FNSP, 1993), 896.
19. Manin, 'Métamorphoses du gouvernement représentatif', 71.
20. Vincent Auriol, *Mon Septennat 1947–1954: Notes de journal*, presented by P. Nora and J. Ozouf (Paris: Gallimard, 1970).
21. Jean Charlot, *The Gaullist Phenomenon* (London: Allen & Unwin, 1971).

5

The European Union, the Political Class, and the People

VERNON BOGDANOR

1

The Maastricht Treaty was ratified with very large majorities in the legislatures of all the member states of the Community.[1] In Belgium it gained in the lower house a majority of 146 to 33 with 3 abstentions, and in the Senate a majority of 115 to 26 with 1 abstention. In France the treaty received a majority of 388 to 43 on second reading in the Assembly, and a vote of 592 to 73 in the joint Congress of both houses needed for constitutional amendments, easily exceeding the three-fifths majority required by the Constitution. In Germany the Bundestag endorsed the treaty by 543 to 17 with 8 abstentions, in Greece Parliament voted 286 to 8 with 1 abstention, and in Spain by 314 to 3 with 8 abstentions, and, in the Senate, by 222 to 0 with 3 abstentions.

Even in the two member states widely regarded as the most sceptical towards membership of the Union—Britain and Denmark—their legislatures endorsed the treaties by large majorities. In Denmark the Folketing, by contrast with 1986, when there was no majority for the Single European Act, voted 130 to 25 in favour of it with 1 abstention and 23 absentees, while in Britain there was a second-reading majority of 244 in the House of Commons in favour of ratification.

Superficially, such large majorities would seem to be in line with the views of the electorates of the member states as reflected in the Eurobarometer surveys which have sought to evaluate public opinion in the European Community since 1974. Writing in 1991 and comparing the trend of public opinion in nine member states, excluding Greece, Portugal, and Spain, which did not join the Community until the 1980s, Inglehart and Reif found that 'a sense of solidarity among the nine nations of the EC has emerged—Today, the prospect of an EC that is united, not only economically, but also politically, is no idle dream. To a surprising extent, the publics of the member nations are already ready to accept it . . .'. Across the twelve nations as a whole, 'supporters of unification outnumber opponents by almost eight to one. Moreover, support for unification outweighs opposition by an overwhelming margin in eleven of the twelve countries. The sole exception is Denmark, and even there 56 per cent of the public are now favourable.'[2]

More specifically, Eurobarometer surveys found that in answer to the question 'In general are you for or against efforts being made to unify Western Europe' asked in 1989, 80 per cent across the twelve member states answered 'Yes', and only 11 per cent answered 'No'. Even in Britain 70 per cent answered 'Yes' and only 18 per cent 'No'. When asked whether they were 'for or against the formation of a European government, responsible to the European Parliament', those favouring a European government outnumbered those who did not by around two to one; 49 per cent said that they did favour a European government, while 24 per cent said they did not, although in Britain and Denmark there were majorities against a European government.

Inglehart and Reif were able to conclude, therefore, on a triumphalist note, 'The parochial nationalism that seemed so pronounced in France under de Gaulle has vanished. Today the French are amongst the most solidly pro-European publics in Europe.' Even in Britain attitudes were changing and so 'If British attitudes continue to evolve as they have during the past two decades, European political unity may come about early in the coming century.'[3]

Yet, whenever the electorates of the member states are required actually to vote on the Union, they have proved that the generalized goodwill and enthusiasm displayed in the Eurobarometer surveys cannot be translated into support for the Union.

During 1992 referendums to endorse Maastricht were held in three of the member states. Only the referendum in Ireland produced a safe majority for the treaty. In Denmark the treaty was narrowly rejected although six out of the eight parties represented in the Folketing, comprising around 80 per cent of the seats in the legislature, supported it. This was a marked contrast to the situation in 1986, when the Folketing rejected the Single European Act but the people endorsed it.

But Denmark had always been regarded as sceptical towards European integration, and so the result there, perhaps, was less of a surprise than the outcome in France, a country believed to be at the heart of Europe, where the treaty was supported by the leadership of all the major parties, with the exception of the National Front, and where media time was slanted in the interests of those favouring ratification of the treaty. The treaty, however, was accepted only narrowly, by a majority of 51 per cent to 49 per cent.

In Britain the government, supported by the official opposition, refused to put the issue to referendum, survey evidence indicating that Maastricht would have been in danger of defeat if submitted to the direct vote of the people. In at least one other member state, Germany, where there was no provision for a referendum, survey evidence indicated that it was by no means certain that Maastricht would be ratified if it were to depend upon a popular vote.

In 1989 there had been an earlier signal that generalized enthusiasm, as expressed in Eurobarometer surveys, was not easy to translate into concrete support for European integration, for the overall level of turn-out for the elections to the European Parliament fell for the third time running. The turn-out in 1989, 58.5 per cent, was lower than it had been in 1984, 59.4 per cent, which was in turn lower than it had been in 1979, 62.5 per cent. In France the turn-out in 1989 was the lowest ever at any national election, and in Spain it was lower than at any time since the return of democratic elections in 1977. In 1994 average turn-out fell to an even lower level than that of 1989, to 56.5 per cent. This time Britain's turn-out of 36.7 per cent was not the lowest, being exceeded by Portugal, 36.4 per cent and by the Netherlands, 35.0 per cent, hitherto regarded as a stronghold of enthusiasm for European integration.

The fall in turn-out between 1984 and 1989 and between 1989 and 1994 has been particularly disappointing for supporters of European integration, for the failure of direct elections to ignite enthusiasm in 1979 or 1984 could easily be ascribed to the lack of powers of the European Parliament. What was the point, it might be argued, of voting for a Parliament which was, in reality, little more than a talking-shop? But that excuse was not available either in 1989 or in 1994. For the European Parliament's powers had been very significantly increased by the Single European Act and the Maastricht Treaty, which had given the Parliament, in practice, if not in theory, the power of co-decision over a wide area of Community legislation.[4] Moreover, the political composition of the Parliament elected in 1989 might have been thought important for the future development of the Union, for it would be called upon to help decide the shape of the internal market: should it be based upon the free market, or upon more interventionist principles? Yet the debate on the future of the Union aroused little interest. Only in Belgium, where voting is compulsory, and in Germany, Ireland, and

TABLE 5.1. *Result of the 1992 referendum on Maastricht in France*

'Yes' Voters	%	'No' Voters	%
Socialists	74	Le Pen supporters	95
Centre-left	72	Communists	92
Génération Écologie	69	Extreme right	83
UDF	58	Extreme left	82
Left	57	Right	68
Neither left nor right	53	RPR	67

Source: SOFRES poll, cited in *Le Monde*, 25 Sept. 1992; *Modern and Contemporary France* (1993), Documents and Resources, 126.

Britain was turn-out higher than in 1984, and in Britain the increase was from the abysmally low level of 32 per cent in 1984 to 36 per cent in 1989. Only in Belgium, Greece, Italy, Ireland, and Luxembourg could the level of turn-out in 1989 be held to constitute a resounding vote of confidence in the Community.

Thus, both the referendums on Maastricht and direct elections to the European Parliament have revealed a very different picture of the state of opinion towards European integration from that obtained through the scrutiny of parliamentary votes or Eurobarometer surveys. The unwillingness of the electorate to endorse Maastricht or to vote in elections for the European Parliament when contrasted with the large majorities for it in the legislatures of the member states showed that the European Union was beginning to give rise to that deepest and most intractable of all political cleavages, a cleavage between the people and the political class.

The existence of such a cleavage was particularly noticeable in France, where it had of course helped to destroy the Fourth Republic. The 1992 referendum pointed to a fundamental divide between moderate France, which was Social-Christian, and a nationalist France of the extremes.

Moreover, in France, the cleavage between the political class and the people had been revealed earlier, in the 1984 European Parliament elections, when they had been the means by which Le Pen's National Front had made its first electoral breakthrough; just as the 1989 elections had been the instrument by which the Republicans in West Germany first won enough votes to attract national attention.

Thus the evidence from actual electoral behaviour as opposed to that from parliamentary decision-making and survey evidence is that a

European consciousness has not yet been created in the member states of the Union. Indeed, it would seem from the evidence of the French and Danish referendums, from the low turn-out in elections to the European Parliament, and from the resurrection of the radical Right in a number of European countries, that nationalism is a rising force in the member states, while enthusiasm for European unity is decreasing rather than increasing.

This has been well understood by the governments of the member states, whose actions, as contrasted with their rhetoric, derive from their understanding that they are still responsible to national electorates with national interests. The two main elements of the Maastricht Treaty, after all, were monetary union and co-operation in foreign and security policy. The effective collapse of the exchange-rate mechanism earlier in 1993 has imperilled the first of these objectives, while the failure of the member states to agree upon policy towards Yugoslavia showed the hollowness of the second ambition. When, in December 1991, Germany declared that she proposed to recognize Croatia and Slovenia within a few weeks, whether other member states of the European Community did so or not, she was supported by Italy, but opposed by France and the United Kingdom. It was natural that, after failure to agree on policy towards the disintegrating Yugoslav state, the Community should be equally unable to agree upon policy towards Bosnia. There was no such entity as 'Europe' capable of formulating an agreed viewpoint. In 1913, by contrast, 'Europe' existed; for the European Concert of Powers was able in that year, for the last time, to impose peace in the Balkans. By 1914 it could not. There is a historical irony in that it was the same Balkan town, Sarajevo, which in 1914 ended one idea of Europe and seventy-eight years later, in 1992, was to end another.

2

In what they do, then, as opposed to what they say, governments seem themselves to accept the thesis that for their electorates national self-interest has a higher priority than adherence to a transnational policy dictated by 'Europe'. How is one to account for this divergence between parliamentary outcomes and opinion polls on the one hand, and the actual behaviour of electors when called upon to vote?

One approach favoured by many European leaders would find the answer in 'fault lines' (to use John Major's phrase) in the Maastricht

Treaty. On this view, the basic need for the Community is to create new monetary institutions capable of overcoming the problems which the ERM has exposed. Others argue that what is needed is a radical push forward, ignoring the set-backs of recent months.

Yet, that was not the approach of the founding fathers of the European Community. When the European Defence Community was defeated in the French National Assembly in 1954, Jean Monnet did not wish to hit his head against a brick wall. Instead, he sought an alternative route to European unity which culminated in the Treaty of Rome establishing the European Community. Similar creative thinking is surely needed today if the whole European enterprise is not to run into the sands.

The Union, as it is at present, is built upon an institutional framework which has for its motivating purpose the economics of self-interest. Pursuit of rational self-interest, so it is argued, on the part both of individuals and states, will lead to the gradual elimination of national boundaries until, almost without peoples and member states being aware of it, a united Europe will spring into being. That, indeed, was why supporters of the Union felt themselves so committed to monetary union. For the setting up of a European central bank would involve the transfer of such massive power over macro-economic decision-making that it would compel Europe's politicians to make provision for a democratic structure to underpin the Union; and the Maastricht Treaty does indeed make some obeisance towards such a democratic structure. For the most important part of this treaty from the point of view of accountability is Article 158, which provides for the term of office of the Commission and the European Parliament to be the same, and for the Commission to be subject to the approval of the Parliament. That, it was believed, would help to establish the Union as a truly democratic structure in which the Commission, an embryonic European executive, would come to be responsible to parliament, as in the classical model of responsible government.

This, however, raises some fundamental questions. The first is whether a parliamentary model of government can work effectively in the absence of a common European consciousness? In those countries where parliamentary government is successful, there is a basic willingness to accept majority decisions, based upon a common consciousness of belonging to the same state. When that consciousness disappears, as with Ireland *vis-à-vis* the United Kingdom after 1885 or Norway *vis-à-vis* Sweden in 1905, parliamentary government cannot work. Is there such a common consciousness in Europe; and, if there is not, can parliamentary government operate successfully in its absence? More generally, can Europe be built on the basis of economics and institutions, or do the institutions follow on from, rather than precede, the creation of a European consciousness; and, if so, how is this European consciousness to be created?

The conventional answer to this last question is that a European consciousness can be created by existing Union institutions, and in particular perhaps by the European Parliament. It is, on this view, direct elections to the European Parliament which can both help to create a European consciousness and allow that consciousness to obtain democratic expression. At first sight, this may appear a plausible view. For direct elections to the European Parliament are, of course, transnational elections; indeed they represent the world's first successful experiment in transnational democracy. Moreover, the party groups in the European Parliament are organized on transnational rather than national lines. They sit in the Parliament divided by political creeds—Christian democrat, social democrat, liberal, etc.—not by national origins—British, French, German. Yet while direct elections may have helped to legitimize the Union, it would be difficult to argue that they have helped to create a European consciousness, or indeed that they are capable of doing so. This is because transnational elections perform a wholly different function from national elections.

At national level, elections normally perform three main functions. They allow electors to choose a government and to help determine the direction of public policy, and they also provide a recognizable human face for government in the form of a political leader—a president or prime minister. This last function has come very much to the fore in an age dominated by the media, which have helped to personalize politics and have made party leaders, even in non-presidential regimes, crucial figures in the creation of a rapport between government and the governed.

Direct elections, however, as they operate at present, can achieve none of these functions. They do not determine the political colour of the Community, how it is to be governed, for they do not affect the composition of the Commission, nor, of course, of the Council of Ministers. Therefore, they do little to help determine the policies followed by the Union; nor do they yield personalized and recognizable leadership for the Union.

For direct elections, although fought by transnational parties, are not at present genuinely transnational elections. Rather, they are a series of separate national test elections whose implications for the domestic politics of the member states are far more important than any consequences they may have for the political direction or government of the Union.

The German political scientist Karlheinz Reif, has characterized direct elections, together with local and other subnational elections, as *Nebenwahlen*, second-order elections, the outcome of which are determined by domestic political allegiances rather than by attitudes towards European matters. The strongest influence upon the outcome of such elections is likely to be the political situation in the first-order arena, i.e. the national arena at the time the second-order elections are held. Indeed, Reif has put forward a model relating the outcomes in direct elections to domestic political allegiances modified by the popularity or unpopularity of the incumbent government in the member state concerned. This in turn will be considerably influenced by the length of time that the incumbent government has been in office. From these factors—domestic political allegiances, the popularity or unpopularity of an incumbent government, and the length of time the incumbent government has been in office—Reif's model enables one to predict, with a considerable degree of accuracy, the outcome of elections to the European Parliament.[5]

The primary purpose of a first-order election is to choose a government. Second-order elections, by contrast, can have a number of very different functions. But, when compared with first-order elections, second-order elections are likely to stimulate a lower turn-out, since there is less at stake. Voters are not choosing a government in elections to the European Parliament any more than they are in local elections. Second, small new parties—'flash' parties—are likely to perform better. In national elections, voters may be chary of 'wasting' their votes on a party which is unlikely to be able to form a government. They will therefore vote tactically. But, in a second-order election, this consideration will not be relevant since the formation of a government is not in question. Finally, the 'protest' element is likely to be greater, and so the model may over-predict the government vote and under-predict the vote for opposition parties. The same is true, of course, if the model is applied to local elections and, in Britain, by-elections.[6] It is the second and third factors which largely explain the success that the French National Front and the German Republicans have been able to achieve in direct elections.

3

Thus, direct elections to the European Parliament, although in form transnational, are in reality an arena for a series of national contests. The most important electoral arena, despite over forty years of 'European integration', remains, therefore, the domestic political system. European Parliament elections are in reality a conglomeration of national elections in the twelve member states.

Looking at the 1989 elections, for example, there seemed only one genuinely transnational feature, an increase in support for the Greens. Since most of the Green parties, if not openly hostile to the Union, are sceptical towards proposals for further integration—the German Greens were the only party represented in the Bundestag to have voted against the Single European Act, while the British Greens favoured withdrawal—the success of the Greens in 1989 could be interpreted as a rejection by European voters of moves towards integration. Yet, it would be highly implausible to interpret the success of the Greens in this way until we have data to indicate that Green voters shared the attitude of their party towards European Union, and that their vote was cast primarily because of the Green parties' hostility to Union. Otherwise, apart from the Greens, it is hardly possible to draw any firm conclusions about the attitudes of electors to issues of European policy, since other transnational trends were conspicuous only by their absence.

In Britain, for example, the Euro-elections were primarily seen as a contest between the Conservative and Labour Parties, the main issue being whether Labour could overtake the Conservatives in a national election for the first time since 1974. Yet, on Community issues, the approaches of the Conservative and Labour Parties were remarkably similar. Both were at that time in favour of a Europe of co-operating and independent sovereign states. Both were against greater powers for the European Parliament. Both were at that time against immediate participation in the exchange-rate mechanism, and both at that time rejected monetary union. A real contest on Community issues should have pitted Labour and the Conservatives together against, on the one hand, the Liberal Democrats, who favoured a broadly federal Europe, and the Greens, who sought British withdrawal. Yet this cleavage on European issues was entirely ignored in the election campaign, and it played no part whatever in electoral behaviour. It was in consequence impossible to derive any clear conclusions concerning British attitudes to Europe from the outcome of the elections. The only conclusions that could have been drawn related to domestic politics, the greater popularity of Labour, and the decline in support for the Conservatives and Liberal Democrats.

One may contrast this situation with that in Denmark, the only member state in which party divisions reflected a European rather than a merely domestic dimension. For Denmark, as Torben Worre has shown, is a striking exception to the generalization made concerning the primarily domestic function of direct elections, in that it is the only country of the Union where a genuine Euro-party system has arisen, coexisting with the domestic party system, but with the two party systems insulated from each other.[7] The development of a separate Euro-party system in Denmark is primarily due to the formation of the People's Movement against the European Community, which competes in European Parliament elections but not in domestic elections. The People's Movement is a coalition of parties hostile to the Union, which seeks to give the Danish voter the opportunity to show his or her rejection of European integration.

In Denmark the Euro-party system allowed for the three basic attitudes towards the Union to be articulated by the parties. The first, that of the People's Movement, the Socialist People's Party, and other parties to the left of the Social Democrats, was one of rejection. The second position, that of a state's rights acceptance of the Community but resistance to further encroachments of sovereignty—roughly the position adumbrated by Margaret Thatcher in her Bruges speech of September 1988—was expressed by the Social Democrats, the Radicals, and Mogens Glistrup's Progress Party; while, finally, support for European integration was the position of the Conservatives, Liberals, Centre Democrats, and Christian Peoples Party.

Thus the Danish electorate could, if it chose to vote on European rather than domestic issues, express its opinion on the future of Europe. But in no other member state, nor in the European Parliament itself, does the party system allow for such a structuring of opinion. Denmark may be contrasted, for example, with Britain, where many shared the Danish states rights philosophy. In Britain in 1989 the election was a left–right domestic battle and it was fought as a plebiscite on Margaret Thatcher's government after ten years in office. The future of Europe is probably as controversial in Britain as it is in Denmark, but the party system inhibited debate on Europe's future direction. The structure of the party system in Britain and indeed in all of the member states except Denmark is such that it does not allow deductions to be made from the outcome of direct elections about the distribution of opinion in the electorate on Europe-wide issues.

Indeed, it could be argued that even to characterize direct elections as 'second-order elections' is to concede too much. For in other second-order elections such as local elections, voters are choosing the government of their locality, either a local council of a particular colour or a mayor with executive functions. Thus, the voter will be able to grasp the connection between his or her vote and local political outcomes. In the European Union, however, the election does not lead to the choice of an executive or of an electoral college which chooses an executive. Therefore, it is extremely difficult for the voter to perceive any connection between his or her vote and the policy of the Union. Direct elections may come to appear as little more than a superior opinion poll, charting the fortunes of the main domestic political forces. It is for this reason that Reif claims that 'European elections are in danger of constituting a category of their own—"third-order national elections" with barely more relevance than that of an official opinion poll.'[8]

4

The standard response made by reformers to these weaknesses in the mechanisms of popular control and accountability in the European Parliament is to suggest that they can be overcome by making the Commission responsible to the European Parliament, just as in parliamentary democracies the government is generally responsible to a chamber elected directly by universal suffrage. They point to the increasing importance of the European Parliament, as shown by the percentage of its amendments now accepted by both the Commission and the Council of Ministers. Further steps towards making the Commission responsible to the European Parliament along the lines of Article 158 of the Maastricht Treaty would emphasize the strengthening of the principle of parliamentary responsibility.

But the analogy with domestic political systems is fatally flawed. The relative success of the European Parliament's amendments is indeed an indicator of the importance of Parliament's role as a scrutineer of European legislation. But it says little about the role of Parliament in determining the general drift of European policy. This is hardly determined by Parliament, but rather, as the genesis of both the Single European Act and the Maastricht Treaty have shown, by élite manœuvres by the heads of government of the member states, and, in particular, of course, by the leaders of France and Germany.

The European Parliament can only exert a strong influence on the direction of European affairs if it is able to sustain (or reject) a party or coalition government against an alternative government comprising either a single party or coalition of parties. In the modern world political conflict in parliamentary regimes is generally not between legislative and executive, but primarily between competing parties alternating in power. What the European Parliament enjoys is, in essence, the power to amend; what it lacks is the power to determine the broad drift of policy in Europe. For it is unable to sustain a party government of the type that rules in almost all parliamentary democracies.

The main reason for this, as we have seen, is that there is, despite the seeming existence of a transnational party system, only a weakly developed European party system. In most democracies, the fundamental cleavage between parties is between left and right and it is based upon the socio-economic dimension of politics. The parties are divided on such issues as the distribution of income and the relative balance between public power and private enterprise. Writing in 1981, Arend Lijphart contrasted twenty-eight democratic party systems with the party system of the European Parliament.[9] He found that the 'most common ideological dimensions of democratic party systems are the socio-economic dimension, present in all systems, and the religious dimension found in half of the party systems'.[10] In the member states of the Union, excluding Luxembourg, the religious dimension was to be found in five of the eleven countries. With the party groups in the European Parliament, however, the socio-economic dimension was less dominant than in domestic party systems. There was a much wider range of deviation on the socio-economic left–right dimension than might have been expected. Lijphart's findings 'partly contradict our earlier conclusion about the dominance of the socio-economic dimension. On the basis of this conclusion, we would have expected the party groups to have small mean deviations on the socio-economic dimension and relatively large variations on the religious dimension.'[11] Admittedly, this surprising outcome resulted in part from the methodology used in determining party group ratings, but it nevertheless remained significant even when this point had been taken into account. Indeed, it was for this very reason, the lack of dominance of the socio-economic dimension, that Lijphart questioned the credentials of the European Parliament to be regarded as a true Parliament, concluding his discussion with the speculation that 'If and when the European Parliament becomes a true legislature, and if socioeconomic problems constitute its principal dimension of ideological conflict, it is likely that drastic party realignments will take place.'[12]

Thus, the domestic party systems in the member states are based primarily upon a socio-economic dimension, while the party system in the European Parliament emphasizes, especially upon issues concerning European integration, a quite different cleavage. Although, in the 1989 elections to the European Parliament, politicians such as Margaret Thatcher spoke as if the Parliament was divided by a left–right cleavage, the Parliament does not in fact operate on such a basis. The left majority discerned by some commentators after the 1989 election is a mere artefact, the result of adding up the results of a series of separate contests. In fact, the socialist group, the largest in the Parliament, rather than work with groups to the left who did not share their enthusiasm for European integration, preferred to work with the Christian democrats, with whom they could secure an absolute majority of votes in the Parliament. Nor could the Christian democrats and the liberals, both committed to a federal Europe, be expected to work with the European right, which includes the French National Front, or with any party such as the British Conservatives or French Gaullists which maintains its serious reservations towards European integration.

Thus, on most matters, and especially on issues connected with European integration, the majority in the European Parliament is not one of 'left' or 'right', but one comprising the two leading party groups, the socialists and Christian democrats (European People's Party), together often with the liberals. The absolute majority which the socialists and Christian democrats can command has been of particular importance after the Single European Act, since, under the co-operation procedure established by this Act, the European Parliament needs an absolute rather than a simple majority to amend or reject the Council's common position on second reading. Thus the Christian democrats do not see themselves as a party of the right, but as put by their then Chairman, Jacques Santer, it 'presents itself as a viable partner for all the political forces in the European Parliament which want to take on the responsibility of continuing the development of the European Community into a political union which responds to the future challenges of internal and external policies. Via its central position, the European People's Party is the guarantor of the realization of the internal market and of its social dimension.'[13] The co-operation between the two dominant groups—the socialists and the Christian democrats—was symbolized in one of the first decisions to be taken by the new Parliament when the socialist Enrique Baron Crespo was elected President of the Parliament on the first ballot, with the Christian democrats abstaining, in return for socialist agreement to allow the election of a Christian democrat President for the second half of the Parliament's term.

The European Parliament, therefore, cannot be understood after the manner of most domestic parliaments as bipolar, with the parties in it seeking to sustain or reject a government, first because it has no control over the 'government' of Europe, and secondly because the Parliament is not bipolar. Rather it bears more resemblance to a consensual legislative model of the Swiss type. For the major groups in the European Parliament—socialists, Christian democrats, and liberals—form a consensual bloc and work together on the policy of European integration. The opposition parties form a motley collection of outsiders. First there is the European Democratic Alliance, comprising primarily French Gaullists and Irish Fianna Fáil. Second, there are the fringe groups both on the left—Greens, and French, Greek, and Portuguese communists— and on the right—the European right. Outside Britain, Denmark, France, and Ireland, therefore, it is difficult for the European voter to call for a change of direction in the European Union without voting for one of the fringe groups—either the Greens or the semi-Fascist European right.

The European party system bears less resemblance to that of the typical democrat legislature than it does to Giovanni Sartori's model of polarized pluralism in which physical occupation of the centre leads to centrifugal drives, with party competition increasingly coming to take place between an immobile centre and two incompatible extremes, so benefiting anti-system parties and irresponsible oppositions.[14] It is a paradox that direct elections, intended to help create the political will for European integration, might actually have served to increase popular alienation from European institutions, since the European party system is unable to act as a vehicle for genuine choice at the electoral level. The only means of protest in many countries seems to be to support parties of the extreme right which leave voters in no doubt about their hostility to European Union. It should thus be clear why direct elections to the European Parliament have provided a platform for such extremist parties.

Admittedly, were monetary union to be achieved, this situation could well change. Left–right issues could then play a crucial role, since macro-economic management would fall within Parliament's purview. But, as we have argued, monetary union is unlikely to come about for the foreseeable future, and indeed probably cannot come about without a much stronger underpinning of European institutions than exists at present. The party system of the European Parliament does not allow for the alternation—or potential alternation—of government characteristic of most parliamentary democracies, and it is difficult to see how any effective challenge to the dominant coalition can be made.

Direct elections, then, as at present constituted, are unable to offer the elector the power to decide the shape of Europe. Direct elections were advocated so that they might bring legitimacy to the Community. But they have been able to achieve this aim in only a limited sense. They can legitimize the major decisions concerning the future of Europe that have already been made; they offer a form of *ex post facto* endorsement; but they do not yield the choice of whether to give or to withhold that endorsement. For this reason, the European Parliament, intended as a counterweight to the bureaucratic and technocratic elements of the Union, has come to be perceived by the electors of Europe as part of that very technostructure. It is seen as an alienated superstructure, remote from the hopes and aspirations of those whom it is meant to serve.

There is thus a striking contrast between the progressive transfer of competences to European level and the growing influence of the European Parliament on the one hand, and, on the other, the lack of popular involvement on the part of the electorate. Direct elections are unable to create the popular support needed to construct a united Europe, and it is the absence of popular support which constitutes the main weakness of the European project. If not checked, this will lead to disenchantment from European Union and alienation from its objectives.

5

The European Parliament, then, is quite unlike any of the legislatures of the member states. It bears much more resemblance to the Swiss Parliament, in which there is also a consensual bloc comprising all of the main parties. Because it has not been able to articulate clear lines of division between government and opposition, the European Parliament has been unable to secure accountability of the institutions of the

Union to the electorates in the member states. This means that it has done little to help arouse a European consciousness without which European Union is unlikely to progress much further.

How, then, is such accountability to be secured? The Swiss model of consensual government suffers from the defect that, with all of the major parties represented in government, there seems no place for any equivalent to a parliamentary opposition. In Switzerland, this problem is solved through the machinery of direct democracy—the referendum and the initiative. The people themselves become in effect Her Majesty's Opposition, and the main hurdle which the Swiss government faces lies not in the legislature, but in the referendum, which takes on the character of a popular check upon government, a substitute for the missing parliamentary check.

In five of the member states—Denmark, France, Ireland, Italy, and Spain—a referendum is required either as the sole method or as one alternative method of changing the constitution. Article 247 of the Treaty of Rome requires amendments to the Treaty to be ratified in accordance with the respective constitutional requirements of the member states. That involves, in most of the member states, ratification by parliament. But, as we have seen, in a number of member states, the decisions made by parliamentarians do not correspond with public opinion. Constitutional theory requires that popular as well as parliamentary endorsement is secured in a democratic polity when sovereignty is transferred. 'The Legislative cannot transfer the power of making laws to any other hands. For it being but a delegated power from the People, they who have it cannot pass it to others' (Locke, *Second Treatise of Government*, para. 141). That constitutional principle was well understood by Altiero Spinelli, who hoped that his proposed European Union could be worked out by a European Parliament which had been granted a constituent mandate for the purpose through a referendum. Even de Gaulle, generally regarded as hostile to European Union, believed that his Fouchet Plan, providing for a confederal Europe of States, should be validated by referendum.[15]

Why, therefore, should not amendments to the Treaty of Rome be ratified in future by referendum? Of course, a simple majority in a referendum would not be sufficient, for that would enable those in the larger member states always to outvote voters in the smaller states. Instead, the Union should follow the procedure of such federal states as Australia and Switzerland and require a double majority for the endorsement of any proposal—a majority both of the voters and of the member states. Perhaps more than a bare majority of member states should be required and a two-thirds majority would be more appropriate. In addition, there might be a requirement for a qualifying majority so that amendments to the treaty were not approved on a low turn-out. That qualifying majority might be 30 per cent of the total electorate of the Union.

Were future amendments to the Union to be ratified by referendum in the manner suggested, this would serve to circumvent the problem of an amendment to which all of the member states but one agreed by large majorities, and yet the one dissenting member state was in a position to veto ratification. That looked at one time to be the fate of Maastricht when it appeared in the summer of 1992 that there were large majorities for it in every member state with the exception of Denmark.

But, of course, the referendum, while it can supplement representative democracy by remedying some of its deficiencies, cannot replace it. Even if the referendum were introduced into the Union as an instrument to validate constitutional change, that would hardly suffice to secure popular accountability for the institutions of the Union.

If the political structure of European Union does not at present yield parliamentary accountability, what alternative mechanism of accountability might there be? A number of Europe's more far-sighted leaders have come to favour the introduction of an element of direct election in European institutions. Ex-President Giscard of France has advocated that the President of the European Council be directly elected by universal suffrage and Jacques Delors has called for the direct election of the Commission President, with, as a first step towards achieving that aim, the election of the Commission President by an electoral college comprising members of national parliaments and the European Parliament.

The difficulty with these suggestions, however, is that European solidarity may not yet be sufficiently advanced for the nationals of one country to be willing to support a national of another as in effect leader of Europe. But the basic premiss behind the proposals—that Europe needs a stronger basis of democratic legitimacy—is surely right. Is there an alternative way in which this might be achieved?

One natural alternative would be direct election of the Commission, the embryonic executive of a united Europe, by the universal suffrage of electors in the member states. Electors would then be voting not for an individual candidate who might be the national of another member state, but for a ticket. Thus there would be a socialist ticket headed by, for example, Piet Dankert as candidate for the Presidency, a liberal one headed by, for example, Simone Veil, and a Christian democrat ticket headed by, for example, Leo Tindemans. Because there is a multiplicity of parties in Europe, a two-ballot system as used in elections to the French presidency would be required, with the choice on the second ballot being between a broadly left-leaning ticket and a rightward one. The election of the Commission by a two-ballot system would probably, as in elections for the French presidency, serve to encourage bipolarity: such a realignment of Europe's party system would clarify the basis of choice for European electors, so helping to secure democratic accountability.

Direct election of the Commission would clearly fulfil the functions of elections as outlined earlier. The election would be seen as fundamental to the allocation of political power in Europe. It would enable electors both to choose the government of Europe and also to indicate its conception of what the future policy of Europe should be. It would therefore give the Commission both a democratic base and a legitimacy which it at present lacks. There would, moreover, be a strong incentive for Europeans to vote in elections genuinely designed to determine Europe's political orientation. Direct election of the Commission would focus popular interest on European issues, giving them glamour and excitement, qualities sadly lacking at present, and help to cure falling turn-out and electoral apathy.

Direct election would be an explicit recognition of the principle of the sovereignty of the people, which ought to underpin the construction of an integrated Europe. For the central challenge which Europe faces is to discover some means of bridging the gap between élite proposals and popular perceptions, to construct a European consciousness, without which 'Europe' can remain but an empty construct.

Yet, neither of these two proposals—introduction of the referendum into the European Union and direct election of a European executive—would meet the immediate crisis of European institutions symbolized by lack of support for the Maastricht Treaty and the lack of enthusiasm displayed in the 1994 European elections. Any referendum held on the future of European Union at the present time would, almost certainly, lead to a rejection of the idea, while both the referendum and direct election of an executive would require further amendments to the Treaty of Rome. These amendments would be unlikely to secure ratification in all of the member states, and they would reawaken the atavistic senti-ments which Maastricht aroused.

There is, however, an alternative method by which electors to the European Parliament could be enabled to choose the Commission. Under Article 138 of the Treaty of Rome, elections to the European Parlia-ment are required to be conducted by a uniform electoral procedure in all of the member states. This uniform electoral procedure has not yet been achieved. There are numerous differences between the systems used in the various member states. The most glaring difference, however, is that Britain alone refuses, except in Northern Ireland, to use a system of proportional representation for European Parliament elections. This is, indeed, the prime source of distortion in the Parliament. After the 1994 elections, use of the first-past-the-post system in Britain had the effect of making the British Labour Party the largest party in the Parlia-ment, and the socialists the largest of the party groups, even though one of the most noticeable transnational trends had been the success of the Right in three of the five large member states: Germany, Italy, and Spain.

If, however, Britain could be persuaded to adopt one of the propor-tional representation systems, then it would be possible to produce common transnational lists for European elections. It might then come to be accepted that the winning list or bloc would have the right to form the Commission, since any Commission which was not to its liking would be rejected by the Parliament. The Commission would then be composed of members of one political colour, and it could offer the political leadership, whether of the Left or of the Right, that Europe so badly needs, leadership which would be genuinely account-able to European voters. Elections to the European Parliament would thus come to fulfil the three functions of democratic elections men-tioned previously. They would help to decide the future policies of Europe, the future government of Europe, and also its future leader-ship. It is in this direction, perhaps, that the best immediate hope lies of helping to arouse a genuine European consciousness.

This European consciousness can only be built with popular support and involvement. Thus, for Europe's leaders, the gap between élite perceptions and popular viewpoint constitutes not only a challenge but also an opportunity. The challenge is to find some means of harnessing popular sentiments to the construction of Europe. The opportunity is that of helping to create a European consciousness without which European Union cannot even be contemplated.

120   *Vernon Bogdanor*

NOTES

1. For the parliamentary votes, see *European Law Review*, 18 (June 1993), 229 ff.
2. Ronald Inglehart and Karlheinz Reif, 'Analysing Trends in West European Opinion: The Role of the Eurobarometer Surveys', in Karlheinz Reif and Ronald Inglehart (eds.), *Eurobarometer* (London: Macmillan, 1991).
3. Ibid. 10, 11.
4. For a brief account of the new co-operation procedure introduced by the Single European Act of 1986 and its effects, see Vernon Bogdanor, 'Direct Elections, Representative Democracy and European Integration', *Electoral Studies*, 8 (1989), 205–16.
5. See, Karlheinz Reif, 'National Electoral Cycles and European Elections 1979 and 1984', *Electoral Studies*, 3 (1984), 244–55, and Reif, 'Ten Second-Order National Elections', in Reif (ed.), *Ten European Elections* (Aldershot: Gower, 1985).
6. Reif, 'Ten Second-Order National Elections', 9.
7. Torben Worre, 'The Danish Euro-Party System', *Scandinavian Political Studies*, 10 (1987), 79–95, and 'Denmark', *Electoral Studies*, 8 (1989), 237–45.
8. Reif, 'National Electoral Cycles and European Elections 1979 and 1984', 253.
9. Arend Lijphart, 'Political Parties: Ideologies and Programs', in David Butler, Howard R. Penniman, and Austin Ranney (eds.), *Democracy at the Polls: A Comparative Study of Competitive National Elections* (Washington: AEI, 1981).
10. Ibid. 41.
11. Ibid. 49.
12. Ibid. 50.
13. Quoted in *Agence Europe*, 26 Mar. 1989.
14. Giovanni Sartori, *Parties and Party Systems: A Framework for Analysis*, pt. 1 (Cambridge: Cambridge University Press, 1976).
15. De Gaulle's proposal for a referendum was in fact dropped in the final version of the Plan, since the Germans objected, their Constitution containing no provision for a referendum. Roger Massip, *De Gaulle et L'Europe* (Paris: Flammarion, 1963), 70.

6

Political Parties and the Public Accountability of Leaders

DAVID HINE

1. Party Accountability and Party Government

Political parties are an essential, though not sufficient, link in the chain of 'accountability' between the political élite and the people. Accountability can be given various meanings and involves not just effective policy and respect for manifesto pledges, but also the probity and honesty of office-holders. In the latter area administrative, constitutional, and even penal law act as constraints supplementary to electoral accountability. However, electoral accountability is the *sine qua non* of representative democracy, and in most of Europe it is still organized along more or less 'party' lines. There are probably few democracies, at least in Europe, where electoral choice is not still conceived, in the minds of voters, primarily in party terms. France has always been a partial exception on this score, and the startling political breakthrough of Silvio Berlusconi suggests a similar process of personalization of politics in Italy, but elsewhere there are few leaders who can, with any confidence, operate far outside the limits of partisan identities.

When it comes to assessing whether office-holders actually implement 'party' policy, however, the situation becomes less clear, and just what we mean by 'party government' varies considerably across liberal democracies. The extent to which, out of the complex circuit of parliamentary, bureaucratic, and interest-group interaction, policy can be described as having been determined by 'party' is much debated.[1] This gap, between on one side what is done in the name of particular parties, and on the other what they have committed themselves to doing—or what voters believe they have committed themselves to doing—is a perennial source of potential public mistrust in parties. Such a gap can exist for different reasons: parties may be ill prepared for office, failing to understand the complexities of policy issues or finding themselves overwhelmed by the ever-present forces of bureaucratic capture and interest-group pressure; or they may simply encounter bad luck, in that circumstances change in ways they could not reasonably have foreseen. A further source of potential mistrust in parties may lie in their own organizations. Parties are not just collections of ideas and policies, but organizations for researching, assembling, and explaining their policies, gathering votes on election day, and placing their members in elective office, and often in areas of non-elective public appointment. Most accounts of the work of modern political parties assign them an impressive range of possible roles that includes selecting and socializing leaders and activists, structuring and articulating ideas, contributing to public debate and thereby educating citizens, as well as formulating precise packages of policy for implementation. Furthermore, as organizations, parties consume resources; in many countries the quantities are prodigious, and paid partly out of public funds. What parties do, and how they present themselves to the electorate, *as quasi-public organizations*, can thus be just as important in the relationship of trust between the rulers and the ruled as how they implement public policy.

The twentieth-century political science literature on parties in liberal democracy shows that neither source of concern about the role of parties in linking the governors to the governed is new. The long period of democratic stability and relative prosperity in most of Western Europe since 1945 conceals the frequency with which, in the past, whole party systems seem to have been unpopular, and to have led commentators to talk of a gap between politics and civil society. The inter-war breakdown of democracy in several key European states was at least partly a failure of parties to adapt to mass democracy, as was recognized by the emphasis placed on strengthening parties by those responsible for democratic reconstruction in Germany and Italy after the Second World War. Even after 1945 the general stability of party systems and the centrality of party government was subject to the one notable exception of the failure of the parties of the Fourth French Republic. More importantly, even where parties and party systems have been relatively stable, democratic theorists have shown a continuing concern for the meaning and effectiveness of party government. Their work has examined not only the dilution of electoral choice at the implementation stage by the impact of parliament, bureaucracy, and interest groups, but also the way in which choice is restricted by imperfect voter information, by barriers to entry against new parties, by distortions of the electoral system, by complexities of coalition-building in multi-party systems, and by structural and behavioural aspects of the lives of the individual parties.

In this chapter, it is impossible to do justice to the richness of this literature, especially since much of it ranges over social changes—in the field of communications, expectations, and life-styles—which go well beyond the parties themselves. Here, the emphasis will not be so much on the evidence of a growing gap between rulers and ruled itself, much of which is considered in Chapter 7 by Rudy Andeweg, as on recent changes in organizational and social changes *inside* individual parties that may affect the way they relate to their social bases. Since the two questions are difficult to separate, however, we should begin by noting some of the methodological issues raised in the debate over the decline of parties, as it has applied to Europe.

2. The 'Decline of Parties': Electoral Volatility and Collapsing Membership Rolls

The thesis of party 'decline' or 'failure' has never been as satisfactorily applied to European conditions as to those in the USA. Nevertheless, arguments about the continuing solidity of European parties have abounded over the last twenty years, and have focused on a number of more or less measurable phenomena: electoral volatility, partisan identification, levels of electoral participation, levels of party membership, and general indices of satisfaction with political parties. Likewise, the emergence of new (frequently single-issue) parties, the rise of new social movements, and the seemingly greater range of interest groups present in many societies have also been taken as indications that long-established parties have less control over the means of communication, articulation, and probably political influence than was formerly the case.

Electoral Volatility

Along with declining party membership this is the subject which most frequently has earned special attention in this debate. It is often argued that a fluid electorate, not linked to parties by enduring bonds of loyalty and identification, preferably backed up by strong organizational support, can be dangerous to governability, or even to democratic stability. Governability is often said to become more difficult when governments, overloaded by distributional demands, are persuaded to off-load the cost on to inflation or future generations of taxpayers through excessive public borrowing. Democratic stability is threatened where voters are potentially available to extremist political parties.

Without doubt some parties that are candidates for the label 'extremist' have made significant gains in recent years. On questions of race and immigration they have looked particularly threatening. They have emerged in Italy, France, Belgium, and Austria with particular force. Other parties which are sometimes ranged under the extremist banner include separatist movements and the sort of anti-tax protest parties which have made their occasional appearance in northern Europe in the last two decades. In general, such changes have occurred on the right rather than the left, and this is understandable given the overall decline of parties of the left during the last decade, and the unfavourable ideological climate for collectivist solutions to structural economic problems, but it is not something which can be counted on to continue if unemployment continues to rise.

To date, however, with the possible exception of Italy, which we shall consider below, there are no cases where the rise of parties with questionable commitments to democracy has brought such parties into government. Changes to date are still at the level of lower turn-out, more frequent switching between parties, and a greater voter willingness to support—at least temporarily—single-issue parties of various types. Assessing whether such developments are attributable to party failure, or whether they are exogenous changes contributing to a more articulated democracy, relieving parties of impossible burdens rather than depriving them of power and influence, is far from easy. Certainly, socio-political developments which are described in terms of a zero-sum competition for influence and for the right to articulate and represent would sometimes be better set in the context of changes in the quality of democracies in which citizens have more information, skills, resources, and belief in their own political efficacy.

To assume that rising electoral volatility necessarily demonstrates voter dissatisfaction with political leadership is to assume a particular theory of voting behaviour in which voters use their votes to react, retrospectively, to party performance in office rather than to respond positively to the attractions of alternative policies by rival parties. While it is possible that many voters do move rapidly between parties because they are dissatisfied with the performance of those parties in office, it is also possible that others do so because parties are becoming more sensitive to complex patterns of voter preferences. This may be the case in party systems where the number of parties available to voters has increased in recent years, through the emergence of special-interest parties pursuing environmentalist politics, ethnic or territorial interests, moral issues, etc. That voters turn to such parties does not necessarily imply that traditional parties have failed. Some voters might simply be recognizing that the choices they face are more complex and articulated than they previously supposed, and that by switching between parties more readily they have a mechanism for more sophisticated transmission of their demands to those in government. Even where the nature of the vote *is* self-evidently a protest, such action can still serve as an effective warning signal on specific issues, persuading established parties to make timely, if painful, policy adjustments (for example, on tax, immigration, environmentalism). It may also contribute to a reworking of the party system that can, in time, lead to a set of party choices more in tune with what voters really want.

This latter possibility is even evident, though by no means guaranteed, in the country—namely Italy—in which a volatile and dissatisfied electorate has gone furthest in the direction of new parties with ambiguous democratic credentials. The extraordinarily rapid reconstruction of the centre-right that has occurred since 1992 has facilitated a large increase for the formerly neo-Fascist movement (now renamed the Alleanza Nazionale). In the 1994 elections it won nearly 14 per cent of the vote. The Northern League won a further 8 per cent, its early separatist and anti-immigrant aspirations casting some doubt over its democratic credentials too. Yet under the expansive umbrella cast by Silvio Berlusconi's entry into politics, both parties suddenly found themselves in government, having hitherto been the untouchables of the political extremes. The doubts and uncertainties, both in Italy and outside, about how to deal with this remarkable transformation underline the ambiguity of electoral volatility. It is possible, despite the evident worries about 'Fascists' in the 1994 Italian government, that Berlusconi may eventually rationalize the Italian right somewhat as de Gaulle did the French right (from equally dubious origins), creating a large, neo-liberal majoritarian movement out of a hitherto deeply fractured range of parties. He may fail abjectly, but if he does succeed, he will have done so on the back of evident dissatisfaction with the old and discredited party system, and exceptionally high levels of electoral volatility, but volatility that did not presage a collapse of democracy itself.

Declining Party Membership

There is little doubt, despite the formidable difficulties in producing meaningful cross-national data on party membership and the almost complete absence of membership figures for French political parties, that, overall, party membership is on the decline almost everywhere. Only in Germany and Belgium is there evidence of a rise in membership over the last three decades, and in the German case party membership in the early post-war period, especially when compared to other Teutonic–Nordic participatory states, was low for obvious reasons connected with the post-war distancing from politics practised by a large part of the population until the end of the 1960s. Even today, as Katz and Mair point out, membership of Austrian parties, when measured as a percentage of the electorate, is five times larger than membership of German parties.[2]

The decline in party membership in some periods, and in some parties, has been quite precipitous. In Denmark, total party membership fell by two-thirds between 1960 and 1988.[3] The collapse of individual membership in the British Labour Party is also striking, and exposed the party to serious strains in the late 1970s and early 1980s as the party in some local constituencies fell into the hands of far-left minorities. Moreover, although we know very little about the *meaning* of party membership, in terms of attendance at meetings, working for the party, raising funds, contributing to policy discussion, there is a general sense in the literature on parties and their membership that the decline in numbers has been accompanied by a decline in meaningful participation, at least outside election times, as well.[4] Nor is such a decline at all counter-intuitive. The social function of parties of mass integration (face-to-face relationships in clubs and societies, insurance systems, co-operatives, unions, etc.) have, as has been so widely noted, been overtaken on the one side by a tendency towards individual solutions to such matters, and on the other by the institutionalized provision of the welfare state. Only where party membership is taken out, on a mass scale, for clientelistic reasons, as in Spain and Italy, might it be said that party membership has been able to find new social functions to replace old ones, but in the long run such clientelism does a party little good in ensuring solid social implantation.

For our purposes, the key question is: if this trend of declining membership participation and commitment is set to continue, does it matter? After all, the variations in membership participation across Europe have always been so great (cf. France and Austria) that some parties have never been other than 'electoral' parties, and others would have to continue to decline at the present rate for many years yet before they reached a similar state of membership exiguity. Is it thus enough for modern political parties to act like high-tech entrepreneurial vote-maximizers—at the limit, sets of rules by which professionalized candidates for office assemble packages of policies for sale to electors? Or does the participatory aspect of political parties still perform some important psychological function in binding leaders to ordinary voters, even if the meaning of membership is largely a formality in terms of day-to-day party work?

Arguably, membership *does* matter, because parties need to be *thought of* by voters as open organizations, and hence be available to ordinary citizens, *should they choose to participate*. It is true that the costs of participation to influence policy are, for any individual, extraordinarily high, but this may be no more important than the belief that political efficacy achieved through participation in party life is at least in principle possible. Naturally, exponents of rational-action theory would object that active participation in party life involves little more real political empowerment than the act of voting, since the effort involved, when discounted by the probability that one person's action would make a difference, would almost never justify itself. However, leaving aside the higher probability involved in the smaller size of party membership compared to total electorate, participation opens up many more possibilities—office-holding, platforms to propagate views, etc.—than does voting. And for the great majority who do not join political parties, there is also the possibility of free-riding on the efforts of others. Perhaps individuals are satisfied simply to know that, should they wish to do so, they could join and become influential, and can identify with the efforts of those who do become active.

There is, of course, a danger in free-riding: that the small numbers who do then participate are unrepresentative of the majority of free-riders. This danger is frequently pointed out by critics of the influence on parties of members who, it is claimed, if committed enough to participate as members, are likely to do so as 'militant extremists', rather than 'militant moderates'. However, low membership participation (and hence of free-riding leading to party unrepresentativeness) is no reason for limiting, as opposed to expanding, the possibility for active membership. If there is a problem of this type, it seems appropriate to seek ways of encouraging participation and widening access. Just as the irrationality (in rational-action terms) of the act of voting would be unlikely to lead any real-life designer of the rules of the political game to abolish voting as one of the fundamentals of representative democracy, so low rates of political participation do not in themselves justify the belief that political participation through party membership is irrelevant in modern democracies.

3. The Organizational Adequacy of Modern Parties

So far, we have concentrated on the objective difficulties parties face in adapting to changed political circumstances. We now turn to the factors inherent in the organization of political parties which may prevent them from meeting standards expected by mass electorates. After all, many—though not all—parties in European liberal democracies are not just agents *in* a democracy; they are also agents *of* democracy. By their example, they help socialize citizens into democratic procedures. Even more centrally, they select leaders and policies by means involving democratic choice. The internal operations of parties ought thus to matter to voters, especially since European parties do not use primaries to select candidates, and European societies still make relatively little use of direct democracy. Voters do not, for the most part, choose their leaders or policies directly; at any given level of election, they choose between candidates for office pre-selected by parties, and between whole packages of policy choices. The remainder of this chapter considers three possible grounds on which modern European parties may be alienating their mass publics:

1. a decline in the standards of probity and honesty amongst the political class;
2. an increase in internal party conflict to the detriment of party morale and public-standing, and a failure in the mechanisms for selecting party leaders and replacing inadequate ones;
3. a failure of modern parties to develop adequate policy-making capacities in a world in which policy goals are set within more tightly circumscribed limits.

Corruption in Contemporary Political Life

Of the various indices of change in party systems considered here, one that tapped standards of honesty among politicians would be the most difficult to construct. Yet recent events in Western Europe suggest that it would contribute much to an explanation of voters' distrust of parties. The recent proliferation of political scandals generally associated with party funding in several European countries has been striking. The Italian and Spanish cases fall into a class of their own for the astonishing size of some of the individual cases of corruption involved. This is not the place to explore how or why a systematic relationship between business and politics based mainly around public-sector contracting came to be exposed so spectacularly and rapidly in both countries. Suffice it to say that in Italy at national level it has not just removed the two main governing parties from office, but has actually destroyed them as credible parties. In Spain to date the Socialist Party survives in office, but the damage done to it seems increasingly likely to be fatal to its chances of remaining in office.

What is striking in both countries is the systematic nature of corruption: the regularity with which it has been practised, and the large number of politicians at all levels of the political system who appear to be involved. Almost a third of the Italian Parliament elected in 1992 was being investigated for corruption by the time it was dissolved two years later. The Cortes has not yet suffered a similar indignity, but the size of the scandals involved in the *Filesa* case, Expo92, the *Juan Guerra* case, and the Banco Bilbao Vizcaya scandal, suggest problems on a comparable scale. What has been revealed in France and even Germany pales in comparison to Italian and Spanish developments, but in these countries too, and even in the United Kingdom, the debate about party funding and finance from big business has become more intense in the face of embarrassing and, for the governing parties in particular, discrediting revelations.

The way in which the debate over probity in public life has been sparked in the United Kingdom in the 1990s is particularly striking, given how far the country has traditionally prided itself on high standards in public life. Three House of Commons committee reports—from Public Accounts, Home Affairs, and Members' Interests—have fed that debate. The Eighth Report from the Committee on Public Accounts[5] details a range of concerns that fundamental changes in the way in which a number of public bodies work—most notably various forms of marketization, the introduction of executive agencies, and the development of stricter targets for performance and value for money—may be eroding traditional public-sector standards of honesty, and ultimately efficiency. It lists a range of failures, including poor monitoring of financial controls, failure to comply with rules, excessive levels of personal discretion in the use of resources, lack of fully open competition in contracting out, failure to secure arms'-length relationships with private-sector consultants, and so on. No less significant is the 1994 (inconclusive because divided) report from the Home Affairs Committee on the funding of political parties.[6] This issue has become highly controversial in the light of allegations about contributions to the Conservative Party, especially from organizations and individuals who benefit in a variety of more of less direct ways (privatization policy, taxation policy, licence concessions in broadcasting, health regulation, the distribution of honours, and so on) from government policy. The trading of allegations between the two major British parties (trade-union sponsorship on Labour's side, and corporate campaign contributions on the Conservative side) is far from new, but the intensity of the debate has never been as great in the post-war period. The contrast between the relatively relaxed and secretive regime under which British parties obtain their funds and the formally much tighter (though not necessarily more effective) rules on contributions and disclosure operating in several other liberal democracies has become striking through the attention which the debate has received. It has also raised a legitimate doubt about whether British political life appears less obviously corrupt because it really is so or because the rules are set up differently.

Providing a systematic Europe-wide explanation for the apparent rise in cases of corruption linked to party funding is beyond the resources of this chapter, and there are no doubt multiple factors at work. One of the most basic is the long-term absence of turnover in government. Where the same parties remain in power for long periods, and where there is no credible alternative to which voters can turn, there is always a serious risk that politicians will grow contemptuous of the risks they run by engaging in corruption, and confident that their control over the means by which they might be brought to justice is foolproof. There is little doubt that this has been a major factor in the growth of corruption in Italy and Spain, but there have also been suggestions that the absence of a credible opposition has had similar effects even in the United Kingdom.

A further explanation lies in the extent to which there is perceived to be a likely penalty attached to the exposure of corruption, whether personally to the individuals involved, or more generally to the standing and re-electability of the parties involved. In this connection the ultimate—and frequently deployed—weapon in some countries has traditionally been legally entrenched immunity from prosecution enjoyed by members of parliament. This weapon had, at least until 1993, a long and disreputable tradition in the Italian context, where politicians accused of corruption invariably enjoyed the benefit of having their case removed from the public court system, only to be held up and then archived by the benign neglect of a court of their parliamentary peers.[7] A related but distinct antidote to police and judicial enforcement is to politicize or publicly discredit the enforcement authorities, or indeed to intimidate them, either physically or through career sanctions. Again, these strategies were resorted to with regularity and considerable effect in Italy throughout the 1980s, though they ceased to operate once the political authorities themselves were weakened after the 1992 election.

What the law is, and what may be expected of the court system, can also affect the more general climate of public morality. Just as in the case of the moral ambiguity surrounding the adoption of market or pseudo-market principles in the allocation of 'public' money, so in the relationship between party funding and public policy, the boundary lines are hard to draw, and moral sensibilities are easily blunted. In the case of Italy, it is clear that the institutionalization of party funding through control of the public sector, the banks, etc. was so complete that those who exercised this control to party advantage appeared at times not to have regarded the system as corrupt at all: merely a way of raising funds for institutions—the parties—which provided a necessary public service under arrangements which were so widespread and so tacitly tolerated that everyone more or less accepted them as a normal part of political life. Linked to this is a second factor, which again clearly operated in the Italian context: the low level of respect for, or commitment to, the law. Paradoxically, that attitude is itself in part a reflection of the excessive 'legalism' of Italian society and the Italian state. The country and its government are enmeshed in a complex maze of legalism, but it is precisely because the mediating powers of political parties have often been necessary to cut through, or at least make more flexible, laws which would otherwise paralyse much important commercial and administrative activity that the real constraining powers of the *stato di diritto* have been brought into contempt.

What is clear about systems of policing and enforcement, then, is that they are *relative* (just because an activity is legal, or difficult to prosecute, does not mean that it does not involve a form of corruption), that they are unlikely to be effective if they are not backed up by a strong culture of probity in public life (the enforcement of sanctions alone is unlikely to be enough), and that they are easily devalued as deterrents once they have to be deployed widely, for the shock effect on public opinion is easily devalued, and resignation or cynicism can easily set in.

However, corruption is apparent even in systems where there is turnover in government and where the law appears to enjoy a less tenuous hold on public morality. There are clearly other, broader factors operating, and two significant ones are the size and complexity of the relationship between the state and the private sector, and the change in the nature of parties from agents of mass social mobilization to catch-all entrepreneurial organizations dependent less on voluntary individual commitment than on mass communications and business-orientated fundraising. Both have major implications for the issue of party finance.

Public procurement provides a significant part of the demand for major European construction, automobile, and defence-related firms, among many others. Because of the need for state underwriting of much large-scale provision of finance to private industry, the relationship between the state and the financial world, even where not one of direct ownership, is nevertheless replete with opportunities for discreet party pressure for reciprocation. The key element is that of political discretion in the award of very large contracts, and the difficulties of assessing when and where that discretion has been abused. Indeed, a direct quid pro quo may not be involved. Large corporations may find it a desirable precaution to provide finance to political parties, if for no other reason than to avoid one day finding themselves at a *dis*advantage, rather than to obtain some immediate illicit commercial *ad*vantage. Furthermore, the notion that donations to political parties can be public-spirited contributions to oil the wheels of democracy is fostered in some countries by a conscious public theory of the collective benefits of political giving. Deutsche Bank, one of Germany's largest contributors, claims it gives money to all parties 'to support democracy'.[8] If this can happen with free agents in the private sector, it is all the more likely to happen where the status of the agent is ambiguous, as is the case in Europe with many public-law agencies like savings banks, housing associations, trading co-operatives, and other commercial organizations, in which post-holders nominated to serve as managers and directors come into office through party patronage. The impact of the new public-sector managerialism discussed in the UK House of Commons Public Accounts Committee referred to above brings the same attendant risks.

The arguments over the most appropriate method of funding political parties generated by extensive cases of corruption have on the whole been inconclusive. Democratic theory might suggest that, at the least, parties should make clear to voters exactly what their sources of finance are, but this often seems, not surprisingly, to drive the financing underground. Most parties seem embarrassed if their supporters are from overseas. Many commercial organizations want to keep their contributions secret for reasons of public image. Thus although several European states have rules requiring disclosure, and indeed rules requiring the publishing of full party accounts, the rules are systematically flouted, front organizations abound, and the accounts often bear little relationship to what parties actually receive and spend.

The obvious place to turn, if doubts persist over the acceptability of private funding, is often said to be the public purse directly. But public funding of political parties, though now extensive, is itself highly controversial since taxpayers who vote for one party will not willingly pay to subsidize all the other parties, of which they may radically disapprove.[9] There are many other theoretical objections to such funding, not least of which is the sense that parties *should* depend on voluntary contributions or they will lose touch with the society from which they spring. They are not, so the argument would run, permanent public institutions, and where they cannot survive on voluntary initiative, they have no claim on the taxpayer.

In any case, experience has shown that even high levels of public funding do not necessarily reduce a party's appetite for private funding. Germany and Italy have both had high levels of public funding, but both have encountered serious problems over illicit private funding. In the Italian case, the 1974 law on public financing was rushed through parliament in response to a series of scandals that had severely damaged the standing of the Christian Democrats (Italy was, not surprisingly, a target for the attentions of the then infamous Lockheed Corporation), but in subsequent years public funding became highly unpopular, and in April 1993 the legislation was abolished by popular referendum. At the very least, there is a strong case, where public funding is to be supplied, for providing the benefits in kind, and ensuring that they are made commensurate, retrospectively, with levels of public support for the individual parties.

The problem of the high cost of operating political parties thus admits of no easy solution. Parties are necessary, and they are expensive. Public law can regulate them and can limit expenditure to some extent, but over time it can be evaded. Collectively, politicians have no interest in escalating the cost of party competition through regular increases in the size of campaign budgets. It increases the strains on themselves, ties their hands, and enhances the risk that parties as a whole will be discredited. Enforcing the logic of this collective interest is, however, likely to suffer regular breakdown under the pressure of inter- and intra-party competition and the size of the potential patronage available to modern parties in the interventionist state.

The Management of Party Conflict and Leadership Renewal

Most parties place some sort of premium on party unity. A party united behind a leader and a set of policies is generally thought of as more fitted to govern than one where internal divisions will make decision-making difficult and complex, and leave voters uncertain about exactly what the party intends to do. However, there are considerable variations across European parties in the strength of the taboo against factionalism. At one end of the spectrum stands—or rather traditionally stood—the British case, where there is a deep-rooted assumption, linked to preferences for strong government, that parties exist to have clear views which they put to voters; they are not there to show how they arrive at those views, or to change them in public through internal debate once in office. Several other European democracies seem more tolerant of internal party division, or at least more used to it.

Much depends on what internal conflict is about and how it is managed. Factionalism may reflect internal divisions over policy, and especially policy towards particular groups or interests that may be represented in the party; it may reflect deep-seated ideological conflict over the whole thrust of party policy; or it may reflect complex battles for personal or group power and preferment which, though dressed up in the language of policy conflict, are really about the interests of the actors themselves. At least in societies with a preference for consensual approaches to policy-making, internal party conflicts that reflect the interplay of sectional interests may be tolerated as long as the demands of the groups themselves are recognized as legitimate. Of course, if the groups are seen as having a powerful voice or even a veto across a wide range of policies (the influence of trade unions in some social democrat parties, especially the British Labour Party, might be such a case) then they are less likely to be looked at tolerantly by potential voters.

There are some reasons for thinking that certain parties have become more divided over the last two decades, though a satisfactory index of internal fragmentation is not readily to hand. Social democrat parties, in particular, have faced quite severe tensions resulting from a more composite and heterogeneous social base, and also from an apparently declining one, which has weakened party confidence and morale.[10] In the United Kingdom the proliferation of identifiable and named groups since the late 1970s in both parties seems to be significant, even by comparison with periods of heightened internal tension in earlier decades. The difficulties the Conservative Party has faced in adjusting to the post-Thatcherite inheritance are especially notable.

Elsewhere, it is probably worth asking whether there is anything to be learned from the limit case, which is again the Italian one. There factionalism among the governing parties is deeply rooted, and goes back many years. Already in the 1960s both the Christian Democrat Party and the Socialists contained several well-defined and highly organized groups, running from leadership to rank and file, and distinguished by rather little in the way of clear-cut policy divisions. The existence of such factions in parties with access to the spoils of public office has been widely documented, and a series of structural incentives in the political system—especially the (recently abolished) 'preference' vote in the electoral system—is generally seen as the root cause. Under the pressures of the intense political crisis that the country experienced after the 1992 general election, these strains reached breaking-point, and the main governing parties, quite literally, fell apart. We would be unwise to extrapolate such extreme conditions on to other European party systems, but it is worth asking whether the basic syndrome of internal competition for the spoils of office, leading to an intensifying and self-sustaining struggle for the resources necessary to secure nominations for election and to get re-elected, is likely to make it more difficult in the future for parties to avoid discrediting factional conflict.

To the extent that factional conflict is endemic, it clearly affects the capacity of the party leadership to lead effectively, and raises the question of the adequacy of mechanisms for selecting and replacing leaders, as well as distributing power between groups. The distribution of internal party power involves not just who holds office and for how long, but also the extent of accountability to their own activists and ordinary members they face. Such issues have been debated throughout the twentieth century, and have been regularly exploited by groups which have found themselves excluded from the levers of power, or whose policies are rejected. As we noted earlier, there is certainly no unambiguous reason why greater accountability to a party's activists, who are potentially unrepresentative of its wider electorate, should make it more popular in the eyes of voters. Likewise, while widening the base of activists who select candidates and leaders may make them more legitimate in the eyes of party members, it may not necessarily lead to the selection of more suitable leaders. Among the various means for selecting a leader destined to occupy the post of head of government, there is room for concern about almost all methods and, given the different coalition, institutional, and party contexts in which leaders have to operate, there is almost certainly no single, universally appropriate model to follow.[11] Worries about the extended methods for selecting American presidential candidates, the impact it has on the type of individual willing and able to run, and the constraints it imposes on him in office are well known. At the other end of the scale, the way in which some little-known figures can be parachuted into prime-ministerial office as a result of coalition dealing, or snap elections inside a parliamentary group, run the risk that the successful candidate's ability to appeal to and communicate with the mass electorate is completely untested.

However, these are by no means new problems for parties, and there is no prima-facie reason why they have become worse in recent years. What has changed, judging from the frequency with which polls nowadays suggest that a particular prime minister or president's popularity is at an all-time low or has dropped at a record rate, is the difficulty leaders have in retaining their personal electoral popularity. However, it is unclear whether this constitutes a recommendation for parties to find mechanisms for changing leaders more frequently. At the very least, it probably does not imply a structural change, since most parties do in fact have a ready mechanism for dispatching their leaders should they wish to do so. The British Conservative Party, that most oligarchic of parties, surprised many voters in 1989 and 1990 when it demonstrated how vulnerable a really unpopular leader could be to the hitherto neglected mechanism of the annual election to the leadership. The Conservative case, moreover, demonstrates the danger of over-familiarity with the potential use of such a weapon, since the very fact that it was used successfully against Mrs Thatcher has reminded commentators of its existence, and the speculation about its renewed use against her infelicitous successor itself appeared to be a factor, albeit not the major one, in his own weakness.

The point is that most parties are actually quite reluctant to change leaders, and not just because the disincentive for rivals to challenge leaders is the potentially high personal cost of failure in such an enterprise, but also because the parties themselves have no guarantee that by ditching a 'failed' leader and selecting another they will actually improve on the status quo. The legacy of internal dispute that such a change may leave, together with the very public acknowledgement that the leader was actually a failure, may be more damaging than the— untested—successor can compensate for through more effective leadership. Conceivably, over time, parties may adjust to a reality in which leaders lose popularity more rapidly, if such a reality proves permanent. In the meantime, it is something with which they will have to live.

Beyond leaders, there is also the possibility that party élites in a wider sense are being selected in the wrong way, or that they are not being renewed in a way that keeps them in touch with their electorates. *If*, as is sometimes suggested, there is a long-term tendency for parties to be populated at parliamentary and possibly other levels by self-perpetuating professionals, who have no other activity (bar nominated office-holding under party patronage) to which to turn should they be voted out of office, then such a political class would have a strong incentive to resist internal processes of turnover and renewal.

The Adequacy of the Policy-Making Capacities of Modern Parties

A final possible area of party inadequacy lies in the area of policy-making machinery. In the light of our discussion of party finance, it might seem odd to ask whether parties have sufficient resources to fulfil their role in policy-making. However, even where parties do dispose of large resources, there is no guarantee that they will be devoted to research and policy elaboration, rather than to keeping the organization in readiness to fight elections.

The difficulty in discussing this subject is, however, that information on exactly how parties make policy is very hard to come by in any systematic and comparable form. Normally, the existence of a party research department is appended to organigrams of party structure, with, at best, a notional figure of the staff within it. However, much party policy is made in voluntary working parties that may be served by a staff member, but rely on outside witnesses, experts who are party sympathizers, and so on. They leave rather little trace once the policy has been formed and has received the stamp of approval by party congresses or by enshrinement in policy statements. Moreover, parties will not generally want to think aloud, especially when the unthinkable is involved. The eventual fate of party policy made in many party research departments is so unpredictable that a healthy dose of scepticism about its relevance to policy output is also in order. By the time policy has passed under the noses of committees writing party manifestos, has been discussed with interest groups, officials, finance ministers, and candidates for ministerial office, and eventually, where appropriate, turned into legislation, it may bear little relation to the early ideological enthusiasm and idealism of its original progenitors.

The possibility that parties may be out of touch in important areas, because their capacity to research and elaborate policy is weak, should not, however, be ignored. This is especially the case where some important area of public life subject to political regulation does not throw up a party's natural supporters: parties of the left and financial regulation, for example, or conservative parties and public-sector management. The possibilities for misunderstanding by parties and their representatives are then considerable. Even when a party has been in office for quite long periods, it is possible for its representatives to become isolated from the policy community in a particular sector. This is not to say that parties should always listen to mainstream policy communities or experts in such areas, for the possibilities of 'bureaucratic capture' are considerable for party research machines, as well as for party representatives who attain ministerial office. Parties need the freedom to think the unthinkable, but should not be allowed to do so in a complete vacuum, or they will make commitments they cannot fulfil and generate tensions between different sources of advice that they cannot manage.

Unfortunately, the way parties make policy, and the sources of information they rely on, seem to vary widely across European parties and make generalization difficult. Some, as in Germany, do appear to have quite sophisticated party research organizations and associated foundations, and these are closely linked to public officials and parliamentary committees. In other countries—both France and the United Kingdom probably fall into this category—there is greater, though often resentful, reliance on the strongly developed *dirigisme* of the state, and the self-confident and evangelistic bureaucratic class. In Italy, where bureaucrats are totally lacking in such evangelism, the reliance is on outside consultancies, and most notably on the elastic reserves of the professoriat, who serve not just behind the scenes but even, professional politicians having been so discredited, in ministerial office as well. In general, however, while public-policy research has in recent years taught us much about non-party policy communities, it has thrown up little evidence of the way in which party research mechanisms mesh with such communities, and in several countries it is worth asking whether they link up with them very closely at all.

An even stronger reason for concern about the policy-making capacities of modern European parties lies in the narrower and more subtle policy agenda that faces all European governments. This is not explored in detail in this chapter, but the narrowing of the parameters within which policy is made in contemporary Europe is one of the most striking political changes in the last decade and a half. Indeed, within the European Community since the late 1970s, it has been elevated into the dominant theme of macro-economic management. Common targets for public budgets, interest- and inflation rates, and common EU-determined rules concerning public intervention and regulation in large sections of the private economy, have placed extensive limits on the freedom of parties to pursue independent economic strategies. We cannot, of course, be sure that these constraints will continue to operate indefinitely, and the strains that they are causing are evident. What is clear, however, is that as long as they do operate, it becomes necessary for parties to have subtle mechanisms for understanding the limits on their action, and much more finely tuned policy instruments for exploiting the remaining margins of manœuvre that are available to them. If not, then differentiation of policy—which is surely necessary in a competitive democracy—will disappear altogether.

4. *Conclusion: Electoral-Professional Parties or Cartel Parties?*

In the literature that has emerged on European political parties in recent years, two common themes appear to stand out:

1. The first is that parties have adapted over time from the movements of mass social mobilization and sharply differentiated interest aggregation that existed in the middle years of the century into the more composite and heterogeneous organizations that Otto Kircheimer referred to in his much-quoted article on so-called 'catch-all' party transformation.[12] The elements of this transformation entail a substantial downgrading of mass party membership and activism, a more eclectic approach to ideology and policy, and an emphasis on the party as an electoral, opinion-driven agency, and on professionals, experts, and technocrats rather than organically linked interest groups as sources of advice.
2. The second is that, though there is some evidence at the electoral

level that the relationship between voters and the traditional parties is under strain, the problems thereby generated are not to date as great as some theorists of party 'decline' or 'failure' have predicted. Party identification has fallen to some degree, and there are some new extremist parties, but, so far, with the possible exception of Italy where the spectacular has occurred, there has been no collapse.

The question which naturally arises from these two observations is whether we should conclude that the transformation of party organization has been successful because the level of electoral breakdown is to date rather modest, or whether we should worry that there is a time-lag inherent in these broad social changes and that catch-all electoral parties are potentially brittle and unstable, and will eventually prove inadequate in structuring the vote and linking leaders to voters. Commentators opt for different prognoses. Some, like Panebianco, are relatively pessimistic.[13] Others, like Mair, who in any case casts some doubt on the thesis of rising electoral instability in his study of long-term electoral change, contemplate possible accounts of how parties adapt which identify elements of considerable stability through the formation of so-called 'cartel' or 'public utility' parties that have grown out of the Kircheimian transformation.[14] Such parties build their strength on a range of publicly generated resources, and survive in office to a large extent because they are already in office. Nowadays, that strength is built on public subsidies, the political patronage that comes from control of the state in its various forms (public employment, public control of credit, public subsidies to various types of economic activity, public control of the media, and so on).

The 'cartel' over political office enjoyed by such parties is assisted, in some countries, by a power-sharing or proportionalist mentality that generates a preference for broad coalitions from which some parties are almost never excluded. Coalition government is certainly the norm in large parts of Europe. Even where coalitions do not operate at national level, or are restricted in scope, the fact that government is, in many countries, now a multi-tiered construction enables parties that are out of office at one level to enjoy considerable leverage (including leverage against national government) at another, lower, level. They have sufficient hold over strategic positions to block out the entry of new political parties. In this light, an apologist of the role of modern parties could almost see them as 'public-utilities': quasi-constitutional bodies,

regulated by law if not by the constitution itself, accepted as necessary features of the political framework, and given special, publicly
subsidized assistance to perform their roles.

The essential danger that is posed by this state of affairs, however,
is that much more than most other formal political institutions, such as
bureaucracies, security, and enforcement agencies, etc., parties almost
certainly enjoy only a *contingent* legitimacy in the eyes of mass electorates. They are not part of the constitutional contract, and for them
to be seen as public utilities with rights to monopolize the representative process may be dangerous, especially where parties are large-scale
users of publicly rather than voluntarily raised resources. The dangers
of corruption, internal factionalism, policy incompetence, and excessive oligarchy and rigidity among leaders and office-holders raised in
this chapter are ever present, and where they are not addressed by
parties that enjoy formidable mechanisms to retain power they can be
deeply corrosive of a party system's long-term legitimacy.

If the main worry about the health of democracy is electoral instability, the operation of a cartel to guarantee the survival of democratically respectable parties may be an acceptable state of affairs. If the
mass electorate came to view the role of the parties in this light, it
would be much more dangerous. Some minimal level of clear policy
differentiation, and certainly some minimal level of real competition
for power, seem necessary to persuade voters that the modern party
continues to grow out of civil society, and remains attached to it, and
is not operating in a cartel looking suspiciously like a conspiracy *against*
society. While there are no clear prescriptions about what form party
government should take in any given European society, this does perhaps
suggest at least certain limitations on post-war party developments.
Parties should not, at least for long, operate broad and all-inclusive
coalitions that admit of no alternatives; parties should not allow consensus politics to restrict political debate to high-level technical discussion suitable only to the initiated; and parties should not allow their
mass organizations—particularly their membership and their policy-
formulating mechanisms—to fall into desuetude.

NOTES

1. For a definition, see R. Wildenmann, 'The Problematic of Party Government', in F. G. Castles and R. Wildenmann (eds.), *The Future of Party*

Government, i: *Visions and Realities of Party Government* (New York: De Gruyter 1986). For efforts to measure 'party' government, see, *inter alia*, R. Rose, *Do Parties Make a Difference?* (London: Macmillan, 1984) and F. G. Castles, *The Impact of Parties* (London: Sage, ECPR, 1982).

2. R. S. Katz, P. Mair, *et al.*, 'The Membership of Political Parties in European Democracies 1960–1990', *European Journal of Political Research*, 22 (1992), 329–45.

3. Ibid. 340.

4. See, *inter alia*, J. Sundberg, 'Exploring the Case of Declining Party Membership in Denmark: A Scandinavian Comparison', *Scandinavian Political Studies*, 10/1 (1987), 17–38; R. S. Katz, 'Party as Linkage: A Vestigial Function', *European Journal of Political Research*, 18 (Jan. 1990), 143–61; and D. J. Hine, *Governing Italy: The Politics of Bargained Pluralism* (Oxford: Oxford University Press, 1993), 111–40.

5. *The Proper Conduct of Public Business*, Committee of Public Accounts, Eighth Report, Session 1993–4 (London: HMSO, 17 Jan. 1994).

6. See *Funding of Political Parties*, Home Affairs Committee Second Report, House of Commons, Session 1993–4 (London: HMSO, 16 Mar. 1994).

7. On these and other issues related to the culture of Italian corruption, see David Hine, 'Party, Personality, and Law: The Political Culture of Italian Corruption', in Peter Jones (ed.), *Party, Parliament, and Personality: Essays Presented to Hugh Berrington* (London: Routledge, 1995).

8. *Financial Times*, 24 June 1993.

9. For an account of public funding in four European states, see K.-H. Nassmacher, 'Structure and Impact of Public Subsidies to Political Parties in Europe: The Examples of Austria, Italy, Sweden, and West Germany', in H. E. Alexander (ed.), *Comparative Political Finance in the 1980s* (Cambridge: Cambridge University Press, 1989).

10. See D. Hine, 'Democracy and Manageability in the Social-Democratic Parties of Western Europe', in A. Thomas and W. Paterson (eds.), *The Future of Social Democracy* (Oxford: Oxford University Press, 1986), 261–90.

11. See R. M. Punnett, *Selecting the Party Leader: Britain in Comparative Perspective* (London: Harvester Wheatsheaf, 1992), esp. ch. 1.

12. O. Kircheimer, 'The Transformation of the Western European Party System', in J. LaPalombara and M. Weiner (eds.), *Political Parties and Political Development* (Princeton: Princeton University Press, 1966), 177–200.

13. A. Panebianco, *Political Parties: Organization and Power* (Cambridge: Cambridge University Press, 1988), 262–74.

14. R. S. Katz and P. Mair, 'Changing Models of Party Organization: The Emergence of the Cartel Party', paper presented to the workshop on Democracies and the Organization of Political Parties, ECPR Joint Sessions of Workshops, Limerick, 1992.

7

Élite–Mass Linkages in Europe: Legitimacy Crisis or Party Crisis?

RUDY B. ANDEWEG

1. A Legitimacy Crisis?

It is difficult to find a democratic country in the Western world where political pundits and politicians have not commented recently on a widening gap between the citizens and the political system. Declining trust in politics is not only reported from East and Central Europe, where the introduction of parliamentary democracy did not prove to be a quick fix to economic and ethnic problems. A gap between representatives and the represented is also offered as an explanation for the large majorities that voted in favour of electoral reform in such different countries as Italy and New Zealand. In the Netherlands, once a paragon of almost boring political stability, an all-party committee of parliamentary leaders suggested a series of wide-ranging reforms to stop the 'legitimacy crisis'. When 'Maastricht' ran into strong popular opposition in the referendums in Denmark (a small majority voting against in June 1992) and France (the small 'Oui' in September 1992), the President of the European Commission, Jacques Delors, was not the only one attributing this adversity to the gap the citizens feel with regard to the government, and especially with regard to the EC.

Such a 'confidence gap'[1] between citizens and politics surfaces as regularly in political commentaries as the Loch Ness monster in other sections of the newspapers. To a certain extent the gap is more real than the monster. It is an inevitable side-effect of any parliamentary, i.e. representative, democracy. Etymologically, Pitkin reminds us, ' "representation" means "re-presentation", a making present of something absent—but not making it literally present. It must be made present indirectly, through an intermediary; it must be present in some sense, while nevertheless remaining literally absent.'[2] This ambiguity creates a tension between the principal and the agent. As Van Gunsteren put it in a recent study on citizenship: 'Representation presupposes a gap, a distance between the represented and the representative, but at the same time also the obligation and the pretension to bridge this gap. However, if the latter would be guaranteed to succeed, representation ceases to exist.'[3] The literature on political representation can be read as an inconclusive and rather abstract debate on the appropriate distance between citizens and politicians. Ever since Burke and Mill, writers have differed on the degree of freedom the representative should have from those he or she represents. Where a theorist stands in this 'mandate-independence controversy', according to Pitkin depends on a number of factors:[4]

1. The more political leaders are perceived as in possession of superior wisdom and expertise, a greater freedom is allowed for; if a relative equality of capacities is seen, less freedom is granted to the politician.
2. The more political problems are seen as having an objectively determinable solution, the greater the freedom for the politician; the more political issues are seen as having value-laden solutions, the less freedom is allowed.
3. The more one believes in a 'common good' or 'national interest', the more freedom is given to leaders; the more one perceives a need for defending particular interests against a threatening central power, the less one is inclined to give freedom to one's representatives.

These factors can easily be transposed from the literature on representation to the world of political commentary and public opinion. The perception of a gap between political élites and ordinary citizens probably fluctuates with the same three factors. Today, all of them seem to result in a desire for a strict mandate, and concomitantly produce perceptions of a wide gap. Higher levels of education have probably decreased the perception of superior wisdom in political leaders; as governments run into the limits of their capacity to solve problems such as pollution or unemployment, the belief in technocratic solutions probably declines; paradoxically, the size of the modern welfare state has raised more fears for a 'Big Brother' than it has produced gratitude to 'Father State' (be it Washington or Brussels). That is why we may be witnessing a widening of the gap as it is perceived, even though today's political leaders may not be more in or out of touch than they were in the past. If it is merely a temporary phase in a cyclical trend that we are witnessing, the current size of the confidence gap is not much to worry about, but it could also point to a more structural problem in élite–mass linkages. When we attempt to diagnose the nature of the confidence gap, it appears to be an ill-defined and elusive concept. The literature provides no clues on how to measure the gap. Terms such as 'gap', 'distance', 'alienation', or 'Verdrossenheit', are used to put a label on a variety of symptoms that are believed to be detrimental to the democratic order: a decline of trust in politics, decreasing political interest, lower turn-out at elections and other conventional forms of political participation, increasing right-wing extremism, etc. It is unlikely that these diverse phenomena would constitute one syndrome: political apathy (lack of interest and participation) and increasing extremism do not seem to be complementary. Some of these phenomena, which are now regarded as threats to democracy, were once seen as necessary to preserve democratic stability. Using the example of Weimar, it has been argued that a high level of political participation may overload the democratic system with highly politicized controversies.[5] We shall briefly examine these more dubious symptoms of a confidence gap, but first we shall discuss the most crucial of the symptoms, the decline of trust in politics.

A Decline of Trust in Politics?

Ever since Almond and Verba's classic *The Civic Culture*, trust in politics is a relatively well-researched theme. Various dimensions have been identified, such as political cynicism, internal political efficacy (or political competence), and external political efficacy (or a belief in the responsiveness of political élites). However, the most important distinction to be made is between trust in the political system as such (regime support), and trust in the incumbent authorities and their policies.[6] If it is true, as we argued above, that some gap between citizens and political élites is inevitable in any representative democracy, we should expect a certain level of distrust in the incumbent authorities. In itself, such mistrust is healthy, even essential, in a democracy: when too many citizens come to share this mistrust, the 'rascals' are voted out of office.[7] Obviously, when citizens mistrust the democratic system itself, when they no longer believe that they can vote the rascals out, the situation is much more serious.

Of course, trust in the regime and trust in the rulers are not completely independent from each other. The two logically distinct types of political trust are highly correlated and often difficult to disentangle empirically.[8]

Jennings and Van Deth found such high correlations in Germany and the Netherlands, where trust in the system was only marginally higher than trust in the authorities, but not in the United States, where, at much lower levels than in Europe, trust in the incumbents was higher than trust in the system.[9] The American exception is puzzling, but it is not reported in other studies, and it may be explained by the fact that the data were collected during the early years of the Reagan administration, when there was a highly personalized and short-lived upturn in trust of the incumbents.[10]

The extent of the overlap between trust in the system and trust in the authorities is important, because a spill-over from distrust of the rulers to distrust of the regime makes such distrust of incumbent politicians less innocuous than we have suggested thus far. A spill-over effect was detected, for example, in a study of the effect of economic crisis, via negative evaluations of the office-holders, on regime support in (West) Germany and Costa Rica, but it was found to be quite small. 'Thus, the existence of high levels of legitimacy acts as a barrier protecting the political system against the potentially deleterious effects of failures in economic performance.'[11]

What remains to be examined is how high this barrier is in Western Europe, and whether it has become lower in recent years. For this purpose we make use of the 'Eurobarometer', a series of cross-section surveys in all member states of the European Community administered on behalf of the European Commission. These surveys have regularly included the question 'On the whole, are you very satisfied, fairly satisfied, not very satisfied, or not at all satisfied with the way democracy works (in your country)?'[12] In Table 7.1 we have combined the percentages 'very satisfied' and 'fairly satisfied' for all EC member states over the 1973–90 period. The bottom row shows the average satisfaction-rate in the Community as a whole (i.e. for what at the time was the EC ten). For a correct interpretation of these figures, it should be kept in mind that to get to 100 per cent we need to add not only the dissatisfied, but also those who gave no reply (5 per cent, on average). Should we exclude the respondents without an opinion from our calculations, the percentages 'satisfied' would be slightly higher.

Through all the sampling-error noise and short-term oscillations in the satisfaction-rates, two things are clear. In the first place, there are important differences between the EC member states when it comes to satisfaction with the way democracy works. Countries such as the Netherlands, Denmark, and Luxembourg show a relatively stable and high satisfaction-rate around 70 per cent. France, and especially Italy, are countries with an equally stable, but dangerously low satisfaction rate under 50 per cent. Secondly, and more importantly than absolute levels, there is no clear downward trend when it comes to satisfaction with the way democracy works. Greece is the only country where satisfaction seems to be on a long-term decline. The most recent years also indicate a decline in some countries, such as (the western *Länder* of) Germany, but it is too early to tell whether this is a structural trend, or the kind of fluctuation that has occurred before in other countries. If there is a growing confidence gap between citizens and politicians, it does not seem to spill over into dissatisfaction with the functioning of the democratic system. Current events in Italy do not surprise in the light of the long-standing dissatisfaction with Italian democracy, but Table 7.1 shows that Italy is the exception to the rule, with France perhaps the only other country with a relatively low barrier against a spill-over effect.

Although we do not have data from identical questions in the USA, the general conclusion appears to be quite similar. Despite a continuous decrease in trust of political leaders since the early 1960s, confidence in the American political system has not declined: 'It appears that the trend of declining trust in government is focused on the performance of government and the behaviour of public officials, and not on the system itself or the institutions and norms associated with it.'[13]

A Decline of Interest in Politics?

A decline of interest in politics is sometimes seen as an indication of a widening gap between citizens and political élites, although it could also be argued to point to contentment. Empirically, however, there can be no argument: there is no decline in political interest. The Eurobarometer surveys have included the question 'To what extent would you say you are interested in politics' several times. In Table 7.2 we have combined the answers 'a great deal' and 'to some extent' to this question. One might argue that subjective political interest is not very high in most countries, but there is no downward trend during the past decade: in ten out of the twelve countries the figure for the most recent point in time is higher than for the time of the first measurement. Other surveys, wording the question slightly differently, confirm this finding. Van Deth presents data showing a steady increase in subjective political interest in (West) Germany and the Netherlands since the early

TABLE 7.1. *Satisfaction with the way democracy works 1973–1992 (% very + fairly satisfied)*

Country	'73	'76	'77	'78	'78	'79	'79	'80	'81	'82	'82	'83	'83	'84	'84	'85
Belgium	62	53	56	56	42	43	47	34	35	44	44	43	53	44	47	52
Denmark	45	55	63	67	64	62	71	60	67	61	57	70	71	68	70	68
France	41	42	45	49	40	41	41	36	53	44	45	36	46	40	38	44
Germany (West)	44	79	78	76	79	80	80	73	70	68	67	71	66	71	73	73
Greece	—	—	—	—	—	—	—	53	52	60	58	59	61	60	57	59
Ireland	54	61	62	71	61	47	57	48	59	56	47	45	43	50	44	49
Italy	27	14	12	25	19	16	21	21	20	21	19	17	20	20	28	25
Luxembourg	52	54	71	67	63	61	73	77	75	63	59	62	60	64	68	72
The Netherlands	52	67	64	67	53	64	61	51	51	59	55	50	53	54	54	58
Portugal	—	—	—	—	—	—	—	—	—	—	—	—	—	—	—	—
Spain	—	—	—	—	—	—	—	—	—	—	—	—	—	—	—	—
United Kingdom	44	51	59	62	51	53	52	51	48	60	58	64	61	60	60	51
EC 10	48	49	51	55	49	49	51	47	50	49	49	49	51	50	51	50

Country	'85	'86	'86	'87	'87	'88	'88	'89	'89	'89	'90	'90	'91	'91	'92	'92	'93
Belgium	58	50	48	53	45	54	48	58	53	63	66	56	65	53	56	53	49
Denmark	72	74	66	70	69	74	53	70	67	61	75	70	82	73	78	80	81
France	39	49	50	52	42	51	42	54	56	54	53	42	61	43	40	47	41
Germany (West)	69	80	71	75	68	77	68	76	78	78	81	81	70	66	66	60	55
Greece	51	56	57	61	26	51	36	52	53	48	34	44	37	34	36	36	34
Ireland	46	52	44	54	46	54	45	59	57	59	65	59	33	57	61	62	62
Italy	28	30	25	30	26	27	36	27	27	29	29	21	33	20	21	12	12
Luxembourg	67	75	67	77	68	70	64	82	76	77	71	71	76	77	74	70	72
The Netherlands	56	58	61	60	61	57	61	66	71	74	73	67	74	63	70	71	68
Portugal	34	52	59	56	70	53	46	57	53	60	70	71	70	75	72	65	54
Spain	51	51	56	49	55	47	45	57	51	60	61	56	61	57	56	41	41
United Kingdom	52	51	53	58	56	57	47	57	56	53	49	50	60	60	59	48	49
EC 10	49	54	50	55	50	54	50	56	56	56	55	51	58	48	49	45	42

Rudy B. Andeweg

TABLE 7.2. *Subjective interest in politics 1983–1990 (%)*

Country	1983	1988	1989	1989	1989	1990	1990
Belgium	23	34	36	26	45	37	35
Denmark	56	61	71	69	66	68	66
France	44	49	38	44	42	40	39
Germany (West)	51	53	61	62	57	57	54
Greece	45	42	53	51	59	55	55
Ireland	36	48	44	38	45	46	41
Italy	21	25	29	25	37	33	29
Luxembourg	47	44	56	45	48	52	48
The Netherlands	51	53	58	58	58	56	50
Portugal	—	7	12	8	15	10	17
Spain	—	28	39	27	53	36	32
United Kingdom	50	57	59	54	51	60	54
EC 10	42	46	50	47	49	49	45

1950s, and strong fluctuations in the USA since the early 1960s.[14] Dalton finds political interest to be expanding from the early 1950s to the early 1980s in West Germany, France, the United Kingdom, and the USA.[15] Even if we would replace subjective political interest with more objective indicators, such as reading political news or discussing politics with others, the conclusion does not change. For example, the percentage who discuss politics 'frequently' or 'occasionally' went up in most EC member states between 1973 and 1987. Italy is the only country where it dropped slightly.[16]

A Decline in Electoral Participation?

I have already mentioned that political apathy can also be interpreted as a sign of political health, of a contented 'silent majority'. However, low levels of participation, and low turn-out at elections in particular, are often seen as an indication of declining legitimacy. Thus, disappointment about turn-out in the direct elections for the European Parliament has been translated into criticism of a 'democratic lacuna' in Brussels. Has turn-out been declining? Flickinger and Studlar argue that there has been a decline during the 1980s, because 'Of the 18 countries in our sample, ten reported the lowest turnout of the decade for the most recent parliamentary election . . .'.[17] This is hardly convincing evidence, and an overview of average turn-out figures per

TABLE 7.3. *Average turn-out per decade in various countries*
(in % of population over 20 years old)

Country	1960s	1970s	1980s
Austria	90.3[a]	90.7[a]	91.6[a]
Belgium	87.4[a]	92.9[a]	91.6[a]
Denmark	83.7	86.6	86.0
France	65.7	77.1	71.9
Germany (West)	87.1	91.0	87.1
Greece	82.2	90.3	83.6
Ireland	73.1	75.7	72.9
Italy	91.8[a]	92.1[a]	89.8[a]
Luxembourg	89.5[a]	89.5[a]	88.1[a]
The Netherlands	87.3[a]	83.1	83.4
Portugal	—	88.3	77.8
Spain	—	72.5	73.4
United Kingdom	76.5	74.9	74.1

[a] Compulsory voting.

Source: Peter Mair, personal communication.

decade (to get rid of short-term effects) over a longer time period does not support their conclusion, as Table 7.3 shows.

Leaving aside elections under compulsory voting, there are countries with declining turn-out (the United Kingdom) and countries with rising turn-out (Denmark), but most countries exhibit trendless fluctuation. Only the three elections for the European Parliament show a linear decline in average turn-out (from 67.2 per cent in 1979 to 62.8 per cent in 1989), but even here there are exceptions, such as a consistent increase in turn-out in the United Kingdom! Whether for national or European elections, the changes in the level of turn-out are very small.

A Rise in Right-Wing Extremism?

There can be no doubt that extreme right-wing parties increased their share of the vote during the 1980s and early 1990s. Although the 'old' right-wing parties are either in decline (such as the Greek EPEN) or are distancing themselves from their Fascist roots (in Italy creating a post neo-Fascist party), all new right-wing parties, such as the French Front National and the Flemish Vlaams Blok made significant inroads.[18] The tide may already be turning: in recent national elections in most EU countries, the extreme right is losing support, and in the 1994 elections to the European Parliament, the extreme right secured insufficient seats to qualify as a parliamentary group. This decline may or may not be temporary, and the real question remains whether we can diagnose these parties as 'anti-system parties', and their support as a sign of disaffection with the political system.

It is difficult to answer that question. In most countries extreme right-wing parties are still very small, and many of their voters are reluctant to reveal their party preference and their motives to interviewers. This leaves us with very small numbers in ordinary cross-section surveys, and it is difficult to arrive at meaningful conclusions on that basis. In addition, there are a number of reasons why any conclusion that the growth of extreme right-wing parties points to a legitimacy crisis is at least premature. In the first place, it is interesting to note that the 'old' extreme right-wing parties are in decline. These parties are often the self-proclaimed heirs to Fascist regimes, and are most clearly in the anti-system category. This is less clear for the new extreme right-wing parties. Le Pen, for example, advocates the introduction of a full presidential system in France, which is hardly a revolutionary thought.[19]

Secondly, analysis of the popular support for the bigger extreme right-wing parties (such as the German Republikaner and French National Front) often reveals a bewildering variety of motives. The scholarly discussion seems to converge on two distinct hypotheses: diffuse protest against the political system, and fears and resentment about (the government's handling of) immigration. However, these may not be rival hypotheses. In studies of the German Republikaner, it is argued that the established political parties did not respond adequately to a new social problem such as immigration and ethnic tension. This lack of integrative capacity within the party system produced a decline of trust in those parties and the institutions they dominate (government, parliament), and a reservoir of potential support for a party which capitalizes on the neglected issue. 'Since the end of 1989, the results of all German opinion polls unanimously indicate that the established parties in Germany have succeeded in the reintegration of the majority of these protest voters, thereby reducing the Republikaner Party to a relatively marginal political force within the German party system'.[20]

Seen from this perspective, the rise of right-wing extremist parties is not a threat to the democratic order, but a safety-valve, alerting the political élites to a neglected issue and giving them an opportunity to act before discontent spreads and spills over into dissatisfaction with the system as a whole. Support for this view can be found in a study of confidence in government in Norway, Sweden, and the USA. In all three countries confidence in political office-holders declined in the late 1960s and early 1970s, after which it recovered in Norway, but continued to drop in the two other countries. In Norway the Progress Party channelled the discontent back into the political arena. 'As the Progress party became institutionalized it provided a voice for a significant minority of disenchanted people . . . thus reducing their feelings of distrust.'[21] The party systems of Sweden and the USA were not so flexible, and many discontented voters remained without representation in the system, further reducing their trust in politics.

As a sideline, and unrelated to the issue of right-wing extremism itself, a similar phenomenon can be observed with regard to the European Union. Direct elections to the European Parliament exist, but there is no European party system to reflect the dimensions of transnational issues or points of view relating to European unification: the voters are confronted with a choice between national parties disguised as European parties, but actually aligning themselves along national cleavage lines. The fact that turn-out is so low in European elections, and the finding that in most member states satisfaction with the way democracy functions in the European Community is considerably lower than satisfaction with the national democracies,[22] may very well be related to the inability of national party systems to address European issues and represent a European electorate. If this analysis is correct, a strengthening of the powers of the European Parliament alone, without the development of a European party system, will not result in higher levels of turn-out and democratic satisfaction.

2. A Party Crisis?

So far, our argument is that the widening of a dangerous gap between the citizens and the political systems of Western democracies is a myth rather than a reality. Although not without significant exceptions, in most countries electoral turn-out is not in a structural decline; political interest is actually increasing; and, while people may have exchanged a deferential naïvety towards authorities for a healthy scepticism, they continue to have confidence in the functioning of democracy. Even the emergence of extreme right-wing parties may serve to bridge any 'gap' some citizens may experience because the established parties have been slow to pick up a new social problem.

This does not mean that there are no problems with élite–mass linkages in contemporary democracies, but rather that the diagnosis of a 'confidence gap' or a 'legitimacy crisis' is too broad and too imprecise. The above discussion of the rise of extreme right-wing parties, and of the mismatch between national party systems and European elections, led to observations about the importance of party systems for the channelling of political demands. What holds true for party systems is also true for individual parties. Political parties are a crucial linkage mechanism between individual citizens and political office-holders. They serve to mobilize and socialize citizens, and to recruit political personnel; to aggregate citizens' interests into political programmes, and to communicate political decisions to the citizens, etc. All these functions parties are supposed to perform, but there is growing evidence that they are no longer effective with regard to many of the linkage functions: that parties are in decline, that there is a crisis of party, or even that 'the party's over'.[23]

The phenomenon of political parties has always been controversial, and Daalder rightly warns that wishful thinking may colour the perception of a waning of parties by those who have always thought parties to 'divide the common good', or who saw parties as a necessary but temporary evil during a period of mass mobilization.[24] Even with that caveat in mind, there can be no doubt that parties are losing functions:

1. In many countries parties and their associated organizational networks once provided services (for example, housing) directly to their members. Such 'political machines' or pillarized networks have all but disappeared, although there are still exceptions (Belgium). The parties' functions in this field have been taken over by the welfare state.

2. Parties once socialized their members into citizenship, and provided education and training for their cadres. This function has been made largely redundant by the much higher levels of education and the inclusion of some form of civics course in most curricula. Parties no longer train their own cadres, but recruit professionals directly from the universities. The educational system has taken over the parties' functions in this respect.

3. Parties were once a major source of political information for their members, through meetings and through the party press. The electronic mass media have taken over this function. The party press has folded

TABLE 7.4. *Party membership as a percentage of the electorate*

Country	First election in 1960s	Last election in 1980s	Difference
Austria	26.2	21.8	−4.4
Belgium	7.8	9.2	+1.4
Denmark	21.1	6.5	−14.6
Germany (West)	2.5	4.2	+1.7
Ireland	n.a.	5.3	n.a.
Italy	12.7	9.7	−3.0
The Netherlands	9.4	2.8	−6.6
United Kingdom	9.4	3.3	−6.1

n.a. = not available.

Source: R. S. Katz and P. Mair *et al.*, 'The Membership of Political Parties in European Democracies 1960–1990', *European Journal of Political Research*, 22 (1992), 334, table 1.

or has seen its circulation drop to insignificance. Party meetings are staged to attract television coverage, rather than to distribute information. To the extent that meetings served to gauge the membership's opinion, opinion polls now perform that function.

4. Parties once served to aggregate citizens' demands into more or less coherent election manifestos and political agendas. We should not be too nostalgic on this score: parties often focused on a particular segment of society, and 'interest aggregation' may often have amounted to little more than an ideological rewording of the articulated demands of this segment. We should also not overestimate the 'end of ideology' or the emergence of the 'catch-all party', which are claimed to have destroyed the aggregating capacity of the parties. However, parties have to cater to a much more fluid and heterogeneous electorate than in the past, which has resulted in less emphasis on party ideology and more attention to specific issues. As one Dutch observer complained: 'The only thing holding party programmes together is the staple.'[25] Royal commissions and 'think-tanks' are supposed to have taken over the aggregating function, although complaints are widespread that interest aggregation has disappeared altogether.

5. Parties once mobilized large segments of the population on a relatively permanent basis. Their decline in this respect is best illustrated by the erosion of party membership. It should be noted that only

communist parties, and traditional conservative and agrarian parties, have suffered losses without exception. Among the social democratic, Christian democratic, and liberal parties, the general pattern of decline is punctuated by a few parties that actually increased their membership, either in absolute terms, or as a ratio of members to voters. Interesting though these exceptions are, they confirm the rule of a declining party membership. This decline is not offset by the emergence of new extreme right-wing parties or environmentalist parties, with extremely low membership figures.[26] Political parties have never mobilized a majority of the population through membership, but if we look at the percentages of loyal party supporters a similar erosion is evident. In the USA, where card-carrying membership has never been of any significance, it was the decline in party identification that first led to diagnoses of dealignment and a party crisis.[27] In Europe the causes of a decline in party attachment may be different in some countries,[28] but the decay of party loyalty is no less evident: 'In an overall perspective, the proportion of EC citizens more or less attached to a particular party has been decreasing over the past decade by about 10 per cent, from below 70 per cent in the mid-1970s to below 60 per cent in the late 1980s. Accordingly, those not aligned with any party have become more numerous, and today constitute about 40 per cent of the EC electorate.'[29]

Parties may have lost most of their functions with regard to the distribution of services, socialization, communication, aggregation, and mobilization, but obituaries are still premature. In most definitions of 'political parties' the presentation of candidates at elections is crucial, and here the parties have maintained their monopoly. Only in the USA has there been a serious threat to this function of parties. In the 1960s and 1970s the parties lost their grip on the nomination procedure when primaries replaced caucuses on a wave of democratization, and when modern campaign technology and federal campaign finance legislation emphasized the candidate rather than the party. From the early 1980s the parties recouped some of their losses when a few states abolished the primary, when 'super-delegates' were added to the nominating conventions, when a 1979 change in the Campaign Finance Law increased the potential role of the parties, and when the parties (the Republicans first) used this potential by developing their fund-raising capacity.[30]

In most European countries parties always maintained, and sometimes even reinforced, their grip on the selection and recruitment of office-holders. Thus, while the parties' links with the electorate weakened, their links with the state apparatus grew stronger. Paradoxically, amidst a growing literature on the 'decline of party', one can hear warnings of a 'Parteienstaat' (Germany), 'partitocrazia' (Italy), 'particratie' (Belgium), 'l'État Mitterrand–Chirac' (France). As a mechanism for élite–mass linkages, the parties have taken up a position closer to the state, which is epitomized by their increasing reliance on public funding, rather than on membership fees.[31]

It may be argued that, because of this change, we are not witnessing a decline of party, but a transformation from the 'parti de masse', or 'mass-bureaucratic party' to a new type of party, the 'modern cadre party',[32] or the 'electoral-professional party'.[33] Even then, this transformation entails a weakening of parties with important consequences for élite-mass linkage: 'Mass bureaucratic parties were strong institutions. Electoral-professional parties are weak ones. The transition from one to the other thus involves de-institutionalization. . . . The historical epoch of strong parties/strong institutions (the mass parties analyzed by Weber and Duverger) seems to be drawing to a close.'[34]

3. Towards New Forms of Élite–Mass Linkage

With the possible exception of interest aggregation, the functions that used to be performed by parties have not disappeared: the state has taken over the distribution of services, the education system has taken over socialization and training, the mass media and pollsters have taken over communication. In the first part of this chapter we have argued that citizens have not turned away from democratic politics, although the chapter's second part implies that they use party channels less. The same causes that have made party membership less appealing to many citizens have also made other modes of political involvement more accessible to them. Foremost among those causes are education and individualization. In the 1990s the average citizen in the Western world is much better educated than his parents were. A higher level of 'cognitive mobilization', as it is often called in the literature, allows a citizen to analyse political situations by him- or herself instead of taking a party view for granted, and provides him or her with the skills to take appropriate political action, without reliance on party officials as intermediaries. Individualization is a gradual process that can be observed not only in politics: many people continue to have religious feelings, but not necessarily to join churches, or they go jogging by themselves instead of playing team sports, etc. They are less inclined to identify themselves in terms of belonging to collectivities, and if they do join collectivities (from marriage to party) these attachments are less permanent than they used to be. In summary: a trend is visible towards a better-educated, more individualistic, and more mobile citizen. This citizen is not less active politically, but avoids being permanently mobilized in a collective organization, and prefers self-initiated, *ad hoc*, single-issue spurs of action.

Evidence for this view can be found in studies of political participation. They often make a distinction between 'conventional' participation (voting, party membership, campaign activities, contacting officials, etc.) and 'protest', or 'unconventional' participation (signing petitions, demonstrating, boycotts, strikes, participating in an action group, etc.).[35] The label '(un)conventional' is unfortunate, as it is too period- and fashion-bound. Perhaps a distinction between 'élite-directed' and 'élite-directing' politics[36] is more apposite. More important than the terminology, however, is the finding that 'conventional' participation is either stable, or slightly declining, while 'unconventional' participation is increasing.[37] And 'conventional' activities such as voting are becoming more volatile (floating voters, ticket-splitting).

'Unconventional' participation has not been a temporary phenomenon of the turbulent 1960s, but has even been institutionalized to some extent in 'new social movements' ('NSMs', in the jargon of some political scientists), such as the women's movement, the peace movement, the environmentalist movement. However, even these new social movements are different from parties in the way they operate: organizations such as Greenpeace and Amnesty International attract millions of supporters, but they consist of professional teams, focusing on a single issue, with few or any members, calling upon their supporters only intermittently. The development towards *ad hoc* single-issue activity is epitomized by events such as the Live Aid concert organized in 1985 by Bob Geldof.

It should be emphasized that we are observing only trends or developments that are incomplete, not uniform across countries, and moving very slowly: parties are weakening as élite–mass linkages, but at the present rate of change, they will continue to dominate democratic politics for a long time. Yet, the trend is an important one to analyse for two reasons. First, given the underlying causes (burgeoning educational opportunities and individualization), a reversal of the trend, while not unthinkable, is unlikely. Second, a shift from parties as élite–mass linkages to *ad hoc* and single-issue organizations may eventually result in the kind of crisis that we claim does not exist today: 'From V. O. Key Jr. to Giovanni Sartori, serious theorists of party and its necessary link to democracy have stressed the vital importance of party again and again. When parties are absent or . . . have become Cheshire cats of which very little is left but the smile, pathologies multiply.'[38]

Already in 1902 Ostrogorski advocated the replacement of mass parties with *ad hoc* single-issue associations[39] but government is not an *ad hoc* or single-issue affair. The 'permanent' political élites find themselves in an increasingly disorientating situation. The traditional élite–mass linkage mechanisms, such as political parties and established interest groups, provide them with less information than in the past, and information about large collectivities that are becoming less relevant at that. The people they are to govern are more fragmented and heterogeneous, more volatile and less predictable: society is more difficult to know and to understand, more difficult to be in touch with.[40]

There are those who see this development not as a threat to democracy, but as an opportunity for democracy. In their view, the ripening of the modern sophisticated and individualistic citizen makes representative democracy redundant at the same time (happy coincidence!) that modern communication technology makes direct democracy possible in the 'global village'. In addition to futuristic Tofflerian impressions, several experiments have been conducted on 'teledemocracy', ranging from computer conferences to electronic town meetings using interactive cable television.[41] If teledemocracy will not prove to be a solution, it is not because of a lack of technological possibilities, but because of the mistaken assumption that the modern citizen is the long-awaited *zoon politikon*, eager to be continuously involved in the affairs of government from behind his television set and personal computer. Above, we have argued that there is a trend towards different forms of political participation, not towards more or less participation. The same fallacy can be observed in arguments for radical decentralization to bridge the gap between citizen and politics.

The challenge seems to be to create or strengthen institutional mechanisms for occasional 'outbursts' of political activity concerning a specific issue, without destabilizing the 'permanent' representative government. This is not the place to speculate on what such mechanisms might be, but developments within the existing democratic structures may point us in the right direction. For example, in many

160   *Rudy B. Andeweg*

countries citizens increasingly turn to the courts when they are angered by the outcome of governmental or parliamentary decision-making. There is some evidence that, along with its increased political role, the judiciary enjoys an increased popularity. Where the role of the judiciary *vis-à-vis* government is still limited, there are calls to strengthen the courts' position, through the adoption of a bill of rights (as in the United Kingdom) or the introduction of judicial review (as in the Netherlands). Referendums are also increasingly frequent and popular. Counting all nation-wide referendums during this century, in all but a few West European parliamentary systems, Morel found that fifty-one of the eighty-nine referendums took place after 1960 (and twenty-four after 1980).[42] Constitutional provisions for referendums are proposed to be introduced (Belgium, Germany, the Netherlands) or to be extended (Austria, France). What the otherwise very different mechanisms of referendums and judicial action have in common is that they integrate *ad hoc* and single-issue activity into the existing representative system.[43] So far, the standard reaction to political crises defined as a 'confidence gap' has been a proposal to change the electoral system (Italy, Japan, Israel, New Zealand, the United Kingdom, the Netherlands). If the confidence gap is a myth, such reforms will prove futile. If our diagnosis of weakening parties and changing forms of political activity is correct, reforms in the direction pointed by referendums and judicial review are more promising.

NOTES

1. S. M. Lipset and W. Schneider, *The Confidence Gap: Business, Labor and Government in the Public Mind* (New York: Free Press, 1983).
2. H. F. Pitkin, 'The Concept of Representation', in H. F. Pitkin (ed.), *Representation* (New York: Atherton, 1969), 16.
3. H. R. Van Gunsteren, *Eigentijds Burgerschap* (The Hague: SDU, 1992), 48; see also A. Schedler, 'Die Demoskopische Konstruktion von "Politik-verdrossenheit" ', *Politische Vierteljahresschrift*, 34 (1992), 430–1.
4. Pitkin, 'The Concept of Representation', 20–1.
5. R. S. Friedman, *Participation in Democracy* (Ann Arbor, Mich.: Michigan University Press, 1973), and, without the Weimar warning, S. P. Huntington, 'Postindustrial Politics: How Benign Will it Be?', *Comparative Politics*, 6 (1974), 147–77.
6. D. Easton, *A Systems Analysis of Political Life* (New York: Wiley, 1965).
7. G. Parry, 'Trust, Distrust and Consensus', *British Journal of Political*

Science, 6 (1976), 129–42 and M. Kaase, 'Political Alienation and Protest', in M. Dogan (ed.), *Comparing Pluralist Democracies: Strains on Legitimacy* (Boulder, Colo.: Westview, 1988), 125.

8. See the debate between Citrin and Miller in the *American Political Science Review*, 67 (1974), 356–7.

9. M. K. Jennings and J. W. Van Deth, 'Conclusion: Some Consequences for Systems and Governments', in M. K. Jennings and J. W. Van Deth *et al.*, *Continuities in Political Action* (Berlin: De Gruyter, 1990), 356–7.

10. J. Citrin and D. P. Green, 'Presidential Leadership and the Resurgence of Trust in Government', *British Journal of Political Science*, 16 (1986), 431–53 and A. H. Miller and O. Listhaug, 'Political Parties and Confidence in Government: A Comparison of Norway, Sweden and the United States', *British Journal of Political Science*, 20 (1990), 361.

11. S. E. Finkel, E. N. Muller, and M. A. Seligson, 'Economic Crisis, Incumbent Performance and Regime Support: A Comparison of Longitudinal Data from West Germany and Costa Rica', *British Journal of Political Science*, 19 (1989), 350. For a less optimistic view, see U. Widmaier, 'Tendencies toward an Erosion of Legitimacy', in Dogan (ed.), *Comparing Pluralist Democracies*.

12. The wording of the question is not ideal. One might argue that it is not sufficiently focused on regime support, and may therefore also tap satisfaction with the incumbent political authorities. However, in July 1987, half of the national samples were administered a different question: 'Some people are for the present government (in your country). Others are against it. Putting aside whether you are for or against the present government, on the whole, are you very satisfied, fairly satisfied, not very satisfied, or not at all satisfied with the way democracy works (in your country)?' The two questions did not produce significantly different results. Another problem may be that respondents may give socially desirable answers, which in this case may produce an overestimation of satisfaction. However, we can assume that factor to be constant, so that we can still look at the long-term trend, even if we have less confidence in the reliability of the percentages at any given point of time.

13. Lipset and Schneider, *The Confidence Gap*, 29; cf. 375–412.

14. J. W. Van Deth, 'Interest in Politics', in Jennings and Van Deth *et al.*, *Continuities in Political Action*, 282.

15. R. J. Dalton, *Citizen Politics in Western Democracies: Public Opinion and Political Parties in the US, Great Britain, West Germany and France* (Chatham, NJ: Chatham House, 1988), 22–3.

16. R. Inglehart, *Culture Shift in Advanced Industrial Society* (Princeton: Princeton University Press, 1990), 355.

17. R. S. Flickinger and D. T. Studlar, 'The Disappearing Voters? Exploring Declining Turnout in Western European Elections', *West European Politics*, 15/2 (1992), 2; cf. 8.

18. P. Ignazi, 'The Silent Counter-Revolution: Hypotheses of the Emergence of Extreme Right-Wing Parties in Europe', *European Journal of Political Research*, 22 (1992), 16–18.
19. K. Von Beyme, 'Right-Wing Extremism in Post-war Europe', *West European Politics*, 11/2 (1988), 4.
20. B. Westle and O. Niedermayer, 'The New Right in Germany: The Transformation of Conservatism and the Extreme Right', *European Journal of Political Research*, 22 (1992), 98.
21. Miller and Listhaug, 'Political Parties and Confidence in Government', 366.
22. Commission of the European Communities, *Eurobarometer: Public Opinion in the European Community*, no. 39. (Brussels, 1993).
23. D. S. Broder, *The Party's Over: The Failure of Politics in America* (New York: Harper & Row, 1971).
24. H. Daalder, 'A Crisis of Party?', *Scandinavian Political Studies*, 15 (1992), 269–88.
25. B. Tromp, 'Het Verval van Politieke Partijen', *Het Parool*, 20 Dec. 1985.
26. R. S. Katz and P. Mair, *et al.*, 'The Membership of Political Parties in European Democracies 1960–1990', *European Journal of Political Research*, 22 (1992), 334–7.
27. M. P. Wattenberg, *The Decline of American Political Parties 1952–1980* (Cambridge, Mass.: Harvard University Press, 1984) and 'From a Partisan to a Candidate-Centred Electorate', in A. King (ed.), *The New American Political System*, 2nd edn. (Washington: AEI, 1990), 139–74.
28. H.-D. Klingemann and M. P. Wattenberg, 'Decaying versus Developing Party Systems: A Comparison of Party Images in the United States and West Germany', *British Journal of Political Science*, 22 (1992), 131–49.
29. H. Schmitt, 'On Party Attachment in Western Europe and the Utility of the Eurobarometer Data', *West European Politics*, 12/2 (1989), 125.
30. J. W. Ceasar, 'Political Parties: Declining, Stabilizing or Resurging?', in A. King (ed.), *The New American Political System* (Washington: AEI, 1990).
31. H. E. Alexander (ed.), *Comparative Political Finance in the 1980s* (Cambridge: Cambridge University Press, 1989).
32. R. A. Koole, *De Opkomst van de Moderne Kaderpartij* (Utrecht: Spectrum, 1992).
33. A. Panebianco, *Political Parties: Organization and Power* (Cambridge: Cambridge University Press, 1988).
34. Ibid. 267.
35. Jennings and Van Deth, 'Conclusion: Some Consequences for Systems and Governments'.
36. Inglehart, *Culture Shift in Advanced Industrial Society*, 335 ff.
37. Dalton, *Citizen Politics in Western Democracies* and Inglehart, *Culture Shift in Advanced Industrial Society*.

38. W. D. Burnham, 'Foreword', in Wattenberg, *The Decline of American Political Parties*, p. xiii.
39. Daalder, 'A Crisis of Party?', 271.
40. Van Gunsteren, *Eigentijds Burgerschap*.
41. F. C. Arterton, *Teledemocracy: Can Technology Protect Democracy?* (Beverly Hills, Calif.: Sage, 1987).
42. L. Morel, 'Party Attitudes towards Referendums in Western Europe', *West European Politics*, 16 (1993), 226.
43. Ibid. 242 and J. L. Waltman, 'The Courts and Political Change in Postindustrial Society', in J. L. Waltman and K. M. Holland (eds.), *The Political Role of Law Courts in Modern Democracies* (London: Macmillan, 1988), 218.

8

Organized Interests as Intermediaries

JEREMY RICHARDSON

1. Conventional and New Channels of Participation

The conventional model of liberal democracy emphasizes the importance of elections, the sovereignty of the legislature, and the role of political parties. This has been modified by a recognition of increased executive power and the decline of legislatures. However, traditional notions of democratic accountability—linking voters, parties, and governments—have retained their importance in political science—hence the increasing concern with the alleged distancing of governing élites from their peoples. Yet by the 1960s advanced industrial democracies had begun to experience the burgeoning of the citizen action movement, the escalation in demands for more 'participation', and the proliferation of new procedures and new institutions designed to facilitate more and 'better' participation. That decade can be described as the start of the participation explosion in Western democracies. New and more effective forms of linking citizens to governing élites have emerged in the context of a very active market for public participation in politics.

This explosion of citizen activity was in part grafted on to existing conventional modes of participation—voting and campaigning for political parties. In fact, the history of democracy is one of expanding participation and of expanding the modes of participation available to citizens. For example, there has been a steady expansion in voting.[1] Voting was the first participation explosion. Participation in campaign activities is an extension of electoral participation beyond the act of voting. Although fewer citizens participate in campaigning, Dalton argues that, 'as a result of this additional effort, this participation mode provides more political influence to the individual citizen and conveys more information than voting'.[2]

These long-established channels or modes of participation are, of course, still enormously important features of the political landscape.

Of central importance to our understanding of political activism today—and particularly to the dynamics of political activism—is the fact that the range and nature of opportunity structures for citizen participation has changed quite significantly. There is a 'political action repertory', consisting of both conventional and unconventional political involvement. At the theoretical level, Kaase and Marsh suggest that both political competence (as discussed originally by Almond and Verba in their early study) and political repertory 'assume that citizens have acquired through social learning, qualifications that will help them respond to political needs and demands to achieve the goods they strive for'.[3] Their focus on longitudinal change is of special relevance to our own study. Despite methodological problems in comparing their data with that from the original Almond and Verba study, they conclude that there has generally been a thrust towards more political competence among the young and that a new set of political activities has been added to the citizen's political repertory—'a set that had little political salience even among the most highly educated strata of the societies examined in the earlier years'.[4] Though they are at pains to emphasize that it is a mistake to see conventional and unconventional participation as mutually exclusive (in practice they are often used together to achieve a desired result), their analysis is consistent with our argument here that the 'market for activism' is now much more open, competitive, and varied (see Section 4, below). Their finding that, as in the Almond and Verba study, education was a key factor in determining political competence is also reasonably consistent with the argument that not only has the number of opportunity structures expanded, but also potential activists are now much more sophisticated in their understanding of the efficacy of different modes of participation in post-industrial societies.

Moreover, participation in what are obviously political activities (such as joining a political party, joining an interest group, or joining a demonstration) and other forms of social activity (such as joining a voluntary sports or cultural organization) are not independent of each other. The multifarious social activities open to citizens in a post-industrial society are all part of a competition for the time, interest, and money of citizens. As M. Lal Goel and David Horton Smith point out, what political scientists call 'political participation' is known as 'social action' to others.[5] Even membership of organizations thought to be non-political such as sports organizations can provide opportunities for political participation from time to time. Thus, we should be cautious, as Olsen suggests, in automatically accepting the argument that there *is* a crisis of representation or legitimacy. For example, he suggests that our models of analyses may be at fault, rather than the institutions of representation themselves, and that 'the legitimacy crisis-hypothesis underestimates the institutional complexity, the many institutional defense lines of contemporary democracies'.[6] Our argument here is that not only have interest groups always played a key role in the processes of representation and legitimation, they have also possibly begun to displace political parties as intermediaries between governing élites and their peoples. It is to the long tradition of interest group mobilization that we now turn.

2. *A Tradition of Interest Groups as 'Linkage' Institutions*

In focusing on interest groups as intermediaries linking élites to the governed, we must also be conscious that the political process is far more complex than merely the interplay between government and groups. As one of the most perceptive observers of the American interest-group system has claimed, public policy is not simply the outcome of group pressure. Thus, he argued that:

A pressure model of the policy making process in which an essentially passive legislature responds to petitions from groups of citizens who have spontaneously organized because of common social or economic concerns must yield to a model in which influences for change come as much from inside government as from beyond its institutional boundaries, and in which political entrepreneurs operating from bases in interest groups, from within the Congress, the president or many private emerging groups, strive to generate support for their own conceptions of the public interest.[7]

The current emphasis on 'the new institutionalism' in political science is also a reminder that institutions do matter. For example, it is impossible to understand the nature of the policy process of the European Union without a proper understanding of the structure, organization, and interrelationship between the institutions of the European Community and the differing institutional settings at the level of the member states. Similarly, one cannot understand the nature of the policy processes in France and the USA without a clear understanding of the quite different roles which the legislatures play in those two countries and of the institutional differences between federal and unitary states. Thus, in this chapter, it is taken as given that governmental institutions do indeed matter.[8] Similarly, it is taken as given that democracies usually contain multiple channels of representation. Our focus is on the linkage process between government and the governed, and especially on the role that interest groups play in that process in developed or post-industrial political systems.

Even a cursory glance at the literature of comparative politics will show that in Western democracies (and now in some of the newly 'democratized' Eastern states) interest groups are universally recognized as playing a key role in the policy process. This is as true for policy implementation as it is for policy formulation. As each issue is processed via the national or international institutional arrangements, it is usual to be able to identify a constellation of interest groups, mobilized to press for particular policy or implementation outcomes. The history of political mobilization (so closely linked to the process of democratization) is, of course, marked by the emergence of two great intermediary organizations—political parties and interest groups. These two institutions have been the main channels of citizen participation and influence, now supplemented (some would say supplanted) by the mass media and opinion polls. The central thesis of this chapter is that over time interest groups have possibly become far more important as a means of directly linking governing élites with their peoples. Indeed, one might claim that the people have managed to become part of the governing élite, via their group representatives. As Olsen argues, 'contemporary western democracies are organised democracies. Policy-making takes place within complicated networks of organised, public and private actors.'[9]

The increased significance (perhaps dominance) of groups in this linkage process was captured by Stein Rokkan, whose main professional concern was the process of political mobilization. In what has now become a classic summary of the characterization of the modern system of representation, he argued that

> The crucial decisions on economic policy are rarely taken in the parties or in Parliament: the central area is the bargaining table where the government authorities meet directly with the trade union leaders, the representatives of the farmers, the smallholders and the fishermen, and the delegates of the Employers' Association. These yearly rounds of negotiations have in fact come to mean more in the lives of rank-and-file citizens than formal elections.[10]

Although he was writing about the development of Norwegian democracy (and before the participation explosion), he does seem to have
captured a central feature of the policy process in West European states.
Thus, in a broad overview of the 'European polity', Martin Heisler and
Robert Kvavik also saw the integration of interest groups in the policy
process as its central feature. They described the 'European polity'
model as a 'decision structure characterised by continuous, regularised
access for economically, politically, ethnically and/or subculturally based
groups to the highest levels of the political system'.[11] In reality, the 'stuff
of politics' is usually about rather detailed and esoteric matters—more
about the 'low politics' rather than 'high politics', to use Hoffmann's
terminology.[12] This is as true for the European Community—despite
the high drama of Maastricht—as it is for politics in Rome or Bonn.
European integration is more about setting common technical standards
for, say, washing-machines and medicines than it is about a grand
design for a new European state. As one director of a European trade
association put it to an audience of British trade associations, his work
in Brussels was very boring! Citizens, too, may be more interested
in the mundane issues of day-to-day living than in some 'vision' of
Europe.

If we take Britain as an example of the state which has perhaps the
longest tradition of accommodating interest groups in the policy process,
it is very easy to demonstrate that groups as intermediaries were
challenging political parties long ago. For example, Patricia Hollis has
captured the essence of the British pluralist tradition in her description
of Victorian politics as follows:

Forty years before, the existence of such pressure was illegitimate, unnecessary
or both; now it was a necessary tool of social reform, a necessary aid to
government, evidence of healthy public concern. Pressure from without had
both stretched the arena of government and access to government, and in the
process had thrown up feminist groups on the rights of prostitutes, evangelicals
on the wrongs of prostitutes, public health groups on the diseases of prostitutes,
Shaftesbury and Gladstone on refuges for prostitutes, and sabbatarians for no
prostitution on Sundays. Victorian life was engagingly pluralist.[13]

Indeed, Mancur Olson, in his analysis of the decline of nations, cites
Britain as the best (or worst) example of the power of interest groups.
He sees what he terms strong 'distributional coalitions' as one of the
main causes of Britain's economic decline. In a telling passage, he
argues that 'with age British society has acquired so many strong organ-

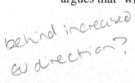

isations and collusions that it suffers from an institutional sclerosis that slows its adaptation to changing circumstances and changing technologies'.[14] In one sense, this implies that governments have become too responsive to opinion and have as a result declined as problem-solving institutions.

The British policy style emerged as one in which consultation (and often negotiation) has been the norm. As a result, any policy reform process tends to stimulate a cacophony of group activity. We need look no further than Mrs Thatcher's administration for the truth of the Mancur Olson theory. If one were to identify only one of the characteristics of 'Thatcherism' (perhaps the only original and genuinely Thatcherite element), it is the enthusiasm to attack the many reform deficits that had developed over many years of a policy style which had generally emphasized the need to accommodate group demands. In essence, Mrs Thatcher set about removing the franchise for public policy which many groups—particularly such professions as doctors, lawyers, and even universities—had secured for themselves over time. This raises the important questions of whether the linkages between at least one part of the governing élite in Britain—the civil service—was perhaps too closely aligned with the specialized publics, as represented by organized interests, and had begun to lose sight of the broader public interest. The irony is that democracies like Britain had emphasized the need to consult what are termed the 'affected interests' in order to *be* democratic. To a considerable degree this had become the yardstick of democracy itself, in a modern version of J. C. Calhoun's 'concurrent majority'.[15] A guiding principle has been that governments should not act without first consulting and seeking the agreement of those most likely to be affected by a proposed policy change. The Scandinavian *remiss* system is very similar and embodies the same notion that mobilizing consensus around policy change is the most appropriate way to proceed. It is perhaps no accident that the country which practised this policy style most enthusiastically—Sweden—now faces the same kind of difficulties experienced by Britain. Similarly, we are also beginning to see the rigidities of the German economy exposed and the same problem of group resistance to policy change, as the German policy style begins to shift to a more 'impositional' mode.

We have argued elsewhere that there is an inherent functional logic drawing governments to consult and negotiate with groups and for governments to see groups as the most effective intermediaries in the policy process.[16] Where groups did not exist, or were badly organized, governments—particularly civil servants—have often been active in creating them.[17] This functional logic to seek out or create intermediary institutions is in part due to the strong sectorization of policy-making in advanced societies. The institutions of governments are themselves sectoral, with quite strong departmental and divisional boundaries, reflecting the specialized and highly technical nature of much of the business of government. This appears to be especially the case at the level of the European Union, with the Commission itself now a classic case of a compartmentalized bureaucracy—a multi-organization with quite serious co-ordination problems. (For example, see the Court of Auditors' Report on the lack of co-ordination between the EU's regional and environmental programmes.[18]) Once public policy becomes concerned with technical detailed issues, it is inevitable that government will talk to and negotiate with a whole series of specialized publics whose primary concern is with quite specific policy problems. Politics at the sectoral and subsectoral level is about implementing Calhoun's recommendation that decisions should be made after taking the sense of each interest or portion of the community.

In part, emphasis on the accommodation of interest groups is also due to the lack of technical expertise within governments themselves. As Sammy Finer correctly observed over twenty-five years ago, the technical expertise of groups is essential if public policies are to stand any chance of being successful.[19] Increasingly, the political costs of not accommodating group demands are considerable, bearing in mind the growing expertise which groups, especially the environmentalists, but also consumer groups, health campaign groups, consumers, women, minorities, etc., have developed in the use of the mass media and in mobilizing broader public support. Interestingly, exactly the same phenomenon is emerging at the level of the European Union. Commission officials have developed an increasingly intimate relationship with both European-level and national groups, as a source of ideas and information, as a means of building successful pan-European coalitions in favour of policy proposals, and as a means of trying to improve the poor implementation record of the EC.[20] So intense has this process become that both the Commission and the European Parliament are now seeking ways of regularizing (though not yet regulating) the Brussels lobbying system, in response to high levels of interest-group mobilization. For Commission officials and MEPs, there seems no lack of linkage mechanisms, informing them of at least organized European opinion.

3. The Broadening of Participation and the Europeanization of Policy-Making

Two broad patterns of interest group–élite relations can be identified in the advanced democracies of Western Europe. First, it is common to see certain types of groups—particularly producer groups—subject to a degree of governmental challenge as the Western democracies begin to bend under the strains of a weak world economy and the increased pace of industrialization in the Third World. Arrangements that were viable in the good times are now seen to be inefficient and uncompetitive. Old 'peace treaties' between government and groups are having to be renegotiated or in some cases simply torn up and new policy regimes instituted. In terms of the long history of group integration, this phenomenon is relatively short-lived and is, therefore, difficult to evaluate. However, it does seem to be a fairly common trend since 1973–4. There have been different time-lags in different countries, but the need to govern, even if policy change has to be imposed, is rather widespread.[21] In a sense, the institutions of government have become more self-assertive in the agenda-setting process, with, again, Britain perhaps being the most striking example. We have seen the destabilization of existing policies and programmes and, more importantly in terms of the focus of this chapter, the destabilization of existing policy communities.[22]

Somehow, the quite strong grip which existing (often rather exclusive) policy communities had exercised has been loosened or broken by governmental initiative and, occasionally, by more general public pressure via the media and via the polls. Yet this relatively recent process of opening up restrictive policy communities by governmental challenge had been preceded by a gradual but much more important change—the steady widening of the network of groups involved in each policy sector and the gradual erosion of boundaries between policy areas. Some twenty years ago it was possible to describe much of policy-making in Britain, for example, as involving rather tightly drawn, restrictive, and stable policy communities.[23] These policy communities generally consisted of civil servants and bureaucrats from those interest groups thought by the relevant government department divisions as having a direct interest in the policy area in question. With increased group mobilization and increased media attention to specific policy issues, these policy communities appear less stable, participation is becoming more fluid, and, above all, the range of actors in each policy area appears to be growing. This trend was first noticed by Hugh Heclo in the USA. He challenged the conventional wisdom of political science that the US policy process was characterized by 'iron triangles' (congressional committees, agencies and bureaux, and the relevant interest groups). His seminal contribution was to suggest that this ordered and stable pattern had, imperceptibly, changed over time. In a much-quoted passage he argued that being too concerned with the 'truly powerful' actors has lead observers to 'overlook the power and influence that arise out of the configurations (of participants) . . . Looking for the closed triangles of control, we tend to overlook the fairly open networks of people that increasingly impinge on government'.[24]

Subsequently, there has been a long and increasingly tedious debate, in Britain particularly, concerning the theoretical distinctions between policy communities and issue networks.[25] For our purposes the debate need not concern us. Its real importance is that most writers now accept that the policy process in Western democracies is a very long way from the (alleged but never proven) corporatism of the 1960s. Under that model, *exclusivity* was a key characteristic. Under the issue network model, *openness* and permeability are the main characteristics. New groups enter old policy areas, old groups from different policy areas demand and get access to sectors hitherto closed to them, and policy-makers often have to contend with a degree of 'overcrowding' which can make problem-solving more difficult. Even the conventional wisdom that British government is a closed and secretive world does not really bear close examination if one examines the way in which the 'consultation lists' of government departments have grown over time. As Finer correctly argued, *pressure* group is quite the wrong term to use in the British case as, historically, groups have been pressing against an open door. Providing the rules of the game are observed, access is generally not a problem. The post-war trend has been to allow greater access to an ever-widening range of groups—hardly consistent with the 'representational crisis' view or with a picture of an élite determined to govern in isolation. Even under Mrs Thatcher, who thought that 'consensus' meant 'fudge', it would be wrong to see groups as having been totally excluded. The policy style certainly changed, but the pattern appears to have been to reincorporate the groups within the new policy frameworks launched by the government.[26] The post-1960s era in the West has been one of greatly increased group mobilization through the formation of conventional interest groups and also of less conventional citizen action organizations and social movements.[27]

For interest groups in the twelve member states of the European Union, there is, of course, an alternative policy-making arena in which they can participate. Indeed, in considering links between élites and their peoples in the EU countries, it is now vital that account is taken of the Europeanization of policy-making. There is now considerable evidence that interest groups are shifting their focus to the European level, especially those groups who are failing to secure what they see as an adequate response at the national level. As the Commission is, above all, a very open bureaucracy, it has proved to be an attractive target for interest groups of all kinds, including many non-producer groups such as women's organizations,[28] environmentalists,[29] the disabled, and a whole network of voluntary organizations.[30] Even weakened producer groups, such as British trade unions, are finding Brussels a more receptive and rewarding area in such questions as the terms and conditions to be granted to state-owned companies under privatization.[31]

One of the more interesting questions to be addressed by researchers is the interrelationship between the linkages between citizens (and groups) and national governments and between citizens (and groups) at the level of the Commission. Because the European Union is still essentially an intergovernmental institution, national linkages remain vital to interest groups and to citizens. Yet national groups can and do directly influence the agenda-setting process at the EU level and, increasingly, are involved in cross-national policy networks. In that sense, the European Union is beginning to see the kind of democratization process, via interest group mobilization, that we suggested earlier has been a central feature of democratization at the national level. This is especially important within the European Union, bearing in mind that the traditional citizen–élite linkages—political parties and elections—are singularly weak elements in the democratic process.

Despite the increasing influence of the European Parliament,[32] it is clear that the European Parliament is even less effective as a channel of representation than are parliaments at the national level in the member states. Moreover, there are no effective European-level parties which citizens can join. Without a well-organized and comprehensive interest-group system within the European Union, the policy process would at present take place in an Executive (Commission plus national administrations)-dominated 'vacuum'. Thus, Lindberg's earlier observations on the role of interest groups in the process of European integration were perhaps somewhat over-cautious. In the 1960s he thought that interest groups were not playing a key role in the process of European integration, as 'the vital interests of relatively few are as yet directly affected by decision of the Community institutions'.[33] Crucially, however, he predicted that

> one can expect that over time the necessity for lobbying will force groups to emphasise collective needs rather than national differences. Such a development can be expected as the central institutions of the EEC become more active, as the types of actions taken involve the harmonization of legislation and the formulations of common policies (rather than the negative process of . . . barriers to trade), and as . . . groups become aware that their interest can no longer be adequately served at the national level alone.[34]

Evidence suggests that groups in all policy sectors have certainly recognized that supranational decisions are now inevitable for many policy problems and that it is often in their interests to engage in anticipatory activity in order to influence the shape and direction of policy solutions at the European level. Groups themselves have recognized the logic and momentum of the greater Europeanization of solutions. They are, therefore, beginning to play a very significant role in the process of European integration, as predicted by the neo-functionalists.

As yet, it is impossible to predict how far this process will go and, therefore, precisely what role interest groups will play in linking the European citizenry to the European-level policy élites. However, following Lehmbruch, it is reasonable to suggest that those linkages will become institutionalized in some way. As he notes, 'in critical junctures state bureaucracies have often played an important and formative part of their own'. Thus, 'interactions of governmental bureaucracies with associations or other corporate economic actors seem to be of crucial importance in linking the macro- and meso-levels and result in the emergence of network configurations which will eventually become institutionalised'.[35] Recent moves by the Commission to regularize the interface between interest groups and the Commission and the ways in which the Commission itself stimulates the development of the interest-group system (often deliberately encouraging 'weaker' groups via direct and indirect funding) appear to confirm Lehmbruch's observations concerning the key role played by bureaucracies in the emergence of comprehensive and institutionalized interest-group systems. As one Commission official has observed, 'lobbies are neither an optional extra nor an occasional irritant but a vital part of the system, with the Community institutions increasingly institutionalising the lobbies' role in a relationship to policy making'. This process has been accelerated by the Danish 'no' and the Edinburgh Council.[36] While we await the emergence at the European level of the other main channel of representation—European parties—the interest groups have arrived and have their feet well under the table!

4. Linking Citizens to Governing Élites: Issues, Participation, and Proliferation

It is possible to construct two quite differing images of modern democracies. The first and now conventional image, reflected in the theme of this volume, is that democratic societies face some kind of crisis caused by a distancing of governments from the governed. The second image is one of societies in which the number and range of opportunity structures for citizen participation has increased quite considerably, particularly after 'participation' became the vogue in the 1960s. Far from lacking 'linkage' processes between governing élites and their people, we see an enormous *proliferation* of linkage structures, sufficient to present a major challenge to political parties. Whichever image is correct, we can usefully remind ourselves of the conclusion of the original 'civic culture' survey published in 1963. In that study, Almond and Verba pointed to the importance of Eckstein's view that a democratic political system requires a blending of apparent contradictions— 'balanced disparities'.[37] A nation consisting of a citizenry all of whom are actively participating in the political process would be ungovernable. For practical purposes, we need a system whereby governing élites are aware of citizen demands, and are willing to respond to some of those demands, but in which these demands are not so excessive or unstructured as to make effective problem-solving impossible. In the end, we need to achieve a balance between governments as consensus-building institutions and governments as problem-solving institutions. Sometimes, governments must govern if problems are to be solved. This should not necessarily be confused with élites distancing themselves from their peoples. The existence of good linkage and representational systems cannot automatically produce universally popular decisions.

The traditional means of achieving this balance has been the political party, campaigning for support and votes via the electoral process. However, even in 1963, before the so-called participation explosion, Almond and Verba found that political parties were probably not fulfilling this role very effectively. Thus, they argued that when it comes to the support that individuals believe they could enlist in a challenging political situation, they think much more often of enlisting the support from the informal face to face groups of which they are members than from the formal organisation to which they belong. In all countries except Germany, less than one per cent of the respondents indicate that they would work through their political party if they were attempting to counteract some unjust regulation being considered by the local government; the German figure is about three per cent. *Clearly, no matter how important the role of political parties may be in democratic societies, relatively few citizens think of them as the first place where support may be enlisted for attempts to influence government.*[38]

These findings were largely confirmed by Kaase and Marsh—hence their suggestion that there is a 'political action repertory' consisting of both unconventional and conventional political involvement.[39] Similarly, Olsen talked of a 'repertory of organised, collective action that at least under some circumstance *increase* the representational quality of the state and facilitates long term change and survival'.[40] The emergence of new forms and institutions of linkage and representation should not be regarded as failure—it might equally be a sign of success. Basically, today's citizens are faced with a rather active and competitive *market* for their participatory needs. A whole range of organizations and processes present themselves to those citizens who decide to participate in the political process. It would be surprising if any policy-maker at the national level or European level today were unaware, on any given issue, of the range of opinions and needs within the citizenry. Indeed, many decision-makers would argue that they are only too well aware of citizen demands. Occasionally, the communication process breaks down—as in the case of the Maastricht Treaty proposals which appear to have been ahead of public opinion in several of the EU states, or in the case of the so-called poll tax in Britain. Even in these two cases, 'corrective' responses followed. Generally, the range of participatory mechanisms is so broad that policy-makers are aware of the political costs and benefits of any course of action, even if they choose to ignore them.

The more sophisticated use of social action for political purposes is a recurring theme in research on participation at the national level. As Dalton suggests, 'participation in citizen-orientated and policy-orientated forms of political activity is increasing'. He argues that these participation modes place greater control over the locus and focus of participation in the hands of the citizenry. Thus:

Political input is not limited to the issues and institutionalised channels determined by elites. A single individual, or a group of citizens, can organise around a specific issue and select the timing and the method of influencing policy-makers. These direct action technologies are high information and high pressure activities. They therefore match some of the participation demands of an increasingly educated and politically sophisticated public for more than conventional participation in voting and campaign activities.[41]

Dalton's reference to the possibility of a trend towards participation around specific issues is an important indicator of why party membership (and possibly degrees of genuine activism with parties) is often in decline. That party membership (though not necessarily support)[42] is in decline in certain countries seems reasonably certain. The British and New Zealand cases are particularly notable. For example, Seyd and Whiteley's study of Labour Party activism argued that 'It is clear that party membership peaked in the 1950s. The decline commenced in the 1950s and continued over the ensuing thirty years.'[43] As they suggest, explanations for the decline vary, but possibly include the changing social composition of the party, the decline of the party as the centre of social and political life at the local level, and the rise of pressure groups. In terms of the latter they cite McKenzie, arguing in 1974 that pressure groups had become a far more important channel of communication than parties,[44] and Moran, in 1985, arguing that 'pressure groups now seriously rival parties in the system of representation'.[45] In particular, the foundation and rise of 'good cause' groups in the 1960s (for example, Shelter, the Child Poverty Action Group, and the Disablement Income Group) were felt to be especially damaging to the Labour Party. In a telling passage they observe that 'by the 1980's, therefore, as a consequence of inertia, inefficiency, and political design, the grass roots of this old established party had withered'.[46]

Similar conclusions can be drawn concerning the Conservative Party in Britain. Thus, in the 1940s and 1950s McKenzie suggested that the Party had approximately 2.2 million members. The Houghton Committee on Financial Aid to Political Parties in 1976 estimated a membership of 1.5 million. More recent work by Whiteley, Richardson, and Seyd, as part of their study of Conservative Party activism, suggests that the current membership of the Party may have fallen to 756,000.[47] Whether this picture is common across the whole of Western Europe is more difficult to establish. Indeed, Gallagher, Laver, and Mair[48] argue that 'despite frequent suggestions that party organisations are declining in Western Europe, no clear trend emerges'. They report 'quite dramatic' falls in some countries, e.g. Denmark and the Netherlands, but stability in others (e.g. Austria, Italy, and Norway) and increases in others such as Belgium, Finland, Germany, Ireland, and Malta. The French case appears, like Denmark and Holland, to be similar to the United Kingdom, however. Thus the French Communist Party's membership has fallen from 700,000 in the 1970s to 200,000 in 1990 and the Socialist Party's membership from 200,000 in 1970 to 150,000 in 1992. Indeed, in a 1990 poll, 60 per cent of respondents expressed 'no confidence' in political parties.[49]

The most reliable data on party membership are reported by Katz and Mair, *et al.* who have surveyed party membership in European parties over the period 1960–90. As with Gallagher, Laver, and Mair, they report that it is incorrect to claim that there has been a universal decline in party membership. Over the period surveyed, 'the number of countries which record an increased party membership exactly equals that which record a decline in membership'.[50] However, they also suggest that this is rather misleading because the data do not take account of the changes in the size of the electorate. Once this is taken into account, a 'quite different picture emerges'. Of the ten countries surveyed, eight exhibited a membership decline in terms of the relationship of membership levels to the size of the electorate. The exceptions were Belgium and West Germany where the proportions were already abnormally low. The so-called M/E ratio (party members as a ratio of the electorate) enables them to assess the relative position of parties in terms of *available* members. Using this calculation, they suggest that it is possible to 'speak of a generalised and more accurate decline, for when one takes into account the initial national values of M/E, the proportionate decline is quite striking'.[51] They conclude that 'in short, the parties of Western Europe have generally failed to maintain their initial shares of the available membership pool'.[52]

These data are very consistent with the main thrust of this chapter, of course. Thus, our argument is that it is useful to view the problem of participation and representation as a market problem. Market conditions change, entrepreneurs see market opportunities, consumers are able to make reasonably rational choices, and organizations have to innovate if they are to retain their market share of those citizens who wish to be involved in the political process in some way. The data produced by Katz, Mair, *et al.* shows fairly convincingly that parties in Western Europe have not maintained their market position in the face of 'the enormous expansion of national electorates in Western Europe over the past thirty years [which] has resulted in a major growth in the available membership pool'.[53] Had a car manufacturer suffered such a relative decline in its market penetration, its share value on the stock market would be derisory.

Just as consumer products and services have become more differentiated and specialized in response to more sophisticated consumer demands, then so, perhaps, participation in the political process is increasingly linked to specialized or 'attentive' publics, specialized issues, and specialized participatory organizations. As policy-making has become more specialized, participation may have become more 'customized'. Moreover, this trend may not be solely due to a more sophisticated and better-educated citizenry. Just as with products and services in the market-place, there are entrepreneurs (or 'movement entrepreneurs', to use Schmitt's term[54]) who see market opportunities for political participation. New issue-related organizations emerge, not just because of existing public concern about an issue, but also because organizational entrepreneurs see opportunities to create new organizations (and careers) by mobilizing public support and funding for interest groups around new issues which they place on the political agenda. It is fair to say that these new entrepreneur-driven organizations are increasingly important in setting the political agenda to which political parties themselves have to respond. For example, it was often not political parties that put such issues as women's rights, environmentalism, and consumerism on the political agenda. These issues were launched by groups (often formed in the 1960s and 1970s) which set out to challenge existing interests—often producer interests—who were closely linked to the traditional parties. The failure of the parties to identify the emergence of new concerns sufficiently early at the national level had the effect of provoking the formation of new participatory organizations and created market opportunities for those unwilling to be constrained by the complexities of party coalitions. A similar phenomenon is evident at the European level. The marked lack of traditional linkage structures has created a special market opportunity for interest groups and other organizations.

Political parties now face a double challenge for the attention, support, and resources of individuals. On the one hand, there are now very many organizations offering *apparently* more exciting and rewarding political participation opportunities, and, on the other, individuals appear to be increasingly discriminating in their choice of political participation. Parties may, therefore, be facing the classic situation of an old 'product' which has been overtaken by innovation in the market-place. Just as with old products, they retain a faithful but ageing clientele, but their market share declines as new products attract new customers. They also find themselves trying to copy the innovator, as in the case of parties taking on board new issues which have been placed on the political agenda by others such as interest groups and the media. For example, the 'greening' of political parties can be seen as a belated response to the challenge from the environmental groups, who, in total, have far more members than the political parties.

5. *Linkage Structures, Democracy, and the Decline of Parties*

As suggested earlier, the challenge to political parties should not necessarily be a cause for concern to those of us interested in maintaining a viable democracy. Moreover, it should not necessarily concern the political parties either, providing they devise new ways of performing those functions which party members have traditionally performed. Thus, rather than concentrating solely on the so-called paradox of participation, Scarrow suggests that we should also focus on the 'paradox of enrolment'. She therefore poses the question 'Why should parties enrol supporters anyway?'[55] As she demonstrates, there are costs as well as benefits to parties in having members. We need to avoid normative assumptions when evaluating different forms of representation. As Heidar concludes from his analysis of Norwegian party members, 'the recruitment and electoral functions of parties may clearly be fulfilled without active members'. The answer to the question 'Does it matter?' depends in part, he argues, 'on whether the point of reference rests with the "idealistic" or the "realistic" conceptions of democracy and in part on which alternative channels for political participation are available'.[56]

Lawson and Merkl suggest at least the possibility 'that the institution of party is gradually disappearing, slowly being replaced by new political structures more suitable for the economic and technological realities of twenty-first century politics'.[57] They also note, however, that the widely observed phenomenon of party decline has got to be explained and that we do not know whether 'major parties are failing because they are ideologically out of touch with their electorates, poorly organized, underfinanced, badly led, nonaccountable, corrupt, overwhelmed by unethical or financial competition, unable to rule effectively, or some combination of these factors'.[58] They do see the main focus of their book—emerging alternative organizations—as possible 'would-be surrogates' for parties.[59] They classify these new organizations into four types—environmental organizations, supplementary organizations, communitarian organizations, and anti-authoritarian organizations. Environmental organizations are seen as a response to today's 'new politics' and are characterized as determined to leave behind what seem to them to be the outdated class or communitarian struggles of the dominant parties. They also have a different participatory style within their organizations, said to be more in tune with the aspirations of the activists who join. Supplementary organizations are more familiar. They are dealing with old issues—such as lower taxes and sectional issues. Their primary characteristic is not that they see their issues as new, nor that they constitute a community distinct from all this, 'but simply a belief *that at the present time there is no way to compel the existing parties to pay adequate attention to them*'.[60] Where parties succeed in incorporating the new issues, as appears to have been the case with the Norwegian Labour Party for example, then their chances of survival are that much greater. One popular view is that one of the major problems facing existing parties is that they still reflect the interests and issues of the original mobilizing élites. As Hans Daalder's perceptive review of the 'crisis of party' debate suggests, this view can be drawn from a particular interpretation of Rokkan's 'freezing' proposition. Rokkan's emphasis on the crucial role of past political alignments could be read as a proposition that parties which represented such alignments would inevitably lose their relevance in the contemporary world, at some point no longer reflecting the 'new politics' of another era.[61]

Lawson and Merkl also see 'communitarian' responses to party neglect as a familiar phenomenon: 'party politics has never successfully aggregated the interests of every religious, racial, ethnic, or caste community in any nation and the non-aggregated have often been ready and willing to form separate political movements to battle for their rights'.[62] Anti-authoritarian organizations—such as Solidarity in Poland—address their attention to the rights and interests of the people at large, especially in hegemonic party systems heavily backed by military leadership. Even in Britain it might be argued that, because of the electoral system, the strong two-party dominance of general elections encourages the use of alternative channels by the (still) minority of citizens who do want to be political activists, via such organizations as the Anti-Racist Alliance and the Anti-Nazi League.

Lawson in fact uses the concept of linkage to suggest possible explanations for the decline of parties and the emergence of alternative organizations. Preferring to use the term 'linkage' rather than the old term 'transmission belt', she suggests that there may be a connection between the failure of political parties to continue to perform a linkage between citizens and the state, and the emergence of new organizations either to replace the linkage when parties fail, or to provide the kind of linkages hitherto lacking in the political system.[63] Her own empirical evidence tends to support the first hypothesis, i.e. the 'replacement' of party linkages due to party failure, rather than the hypothesis that the new organizations are providing new linkages.[64] Some of the new organizations are, of course, new parties, rather than new interest groups. As Poguntke argues, these new parties should be clearly identifiable as a product of conflict over the dominant political paradigm and political style.[65] In France, for example, Machin suggests that there has been a growing importance of other forms of political participation (demonstrations by doctors and travel agents, supporters of private schools, sit-ins by lorry-drivers). Also, new movements and parties have emerged —SOS Racisme, ecology parties—which claim to be qualitatively different in terms of organization and political style. Indeed the Socialist Party has sought to develop links with these social groups and networks in order to retain a broad electoral appeal.[66] Similarly, in Britain the Labour Party, particularly at the local level in London, has often been accused by its critics of trying to create a 'rainbow coalition' of newer groups in order to maximize its support.

As better-informed consumers of participation with perhaps a much keener sense of opportunity cost in the use of their time and money, citizens now have an active market-place of participation in which to shop. In deciding whether or not to participate and, if so, in what type of organization, citizens may perceive parties as especially problematic, because of their 'catch-all' nature. Discerning citizens may be less likely to opt for joining an organization which offers a wide-ranging programme of policies which is bound to include some polices to which the individual is opposed or is at least unsympathetic. An alternative is to join a pressure group, espousing either a single issue or a coherent group of issues, thus avoiding the need to accept policies and programmes to which one is opposed. This rather 'sectorized' view of individual participation is a reflection of the increasing sectorization of policy-making in the real world. If the bigger issues for society have been decided in broad terms—such as universal education, universal health care, extension of the franchise, freedom of association, etc., then it is easier to concentrate one's efforts on specific *ad hoc* issues or on particular causes which have some special, if temporary, appeal. By so doing, the individual can join a group of genuinely like-minded people, can generally avoid the typical left–right ideological splits common in parties, and also may be more likely to see more immediate results of his or her participation in, or financial support for, the organization. In terms of selective benefits and selective disbenefits, an environmental or women's group, say, often presents a much more attractive portfolio than do political parties.

Thus, the rewards system in pressure groups may be much more effective than in political parties. Even if one takes the genuine activists within the party membership and compares them with the genuine activists, rather than just ordinary members, of, say, environmental or cultural groups, then the latter may be more likely to gain access to the corridors of power in meetings at government departments, governmental advisory committees, and quangos, etc. than are party members. This is especially the case at the European level where the various policy-making forums surrounding the Commission tend not to involve political parties or MEPs. Just as it has often been argued that it is irrational to become an MP if one wants to affect public policy (better to be an interest-group leader, so it is argued), so it is more rational to join and support a group if the individual wishes to see specific policy change. The increased level of group mobilization means that modern societies are perhaps best characterized as interest-group societies rather than as societies dominated by mass political parties.

As Parry, Moser, and Day suggest, there may be a trend for 'single issue groups to defend or promote interests and values (to) become even more frequent'.[67] They see this as possibly enhancing participation, even though it 'need not imply a nation of regular activists, noisy and restless'. Borrowing the terms 'sporadic interventionists', they envisage the possibility of a highly mobilizable population. Taking a very positive view of this potential, they see what may be a rather reactive form of participation as an important element in the civic culture and reflecting a considerable confidence in the ability of groups to affect outcomes. Thus, 'this perception of collective political efficacy, coupled with the existence of a network of group allegiances (even if normally apolitical), suggests the presence of latent participation ready to emerge in episodic and reactive forms'.[68] Interest groups will be as subject to this sporadic intervention as are often intermediary organizations.

Thus, many groups exhibit the phenomenon known in the 'group industry' as credit-card participation—individuals making a donation as an expression of support, but playing no further part in the activities of the organization to which they 'belong'. Indeed Greenpeace advertisements refer to donations and not membership as such. Studies of party 'activism' in Britain suggest party membership may be similarly low-key on any scale of activism—most party activists are more accurately described as party inactivists. We should, perhaps, not be too cynical about credit-card membership. It can be seen as some kind of surrogate activism in which individuals support a particular cause— often single-issue—but leave the formulation and delivery of the campaign to organizational professionals or to the few genuine activists within the organization. An increasingly educated electorate has sufficient information and understanding of the workings of the political system to know that single-issue groups regularly influence both the political agenda and the formulation of policy options. Having paid one's contribution, one can rest in the knowledge that the organization will campaign on one's behalf or on behalf of one's pet issue. Like other forms of activity in a post-industrial society, it is easy to 'contract out' the tasks one does not want to, or need to, perform oneself.

The experience of credit-card participation in certain kinds of interest groups (Greenpeace being the classic example) may have some important lessons for political parties. Just as we have suggested that it might be necessary to turn the usual definitions of conventional and unconventional participation on their head, so it may be necessary to challenge the assumption that mass-membership parties are a necessary, if not sufficient, condition of democratic society. Should we necessarily worry if parties are no longer the main channel of political participation? There are many organizations which survive—indeed thrive—on either a very small membership base or with 'members' that are little more than a financial resource, leaving the entrepreneurial leaders of their organizations free to set agendas, formulate policies, and influence the policy process. Indeed, Seyd was reported as describing the British Labour Party as a 'de-energised credit card party'.[69] Here, Mulgan's study of the almost seismic changes to the New Zealand political system are instructive. Following the collapse of party membership, he argues,

both major parties have relied increasingly on a small number of wealthy donors for their campaign funding and on computerised mailouts to groups of targeted voters rather than on labour intensive door knocking as the main means of getting out the vote. This has reinforced the new pattern of electoral politics in which party elites use mass marketing techniques to communicate with the public and are *freed of the obligation to answer to an active rank and file.*[70]

In some states, of course, getting out the vote is not a problem for political parties, as there is compulsory voting. In Australia part of the explanation for the comparatively small membership of political parties is that state regulation performs the work of the parties for them. Thus, there has been a degree of 'regulatory capture', in order to rig the workings of the market by changing the rules.

The argument here is *not* that parties are unimportant political actors or that we will *necessarily* continue to see a decline in party membership. As Mair argues, there has been a general *increase* in the number of votes won by the old parties in Western Europe.[71] His findings are not inconsistent with our argument. Thus, in elections where governments are being chosen by the voters, parties are likely to remain the focus of citizen's attention. Voting is a minimal level of participation, it is very easy and costless, and voters know that a government will emerge from the electoral process anyway. Not to participate would be somewhat irrational bearing in mind the low cost of voting. Citizens can have it both ways. They can continue to participate as voters in the electoral process and continue to support the stability offered by existing party systems. Once this has been resolved they have an array of participatory opportunities, including party membership. I argue that interest groups have come to present a major challenge to parties in linking citizens to their governing élites. The two types of organization perform different and perhaps increasingly specialized functions, possibly operate in different markets, with the main function of parties being to structure the vote and the main function of interest groups and social movements to perform the 'linkage' function. (Indeed Katz goes so far as to suggest that parties may perform only a vestigial linkage function.[72]) It is not surprising that modern citizens are perfectly capable of distinguishing between the two.

In trying to predict the collective outcome of these individual 'consumer' choices over time, we would need to anticipate the reaction of political parties to the challenge and the ability of parties to 'reposition' themselves in the market-place for participation and activism. They face the same problems as do the new 'movement entrepreneurs'. Organizational success (in terms of members) ultimately depends upon whether leaders of these organizations can deliver what members and potential members want. It also depends upon the general market 'image' of the organization. Just as large firms need to produce the right product, they also make great efforts to create a favourable 'image' for themselves (oil companies being a classic example). Party leaders are not stupid. We might expect them to develop organizational responses to market challenge. This might mean a further extension of state funding or even compulsory voting. In the short term it is likely to mean the adoption of new marketing techniques bringing parties, interest groups, and social movements closer together in terms of organizational design. We may conclude by suggesting that the intensity of group activity is such that, in many societies, there is little chance of élites losing touch with their peoples. Modern politics is about organization. Modern citizens have demonstrated that they know how to organize.

NOTES

1. Stein Rokkan, *Citizens, Elections, Parties* (Oslo: Universitetsforlaget, 1970).
2. Russell Dalton, *Citizen Politics in Western Democracies* (Chatham, NJ: Chatham House, 1988), 41.
3. Max Kaase and Alan Marsh, 'Political Action Repertory: Changes over Time and a New Typology', in Samuel H. Barnes and M. Kaase (eds.), *Political Action: Mass Participation in Five Western Democracies* (Beverly Hills, Calif.: Sage), 137.
4. Ibid. 149; cf. Gabriel A. Almond and Sidney Verba, *The Civic Culture: Political Attitudes and Democracy* (Boston: Little, Brown, 1963).
5. M. Lal Goel and David Horton Smith, 'Political Activities', in David Horton Smith, Jacqueline Macaulay, and Associates (eds.), *Participation in Social and Political Activities* (San Francisco: Jossey Bass, 1980), 76.
6. Johan P. Olsen, *Organised Democracy: Political Institutions in a Welfare State: The Case of Norway* (Oslo: Univertitetsforlaget, 1983).
7. Jack L. Walker, 'The Origins and Maintenance of Interest Groups in America', *American Political Science Review*, 77 (1983), 403.
8. Kent Weaver and Bert A. Rockman, *Do Institutions Matter? Government Capabilities in the US and Abroad* (Washington: Brookings Institution, 1993).
9. Olsen, *Organised Democracy*, 7.
10. Stein Rokkan, 'Numerical Democracy and Corporate Pluralism' in Robert A. Dahl, *Political Opposition in Western Democracies* (New Haven: Yale University Press, 1966), 107.
11. Martin Heisler and Robert Kvavik, 'Patterns of European Politics: The "European Polity" Model', in M. Heisler (ed.), *Politics in Europe: Struc-*

tures and Processes in Some Post-industrial Societies (New York: David & Charles, 1974), 48.

12. Stanley Hoffmann, 'Obstinate or Obsolete: The Fate of the Nation State and the Case of Western Europe', *Daedalus*, 95 (1966), 862–915.
13. Patricia Hollis, *Pressure from Without in Early Victorian England* (London: Edward Arnold, 1974), 25.
14. Mancur Olson, *The Rise and Fall of Nations* (New Haven: Yale University Press, 1982), 78.
15. J. C. Calhoun, *Disquisition on Government* (New York: Peter Smith, 1943).
16. Grant Jordan and Jeremy Richardson, 'The British Policy Style or the Logic of Negotiation?', in Jeremy Richardson (ed.), *Policy Styles in Western Europe* (London: Allen & Unwin, 1982).
17. Gerhard Lehmbruch, 'The Organization of Society, Administrative Strategies and Policy Networks', in Roland M. Czada and A. Windhoff-Heriter (eds.), *Political Choice-Institutions, Rules, and the Limits of Rationality*, (Frankfurt: Campus Verlag, 1991).
18. Sonia Mazey and Jeremy Richardson, 'Policy Coordination in Brussels: Environmental and Regional Policy', *Regional Politics and Policy*, 4/1 (1994), 22–44.
19. S. E. Finer, *Anonymous Empire* (London: Pall Mall, 1958).
20. See J. Greenwood, J. Grote, and K. Ronit (eds.), *Organised Interests and the European Community* (London: Sage, 1992); S. Andersen and K. Eliassen (eds.), *Making Policy in Europe: the Europeification of National Policy-Making*, (London: Sage, 1993); and Sonia Mazey and Jeremy Richardson (eds.), *Lobbying in the European Community* (Oxford: Oxford University Press, 1993).
21. Eric Damgaard, Peter Gerlick, and Jeremy Richardson, *The Politics of Economic Crisis* (Aldershot: Avebury, 1989).
22. Jeremy Richardson, 'Doing Less by Doing More: British Government 1979–1993', *West European Politics*, 17 (1994), 178–97.
23. Jeremy Richardson and Grant Jordan, *Governing under Pressure* (Oxford: Martin Robertson, 1979).
24. Hugh Heclo, 'Issue Networks and the Executive Establishment', in A. King (ed.), *The New American Political System* (Washington: AEI, 1978), 88.
25. For a sensible review, see David Judge, *The Parliamentary State* (London: Sage, 1993).
26. Jeremy Richardson, 'Interest Group Behaviour in Britain: Continuity and Change', in Richardson (ed.), *Pressure Groups* (Oxford: Oxford University Press, 1993).
27. Sydney Tarrow, 'Social Movements', in A. Kuper and J. Kuper (eds.), *The Social Science Encyclopedia* (London: Routledge, 1994).
28. Sonia Mazey, 'The Development of EC Equal Opportunities Policies: Bureaucratic Expansion on Behalf of Women?', in H. Kassim and A. Menon

188   *Jeremy Richardson*

(eds.), *Beyond the Market: The European Union and National Social, Environmental and Consumer Protection Policies* (London: Routledge, forthcoming).

29. Sonia Mazey and Jeremy Richardson, 'Environmental Groups and the EC: Challenges and Opportunities', *Environmental Politics*, 1 (1993), 109–28.
30. B. Harvey, *Networking in Europe: A Guide to Voluntary Organisations* (London: National Council for Voluntary Organisations, 1992) and B. Harvey, 'Lobbying in Europe: The Experience of Voluntary Organisations', in Mazey and Richardson (eds.), *Lobbying in the European Community*, 188–200.
31. Bryan Wendon, 'British Trade Union Responses to European Integration', *Journal of European Public Policy*, 1/2 (1994), 243–62.
32. D. Judge, D. Earnshaw, and N. Cowan, 'Ripples or Waves: The European Parliament in the European Community Policy Process', *Journal of European Public Policy*, 1/1 (1994), 27–51.
33. Leon Lindberg, *The Political Dynamics of European Integration* (Stanford, Calif.: Stanford University Press).
34. Ibid. 101.
35. Lehmbruch, 'The Organization of Society, Administrative Strategies and Policy Networks', 136.
36. Martin Westlake, book review, *Political Studies*, 42/1 (March, 1994), 153.
37. Almond and Verba, *The Civic Culture*, 476.
38. Ibid. 192, emphasis added. For recent British data, see Geraint Parry, George Moser, and Neil Day, *Political Participation and Democracy in Britain* (Cambridge: Cambridge University Press, 1992).
39. Kaase and March, 'Political Action Repertory', 137.
40. Olsen, *Organised Democracy*, 14.
41. Dalton, *Citizen Politics in Western Democracies*, 71, emphasis added.
42. P. Mair, 'Myths of Electoral Change and the Survival of Traditional Parties: The 1992 Stein Rokkan Lecture', *European Journal of Political Research*, 24/2 (1993), 121–33.
43. Patrick Seyd and Paul Whiteley, *Labour's Grass Roots: The Politics of Party Membership* (Oxford: Clarendon Press, 1992), 16; cf. 17.
44. Robert McKenzie, 'Parties, Pressure Groups and the British Political Process', in R. Kimber and J. J. Richardson, *Pressure Groups in Britain* (London: Dent, 1974).
45. M. Moran, *Politics and Society in Britain* (Basingstoke: Macmillan, 1985).
46. Seyd and Whiteley, *Labour's Grass Roots*, 19; cf. 18.
47. P. Whiteley, J. Richardson, and P. Seyd, *True Blues: The Politics of Conservative Party Membership* (Oxford: Clarendon Press, 1994).
48. M. Gallagher, M. Laver, and P. Mair, *Representative Government in Western Europe* (New York: McGraw Hill, 1992).
49. *L'Etat de la France 1993–1994* (Paris: La Découverte, 1993), 469–71.
50. R. S. Katz, P. Mair, *et al.* 'The Membership of Political Parties in Euro-

pean Democracies 1960–1990', *European Journal of Political Research*, 22 (1992), 332.
51. Ibid. 333.
52. Ibid. 334.
53. Ibid. 333.
54. R. Schmitt, 'Organisational Interlocks between New Social Movements and Traditional Élites: The Case of the West German Peace Movement', *European Journal of Political Research*, 17 (1989), 583–98.
55. Susan E. Scarrow, 'The "Paradox of Enrolment": Assessing the Costs and Benefits of Party Memberships', *European Journal of Political Research*, 25 (1994), 42.
56. K. Heidar, 'The Polymorphic Nature of Party Membership', *European Journal of Political Research*, 25 (1994), 84.
57. Kay Lawson and Peter Merkl, 'Alternative Organisations: Environmental Supplementary, Communication and Authorisation', in Lawson and Markl (eds.), *When Parties Fail: Emerging Alternative Organisations* (Princeton: Princeton University Press, 1988), 4.
58. Ibid. 3.
59. Ibid. 5.
60. Ibid. 7, emphasis added.
61. Daalder, 'A Crisis of Party?', 282.
62. Lawson and Merkl, 'Alternative Organisations', 8.
63. Kay Lawson, 'When Linkage Fails', in Lawson and Merkel, *When Parties Fail*, 17.
64. Ibid. 30.
65. Thomas Poguntke, 'New Politics and Party Systems: The Emergence of a New Type of Party?', *West European Politics*, 10/1 (1987), 81.
66. H. Machin, 'Changing Patterns of Party Competition', in P. Hall, J. E. S. Hayward, and H. Machin (eds.), *Developments in French Politics* (London: Macmillan, 1990).
67. Parry *et al.*, *Political Participation and Democracy in Britain*, 422.
68. Ibid. 423; cf. R. Dowse and J. Hughes, 'Sporadic Interventionists', *Political Studies*, 25 (1977), 84–92.
69. *Guardian*, 7 Aug. 1993.
70. Richard Mulgan, 'The Democratic Failure of Single Party Government: The New Zealand Experience', paper presented to a Conference on Consensual Policy-Making and Multi-Party Politics, Australian National University, 25–6 Nov. 1993, 20–1, emphasis added.
71. Mair, 'Myths of Electoral Change and the Survival of Political Parties', 127.
72. Richard S. Katz, 'Party as Linkage: A Vestigial Function?', *European Journal of Political Research*, 18 (1990), 143–61.

9

Mediating between the Powerless
and the Powerful

GIANFRANCO PASQUINO

1. Some Preliminary Doubts

It is questionable whether organized interests mediate between the powerless and the powerful. In all likelihood, this function is still better fulfilled by political parties. Indeed, this may be the real problem. Organized interests do not really mediate, even where they organize their interests more or less successfully. Most of the time, they just put pressure on parties and office-holders on behalf of their most powerful members, leaders, and functionaries. Political parties are supposed to activate themselves in order to aggregate a wider spectrum of interests, but, according to some authors, they show a declining capability to do so; for their part, organized interests usually aim selectively at special and specialized constituencies. For electoral and political, in some cases even for ideological, reasons, parties may try to organize the powerless; organized interests may prefer to organize those already enjoying some power and possessing some resources.

The powerless and the resourceless own only their vote, but they are therefore of special interest to the political parties. Only those voters, groups, and interests who are capable of mobilizing on the basis of some shared interest and goal may become the target of organized groups. Exceptionally, social movements will appear capable of drawing into the political arena even the powerless. Though more restricted, public-interest movements will enjoy some mobilizing capabilities and acquire some political influence. They will be led by individuals who start with some important resources: organizational capabilities, socio-political visibility, information, and centrality in their sphere of action. The powerless seem to be destined to remain pawns in a complex political game and to be left aside whenever it may appear appropriate to the (relatively) powerful: the organizers, the leaders.

This chapter explores three issues and advances some tentative conclusions. First, it will briefly evaluate the two most important theories concerning the activity of organized interests. Second, it will analyse the political space available to organized groups when mediating between the powerless and the powerful. Third, it will explore which features of organized interests promote or hinder the task of intermediation. Finally, I will put forward some tentative conclusions related to the theory and practice of democracy in contemporary Europe. I will keep the analysis at a fairly high level of abstraction in order to construct an analytical framework capable of taking into account a variety of phenomena.

2. The Weaknesses of both Pluralist and Corporatist Theories

I think I am justified in stating that there are two main bodies of theories dealing with organized interests, though accompanied by several appendices or corollaries: pluralism and neo-corporatism. Pluralism, classic and neo-, and corporatism, neo-, liberal, and societal, offer two quite different explanations for the dynamics of interest politics. However, neither has really confronted squarely the question of whose interests are articulated and aggregated. Neither provides an assessment of whether organized interests perform the task of intermediation between the powerless and the powerful or whether they create, represent, and satisfy their own organizational interests.

According to the pluralists, in a democratic political regime all interests have a fair chance of getting organized, obtaining access to decision-makers, and influencing decisions. Obviously, their impact on the decision-making process will be graduated according to the representativeness of their interests, and perhaps to their legitimacy as well. If this is really the case, then the powerless, who are many, will indeed get organized. The legitimacy of their interests will not be questioned. Their sheer number will put pressures on the decision-makers. The outcome of the political process will accordingly take into account their demands. Indeed, the political process will be satisfactorily explained, as Arthur Bentley put it, just by looking at the dynamics of the various interest groups, all more or less being on the same footing, all enjoying equality of opportunity. Structural advantages and disadvantages, institutional preferences or blockages, political-culture, privileges or handicaps are rarely considered to be important factors in conventional pluralist explanations. In any case, at the end of the political process in pluralist theory one will find a satisfactory outcome: the common good. Organized interests will have performed their task: reducing the gap between the powerless and the powerful, or even filling it.

Leaving aside some of its many complexities, the neo-corporatist theory puts the emphasis from the very beginning on the existence of disequilibria, of structural and structured advantages, on long-term privileges, on decision-making and institutional biases. Some of its variants almost explicitly deny the possibility that at the end of the political process one will find the common good. On the contrary, the neo-corporatist political process will accommodate and reflect the power of the competing groups. Negotiations and agreements among powerful organized interests may produce political stability and decision-making efficacy. They may result in governability. Hence, there may be some positive spill-over effects for the powerless. There is no guarantee, however, that organized interests in a neo-corporatist situation will mediate between the powerless and the powerful. Indeed, according to some authors, it is more likely that all organized interests participating in corporatist arrangements and agreements will just represent powerful groups. Unable to get organized, to mobilize actors, allies, and resources, the powerless will inevitably be left behind. A society will emerge in which two-thirds of the members are sufficiently well off not to care about the plight and destiny of the remaining one-third. There may be no incentive at all for some organized interests to mobilize the powerless one-third. Any mobilization of this kind may even appear counter-productive if it destroys the possibility of satisfactory agreements among existing powerful organized interests—it may jeopardize profitable exchanges and predictable gains. Again, political parties are, or should be, more interested than organized interests in mobilizing even power-less voters because, after all, these voters have a resource of major and fundamental interest to them: their ballot. (Incidentally, neo-corporatist theory largely neglects and almost dismisses the role of political parties in the political process and in the articulation, aggregation, and rep-resentation of interests.) Along the same lines, one can argue that some organized groups have an interest in reaching out to and mobilizing all their potential supporters because the number of members promises to be an asset for them.

All this said, three questions deserve special attention in pluralist and neo-corporatist theories alike: first, whether numbers really count and are effectively taken into account when organized interests mediate between the powerless and the powerful; second, whether there exists systematic mobilization of members from below or whether there is erratic and episodic mobilization from above; finally, whether there is any chance for the powerless, if not to become powerful, at least to obtain access to the powerful, to exert some influence on the decision-making process, to redistribute political and socio-economic resources, or whether the powerless are stuck in their condition and the powerful become even more powerful.

As to the first question, there is little doubt that for organized groups sheer numbers count less than in the past. The decline of the political and socio-economic influence of the trade-union movement is certainly due to factors other than just the decline of their membership. Trade-union fragmentation is also the product of the differentiation of the labour force. Massive demonstrations and strikes, in which numbers count, have become very rare in European politics and have usually been rather ineffective. Although party leaders and institutional office-holders are still willing to pay lip-service to the mobilization of large numbers of workers and citizens, the impact of these mobilizations on the decision-making process remains rather limited. It can easily be circumscribed and diverted. Moreover, the information deriving from a strike or from a mass demonstration is quite vague: it cannot be translated immediately—that is, without mediation—into public policies; it has to be decodified. Hence, the representational game will pass into the hands of relatively powerful actors, who may, or may not, include interest-group organizers and leaders, but who will definitely exclude the rank and file.

If numbers do not count, then which are the resources most likely to bridge the gap between the powerless and the powerful? The perceived overriding legitimacy of the interest to be promoted is one such resource. Legitimacy in the eyes of all the participants is very rare indeed. The nature of a completely legitimate interest is almost never economic. The preservation and the promotion of peace and the protection of the environment qualify as the most legitimate of the interests around which numbers may rally. However, these interests seem to escape both theories, pluralist and neo-corporatist. It may be questioned whether, when these interests are translated into public policies, they provide a successful case of intermediation by organized interests between the powerless and the powerful. In any case, most of the time, in most places, special interests will take precedence over the interests supposedly shared and somewhat promoted by large numbers of individuals.

In general, the most important weapon of organized interests is usually neither legitimacy nor numbers. It consists in the control of some strategic resource such as information, money, competence, and specialized activity. It is made up of their capability to inflict damage on society at large. Organized interests of this type do not need numbers. They are not counted, though they are taken into account because of their power. Therefore, they do not mediate between the powerless and the powerful: they already belong to the ranks of those who are powerful. They may also be sufficiently well financed to be able to bribe the decision-makers. This is another story, though not an entirely different story. In the light of what is known about the real functioning of contemporary democracies, the availability of money to organized interests and their resort to corruption must be taken seriously, as the accumulating evidence in the 1990s amply demonstrates.

As to the second question, mass mobilizations have become extremely rare. The fragmentation of the industrial working class, due to the division of labour and its specialization, has created several groups competing with each other or, anyway, not sharing the same interests. Systematic and frequent mass mobilizations appear impossible to revive, and selective mobilizations are the norm. The fact is that systematic mass mobilizations created a sense of solidarity among the powerless and between the powerless and some sectors of the powerful, while, in contrast, selective mobilizations are not conducive to solidarity. In the best cases, they may leave things as they are; in the worst, they produce envy, jealousy, and confrontation. Automatically, selective mobilizations reward those already possessing some power. Worse, they may pit the interests of some groups of powerless against those of other similar groups. What follows will not be solidarity or upgrading of the powerless, or any reduction of the gap between them and the powerful. Some types of mass mobilization—peace movements, anti-nuclear demonstrations, pro-environment activities, and anti-racist rallies—tend to recur here and there. However, rarely do they maintain enough impetus to transform themselves into organized interests. Even more rarely can it be said that they have produced significant changes in the relations between the powerless and the powerful. These public-interest movements are interested in issues and not in individuals *per se*. This is not to discount the importance and the activities of the several public-interest groups, common-cause organizations, *Burgerinitiativen*, and so on, but on the whole they are more successful in protecting communities and ideals than in promoting interests and improving the plight of individuals and particular groups.

It is worth highlighting the very different levels of importance that the pluralist and the neo-corporatist theories attribute to the activity of these public-interest movements. For the pluralists, to a large extent they are almost indispensable to the political process. They provide information and ensure the smooth functioning of the system. They participate in the definition and construction of the geometry of the common good. For the neo-corporatists, these unstructured and intermittent organized interests represent a challenge to the functioning and even the very existence of corporatist arrangements and agreements. For the purposes of my analysis, they usually indicate that the decision-making process is not functioning smoothly, representing a more or less significant protest against the political process as it stands. It is, of course, doubtful whether public-interest movements reduce the gap between the powerless and the powerful. None the less, they may have a more or less lasting impact on the agenda of the system, on its procedures, and on the decision-makers. Certainly, Green movements throughout Europe have produced several effects of this kind. Sporadically, other public-interest movements have partially affected governmental decisions without producing any structural change in the distribution of power. Finally, any chance for the powerless to obtain access to decision-makers, to exert some influence on the decision-making process, to succeed in redistributing resources, must be evaluated according to the definition of the political space and the nature of the groups. It is time to turn to these issues.

3. The Competition for Political Space

Organized interests are engaged in competition with political parties and institutions for the conquest of political space. Citizens' groups and initiatives and social and public-interest movements also participate in this competition, though more sporadically. The amount of political space occupied by organized interests in democratic regimes varies according to time and place. It is relatively safe to say that organized interests have conquered more political space in European societies in recent times due to a series of events, the most important of them being the stabilization of democratic regimes and the continuation of economic and social development. None the less, the competition is still going on, and its outcome is not determined. Several redefinitions are still possible. For analytical purposes, it may be useful to explore, first, the relationship between organized interests and political parties; next, the relationship between organized interests and institutions; and finally, the relationship between organized interests and citizens' initiatives.

In the light of the many stern declarations concerning the decline of European political parties, it may be difficult to state the case for their persistence and power. Be that as it may, there is no doubt that organized interests have always entertained a significant relationship with political parties. In some cases, as with trade unions *vis-à-vis* Labour and socialist parties, this relationship was almost symbiotic and organized interests almost dominant. Slightly less intense was the relationship between the national confederations of entrepreneurs and conservative parties. In Western Europe, on the whole, political parties were in a position to decide which organized interests could have access to them and, in some cases, to the institutional arenas. They could filter the demands of organized interests and act as gatekeepers. In recent times, parties have been obliged to be more open to organized interests and more hospitable to their demands. To some extent, many political parties have tried to combine the representation of the interests of the powerless with the representation of the organized interests of the powerful.

Even though organized interests were not necessarily of the powerless in their relationship with political parties, with a few exceptions they remained for a long time in a relatively subordinate position. Organized interests could finance party campaigns; they could put some of their representatives on party lists and have them elected to Parliament; they could influence some decisions through a complex exchange in which political parties retained the overall control of the decision-making process.

Even without exaggerating the control exercised in the past by the parties, it is now relatively clear that the situation is significantly changed. On the one hand, the fragmentation of once powerful and cohesive organized interests has made it very difficult to maintain that quasi-symbiotic relationship that existed for several post-war decades. Moreover, the disappearance or blurring of ideological differences among parties has allowed, or obliged, organized interests to emancipate themselves from the tutelage of some parties. Finally, the multiplication of organized interests of all kinds, due to the development and differentiation of European societies, has redefined the role of parties and interests and, in all likelihood, has reduced the political space of parties. On the other hand, parties themselves are obliged to compete without exclusive reference to a *chasse gardée*, to attract as many voters as possible. Therefore, they cannot tie their electoral destinies to specific organized interests representing the past, albeit a glorious one.

These two sets of changes suggest that the political space between organized interests and political parties has been redefined as follows. Organized interests and their representatives keep political parties at a distance, do not join them, and do not look for any privileged relationship. They try to acquire influence by putting pressures on the various political parties, resorting if possible to the force of numbers, and otherwise to the provision and diffusion of information, even to the general public, in order to obtain its support. Finally, they have engaged themselves in influencing public opinion and in attempting to shift votes between competing party alternatives. If one adds to all this the fact that political parties have shifted their attention away from society and towards the institutions of government, a sweeping generalization may become acceptable and will probably prove valid. Organized interests have occupied some of the socio-political space left free by political parties. More, they have conquered some political space at the expense of political parties. This development goes some way towards explaining the difficulties of European political parties, as well as the current adjustments and problems appearing in the institutional sphere.

If parties are no longer considered indispensable or useful vehicles for representing interests, what additional political space do organized interests occupy or seek to occupy? Obviously, under certain conditions organized interests will try to occupy the political space of representative and governing institutions. The neo-corporatist theory tells us that this, and more specifically the expropriation of Parliament, has often been the case for some countries, less frequently for other countries, and almost never for a few 'pluralist' democracies. The question is whether the attribution of the status of officially recognized groups has become more frequent in recent times or not; whether, indeed, organized groups have sought this status or opted out of it. According to most authors, in the 1980s all existing neo-corporatist arrangements were subjected to severe strains: none of them has survived fundamentally intact; a few have retained some bargaining agreements, though not the overall negotiating structures. This development should not be read as a shrinking of the political space available to organized groups but as its redefinition. No longer enticed or obliged to engage in a long-lasting collaboration among themselves and with the executive, organized groups now feel free to float in the institutional environment. They bargain directly with Parliament, the executive, and the bureaucracy at all levels.

There is not room here to present a more convincing picture through an in-depth analysis of the various institutional systems of European democracies and the space they grant to organized groups. Suffice it to say that the degree of bargaining power of organized groups will very much depend on three factors: the role of Parliament, the composition of the government and its decision-making powers and effectiveness, and the nature of the bureaucracy. There has also been a shift in the locus of activity of most organized interests. They are less active on the input side and more incisive on the output side; that is, they are in a position to bypass Parliament and MPs, even in those political systems where the latter still possess some decision-making powers, and focus their attention and pressures on the government and on the bureaucracy. Organized groups will try to influence a decision where it is actually taken, as well as where it will have to be implemented. Understandably, only a few organized groups have easy access to the government and to the bureaucracy since there are inherent and ineliminable political and social biases discriminating among them. Clearly, organized groups representing the powerful in the socio-economic system are far more successful in gaining access and exerting influence than even large organized groups representing the powerless. One may hypothesize that the enhancement of the areas of decision-making and implementation obliges organized groups capable of doing so to transfer their activities to the institutional sphere.

In contrast, public-interest movements will still find it necessary to reach, through public opinion, Parliament and individual MPs and put pressure on them. Direct appeals to executive decision-makers, though rare, are a last resort, especially to prevent decisions from being made and implemented. Finally, it is not far-fetched to underline that governments and bureaucracies will deliberately produce and implement decisions in such a way as to reach out to some specific, even special organized groups. Not only is a direct relationship established between institutional office-holders and organized groups, but this relationship tends to be exclusive, that is to cut off many of the less organized groups. Therefore, one may tentatively conclude that the political space has been effectively redefined in favour of those organized groups capable of making incursions into the institutional realm and of acquiring some independent staying-power.

There are two countervailing tendencies to this development. The first is that in some political systems both executives in office and challengers will tend to appeal to the common citizen in order to win elections and to implement their programmes, as vague and all-encompassing as they may be. Denunciations of the exaggerated and undemocratic power of organized interests are anything but rare. Rhetorical accusations and populist appeals characterize the style of some executive office-holders, and even more the style of some opponents. Organized interests are accused of representing special socio-economic sectors, creating social rigidities, maintaining economic privileges, even subverting the democratic political process, which may often be the case.

This realization explains the appearance of the second countervailing tendency: the quest for institutional reforms. To a varying degree in all democratic countries the issue of institutional reforms has been and still is widely debated. To bring democracy closer to the people, to get rid of intermediate organizations, to increase the power of the voters all seem reasonable requests. They are all aimed at reducing the political space and power of organized interests. Since one of the most important declared goals of institutional reform is often the reduction of the power of organized interests, one can legitimately infer that this is because organized interests are perceived as not mediating between the powerless and the powerful. They are seen as serving their own selfish interests and considered part and parcel of the powerful. This conclusion must lead the analysis towards an identification and exploration of the factors responsible for this reversal of roles. I will first devote some attention to the inherent organizational features of organized groups and then to the democratic process itself.

4. How Organized Interests Promote or Hinder Mediation

The construction of organized interests requires not only a favourable environment, but above all political entrepreneurs and socio-economic resources. Following Mancur Olson, it is also well known that the construction of such groups, especially those pursuing collective goods, may be seriously hindered and even fatally impaired by the existence of free-riders.[1] Again thanks to Olson, we know that powerful organized groups may create with the passing of time social rigidities which will reduce the economic rate of growth and, in the end, damage the pursuit of the common good. Assuming that the construction of organized interests aiming at the production, acquisition, and distribution of collective goods has been successful, we also know, following Roberto Michels, that their functioning is exposed to the iron law of oligarchy;[2] more precisely, that even organizations made up of a large number of members belonging to more or less the same social stratum, enjoying more or less the same personal resources, sharing the same goal, may lapse into an authoritarian situation. Because of the necessary division of internal labour and specialization of activities, a stratum of leaders and functionaries is very likely to emerge who will displace, and even subvert, the original goals of the membership. The ordinary members' influence on the internal decision-making process will correspondingly be reduced, while the functionaries' influence on the goals of the organization will become overwhelming. Among these goals, the preservation of the leaders' and functionaries' offices and perks is likely to become paramount and take precedence over the collective goals. The functionaries can be dismissed if they do not perform their task effectively; the leaders can be voted out when no longer representative of the rank and file and not capable of reaching the goals of the organization. In practice, however, for different reasons and to different degrees, functionaries and leaders alike control some resources such as information, time, and personal ties which make them very difficult to remove.

Even when the process of internal control by the functionaries and the leaders is only partially completed, organized interest groups of this type will no longer mediate between the powerless and the powerful. They will have adjusted themselves to a rewarding role among the relatively powerful. Moreover, in stable contemporary democracies, there is a relative dearth of political entrepreneurs and existing organized interests thrive on their accumulated resources. It is therefore very difficult to produce a situation in which new political entrepreneurs will be capable of identifying an emerging interest, amassing enough resources, and mobilizing enough individuals in the pursuit of a common goal. It is not that there is a conspiracy against new organized interests or against dispossessed social sectors; simply that, in stable democracies, it is more difficult to break the albeit loose coalition of existing organized interests to obtain access to decision-making arenas and to gain political influence. Phases of collective effervescence provide the initial opportunity for the emergence of new interests and groups, but these phases are rather rare in changing societies. More frequently, new organized interest groups are the product of conflicts among existing political entrepreneurs and splits within long-established organized interests. For a while, conflicts and splits are likely to produce some competition among leaders and interests, which will translate itself into the mobilization of additional social sectors. Conflicts and splits represent a splendid opportunity for disadavantaged sectors to acquire some political influence in tilting the balance of power in favour of some specific organized interests. Understandably, these circumstances are relatively exceptional, particularly in stable political systems. Moreover, they may not be exploited successfully. Still, the powerless are such exactly because it is difficult to mobilize and to organize them.

Keeping these considerations in mind, we may ask ourselves not why the powerless are so disorganized and poorly mobilized, but how come that at certain points in time they did get mobilized and organized, and in some cases they even get partial satisfaction for their demands. Unstructured societies in which the organizational network was not yet very dense offered many opportunities. These political and organizational opportunities were favoured and enhanced by socio-economic changes. What used to be the case is now no longer possible nor feasible. That is, most contemporary democratic societies are extremely dense from an organizational perspective. The rate of their socio-economic change does not offer new organizational opportunities. The powerless are therefore not in the position to create their own organizations to represent, protect, and promote their interests. Existing organized interests appear to reflect faithfully the structure of opportunities and power of most given societies. The pluralist game reproduces the prevailing configuration of power. It does not seem to be conducive to the common good. The neo-corporatist solution is no longer viable. In any case, it was rarely in a position to filter down to the powerless all the resources its structural arrangements and bargaining procedures could in fact produce. It always favoured organized interests, conferring on them the task selectively to reward their members. In sum, the practice of organized interests challenges the theory of democratic pluralism.

5. Democracy in Theory and European Practice

Democratic theory cannot reject one of its most fundamental and cherished tenets, which is the possibility for all citizens to get organized, to mobilize support, peacefully to pursue individual and collective goods. Moreover, the common good is the desired and welcome outcome of a free competition among groups. In this reiterating competition, no group wins all the time, no group loses all the time, all groups obtain enough resources to survive and indefinitely continue the competition. All this said, however, democratic theory cannot remain indifferent when the activity of organized interests does not reduce the gap between the powerless and the powerful, when the powerless do not have access to the decision-making arenas, cannot make their interests heard, cannot influence the outcome of the decision-making process. One can find temporary relief from this sad state of affairs in the various arenas in which individual citizens may exert some influence. In particular, one may want to stress the persisting importance of electoral politics and governmental turnover. One may want to draw attention to the process of political decentralization and power devolution to regional communities. One may underline the constant possibility of the emergence of collective movements and the likelihood of their gaining resources and obtaining favourable decisions. Finally, one may suggest that most democratic citizens have conquered a socio-economic condition, allowing them to exert some political influence even without relying on organized interests. They do so through the impact of public opinion on governmental activities as well as by creating single-issue and public-interest movements. All this does not divert from the sorry reality that organized interests are for the most part unable, and unwilling, to mediate between the powerless and the powerful. In addition, state apparatuses do not appear able to favour a redistribution of opportunities and power.

The malaise of European politics may be attributed to this widespread realization and the demand for institutional reforms may derive from it. Political parties are less capable than in the past to aggregate interests and to transform them into policies. Institutional office-holders are not well equipped to mediate, though they may be in a better position to decide and to implement. If organized interests do not reduce the gap between the powerless and the powerful, the democratic process will remain skewed. Social tensions and political conflicts will periodically emerge. In fact, in European politics they are growing in frequency and intensity. The quality of democratic life deteriorates. Authoritarian solutions will be increasingly entertained.

NOTES

1. Mancur Olson, *The Logic of Collective Action: Public Goods and the Theory of Groups*, rev. edn. (Cambridge, Mass.: Harvard University Press, 1971).
2. Roberto Michels, *Political Parties* (1911; Glencoe, Ill.: Free Press, 1949).

10

Public Demands and Economic Constraints: All Italians Now?

NICHOLAS BOSANQUET

In some terms the debate about democracy and stable public finance is an old one. Tocqueville and Dicey before 1914, Colin Clark, Schumpeter, and the Chicago School of Economics later, developed the theme of inconsistency. Tocqueville was eloquent on how political sentiments would lead to political centralization and growing public expenditure.[1] The practice of democracy could release forces which would waste enormous amounts of resources, retard economic growth, and poison the atmosphere in society. There would also be a new class of subsidy-chasers and *rentiers*. Jomini wrote of how false values might eclipse public esteem for more legitimate professions in favour of those who 'fatten on the public miseries by gambling on the vicissitudes of the national credit'.[2]

There is also little new about vigorous rebuttals affirming the gains to society and the economy from growth in publicly financed programmes. Tawney's lectures on equality supplied one powerful defence of the growth of the social services:[3] but at this stage it was not only the left which supported the growth of social services. The national efficiency school provided strong support. Within the United Kingdom the editors of *A Century of Municipal Progress 1835–1935* included the Conservative Sir Ivor Jennings as well as the archetypal socialist professor Harold Laski.[4] 'If we compare the state of the English towns in 1835 with their state in 1935, we might well conclude that the creation of our modern system of local government is the greatest British achievement in the last hundred years. . . . Nothing surely that the British people have done in the world in these hundred years is more important than the revolution it has effected in its local government.' Two decades later Galbraith was to stress the contrast between private affluence and public squalor and the complementarity between public

Nicholas Bosanquet

and private goods.[5] Others on the left, such as O'Connor in *The Fiscal Crisis of the State*, were more critical.[6]

There is a distinctive literature from Germany with an early consensus for state action and public expenditure. Wagner's Law still appears in textbooks of public finance as a first attempt to explain the growth of public expenditure in statistical terms. Adolph Wagner argued that public expenditure would show an inevitable tendency to grow faster than national income reflecting changing needs in society. The early French experience was of relatively slow development in the social services but of strong commitment to an economic role for the state.

There was also a distinctive contribution from Italy where writers such as Puviani first developed the concept of fiscal illusion. He developed a hypothesis that government always acts to hide the burden of taxes from the public and to magnify the benefits of public expenditure. This thinking has influenced later US writings through Professor James Buchanan of the Virginia School. One of his earliest papers was on the Italian tradition in fiscal theory praising the realism of the view that 'Decisions as such were usually made on pragmatic grounds and each was reached on the basis of causing the minimum of social friction.'[7] Even in those times there was a significant difference between the Woodrow Wilson view of a disinterested élite doing good through their stewardship of government programmes and the realistic assessment of how decisions were actually taken.

There is now a new period of intense concern about contradictions and inconsistencies between public demands and economic resource constraints. The aims of this chapter are (1) to point up the distinctive elements in this current concern especially in terms of contrast between the USA and Europe; (2) to provide a preliminary assessment of the future European policy agenda.

'Public demands and economic resource constraints' cover a very broad territory. It may be helpful to divide this up into a number of subissues. Public demands could arise from some or all of the following sources:

- pressure on a direct basis through demonstrations or mass action;
- interpretation by representatives of public moods;
- pressure from key provider groups within the public sector including doctors, teachers, public officials, and employees of state-owned companies;

- pressure from intense minorities or pressure groups with special interests in issues such as the environment;
- advocacy by sections of the élite—public-health doctors and officials were an important pressure group for spending on preventive health services;
- pressure from the business sector for public-spending programmes to improve infrastructure, subsidize investment, or pay for costs which would otherwise be internal to the firm.

Economic constraints could reflect some or all of the following subissues:

- financing problems in terms of the saleability of public-sector debt;
- the possible impact of public expenditure and taxation on the growth-rate of gross domestic product (GDP);
- impact on the labour market and unemployment;
- impact on investment and industrial competitiveness;
- impact on household real incomes and living-standards.

The nature of the conflict between public demand and economic constraints has varied. The inter-war period saw crises mainly around the short-term financing and debt-funding of the public sector. These were triggered by falling economic activity during the Great Depression and the rise of debt interest as a result of war finance. There was also some concern about the impact of taxation on labour costs and competitiveness shown in Britain by controversy over the role of domestic rates in the 1920s but this was a fairly minor theme: it was the immediate pressure of debt repayments and their effect on financial confidence and stability which were the heart of the issue.

In the 1970s there was local controversy within the United Kingdom about the level of public spending mainly stimulated by work done in Oxford by Bacon and Eltis.[8] Here the main focus was on the impact of public spending on the growth of GDP. In their analysis Britain was affected by a reduction in numbers of producers and the rise of a larger non-market sector involving higher rates of taxation on the market sector. Later more formal analysis on a cross-national basis showed that there was an association between the increase of the public sector and the growth-rate but that the relationship was stronger for public expenditure on services. High levels of public expenditure on social security and transfer payments seemed to make little difference to the growth-rate.

More recently concern about the general issue has spread across the

European Community. One British leader announced in a celebrated phrase in 1975 that the 'party was over': now similar sentiments are to be heard across the EC. Recently the German Finance Minister has set the end to the era of rising public spending. In France the Trente Glorieuses, or thirty glorious years, are seen to have ended.[9] In summary, the main issues of concern in the current European debate can be seen as the impact of public expenditure on industrial competitiveness and on unemployment.

For the USA, on the other hand, the key issue has been that of impact on household real income. There are arguments about the funding of the social security programme and its effect on capital formation, but concern has been mainly about the impact of taxation and health-care costs on the real incomes of Middle America. In effect Middle America has had little gain in real income over the past two decades, as any increases have been used to finance gains in health-care costs. There has also been some concern about the impact of health financing on industrial investment with General Motors now alleged to spend more on health insurance than on steel.

1. Public Attitudes in the 1990s

For many years in the post-war period economic growth had taken the edge off conflict about the role of the public sector. Now there was developing a sharper conflict between economic concerns and public attitudes. For this chapter Social and Community Planning research has carried out some special tabulations on its comparative study for West Germany, Ireland, Great Britain, Italy, and the USA, the data for which was collected in 1990–1. These results show deep-seated collectivism and interventionism covering a whole range of attitudes.

Among the most obvious is support for substantial extra taxation on people with higher incomes. A substantial majority in all countries, including the United States, think that people with high incomes (undefined) should pay a larger or a much larger proportion of their income in tax. In West Germany, 83.7 per cent of respondents think that high incomes should be taxed more strongly compared to 58.7 per cent of respondents in the USA. The market for proportional taxation is small, and for regressive taxation—such as exists through the net effects of direct and indirect taxation—is non-existent. (See Table 10.1.)

There is also an awesome level of support for government intervention to improve economic results. Most citizens want governments to

TABLE 10.1. *Public attitudes to the apportioning of taxation*
1990–1991 (%)

Question: Some people think those with high incomes should pay a larger proportion (percentage) of their earnings in taxes than those who earn low incomes. Other people think that those with high incomes and those with low incomes should pay the same proportion (percentage) of their earnings in taxes. Do you think those with high incomes should . . .

	West Germany	Ireland	Great Britain	USA	Italy
n.a.	—	—	1.0	0.9	—
Pay a much larger proportion	38.4	31.6	21.0	17.9	30.8
Pay a larger proportion	45.3	49.0	61.4	40.8	52.2
Pay the same proportion as those who earn low incomes	11.5	16.7	13.8	34.9	15.5
Pay a smaller proportion	0.5	0.3	0.4	0.8	0.5
Pay a much smaller proportion	0.2	—	0.3	0.4	—
Can't choose	3.3	2.3	2.2	4.2	1.0

n.a. = no answer.

keep prices under control, to provide health care for the sick, and to provide a decent standard of living for the old. They want government to 'provide industry with the help it needs to grow', provide a decent standard of living for the unemployed, and 'reduce income differences between rich and poor'. The numbers who take the opposite view that governments should not do these things is very small, even in the USA. (See Table 10.2.)

The most significant international difference is between the USA and Europe on government approaches to unemployment and income differentials. Amongst American respondents 50 per cent think— somewhat inconsistently, given their views on taxation—that it probably or definitely should not be government's responsibility to reduce income differences between rich and poor; 43 per cent of Americans also consider that it should not be the government's responsibility to provide a decent standard of living for the unemployed.

A third group of questions concerned the attitude of respondents to specific programmes in public spending (see Table 10.3). There

TABLE 10.2. *Public support for government economic intervention 1990–1991* (%)

Question: On the whole, do you think it should or should not be the government's responsibility to....

(a) provide a job for everyone who wants one

	West Germany	Ireland	Great Britain	USA	Italy
Definitely should be	28.4	36.9	22.5	14.6	38.1
Probably should be	42.8	32.2	37.7	25.6	46.4
Probably should not be	20.6	16.3	21.0	30.8	9.2
Definitely should not be	4.2	12.0	13.6	20.8	5.2
Can't choose	2.5	1.6	3.5	4.5	4.8
n.a.	1.5	0.2	1.6	3.6	0.1

(b) keep prices under control

	West Germany	Ireland	Great Britain	USA	Italy
Definitely should be	19.7	58.9	47.4	23.7	66.6
Probably should be	47.3	32.3	39.1	47.4	29.2
Probably should not be	22.5	6.5	6.8	15.6	2.3
Definitely should not be	6.7	1.4	3.5	6.6	1.6
Can't choose	2.2	0.5	2.0	3.1	0.3
n.a.	1.6	0.4	1.1	3.6	—

(c) provide health care for the sick

	West Germany	Ireland	Great Britain	USA	Italy
Definitely should be	55.5	79.7	83.6	38.1	87.6
Probably should be	37.7	18.7	13.9	46.2	11.5
Probably should not be	3.6	0.9	0.6	7.6	0.3
Definitely should not be	0.8	0.1	0.3	2.7	0.2
Can't choose	0.7	0.2	0.9	2.2	0.3
n.a.	1.7	0.4	0.7	3.2	0.1

(d) provide a decent standard of living for the old

	West Germany	Ireland	Great Britain	USA	Italy
Definitely should be	52.9	77.4	77.2	37.8	80.9
Probably should be	39.7	20.3	20.1	44.8	18.1
Probably should not be	4.7	1.7	0.9	9.8	0.6
Definitely should not be	0.5	0.2	0.3	2.0	0.3
Can't choose	0.8	0.2	0.9	2.6	0.1
n.a.	1.5	0.2	0.5	3.0	—

(e) provide industry with the help it needs to grow

Definitely should be	10.9	53.3	41	16.8	28.0
Probably should be	38.1	36.0	49.6	47.0	53.0
Probably should not be	33.7	8.4	4.9	22.4	13.3
Definitely should not be	11.1	1.3	1.1	4.4	3.5
Can't choose	4.6	0.8	2.5	6.1	2.0
n.a.	1.7	0.2	1.0	3.3	0.1

(f) provide a decent standard of living for the unemployed

Definitely should be	18.1	47.9	30.3	12.7	32.1
Probably should be	56.2	41.6	46.4	35.6	45.5
Probably should not be	16.2	7.5	14.2	31.1	15.6
Definitely should not be	4.3	1.8	4.3	11.9	4.9
Can't choose	3.3	1.1	4.2	5.5	1.9
n.a.	1.8	0.2	0.7	3.3	—

(g) reduce income differences between the rich and poor

Definitely should be	20.5	50.0	40.2	15.3	37.2
Probably should be	38.8	28.9	30.4	25.0	40.8
Probably should not be	26.5	12.9	15.2	27.1	14.8
Definitely should not be	7.4	4.9	9.4	23.3	5.8
Can't choose	5.0	3.1	4.5	5.9	1.3
n.a.	1.7	0.2	0.3	3.5	0.1

n.a. = no answer.

TABLE 10.3. *Public support for public expenditure 1990–1991* (%)

Question: Listed below are various areas of government spending. Please show whether you would like to see more or less government spending in each area. Remember that if you say 'much more', it might require a tax increase to pay for it.

(a) The environment

	West Germany	Great Britain	USA	Italy
n.a.	1.3	4.1	3.4	0.1
Spend much more	59.2	13.7	14.6	24.3
Spend more	29.1	45.5	41.9	48.7
Spend the same as now	8.7	31.6	27.9	19.1
Spend less	0.7	2.4	7.0	5.5
Spend much less	0.1	0.3	1.9	0.6
Can't choose	0.8	2.3	3.4	1.7

(b) Health

	West Germany	Great Britain	USA	Italy
n.a.	1.1	1.3	3.5	0.3
Spend much more	35.1	35.0	19.1	39.2
Spend more	36.5	53.4	48.9	45.3
Spend the same as now	23.6	9.2	23.4	10.7
Spend less	2.5	0.4	2.1	3.0
Spend much less	0.4	0.1	0.7	1.2
Can't choose	0.9	0.7	2.3	0.4

(c) The police and law enforcement

	West Germany	Great Britain	USA	Italy
n.a.	1.7	2.1	3.1	—
Spend much more	11.1	9.8	10.8	16.7
Spend more	19.6	38.4	41.8	40.0
Spend the same as now	1.4	44.5	36.3	33.7
Spend less	15.3	3.5	4.1	5.9
Spend much less	9.1	0.4	1.2	2.0
Can't choose	4.4	1.3	2.6	1.6

(d) Education

	West Germany	Great Britain	USA	Italy
n.a.	1.5	2.1	3.0	0.1
Spend much more	19.6	25.4	24.7	22.3
Spend more	37.3	51.9	45.7	42.7
Spend the same as now	33.1	17.8	21.9	31.3
Spend less	5.1	1.3	1.6	2.4
Spend much less	1.6	0.4	0.7	0.6
Can't choose	1.9	1.0	2.2	0.7

(e) The military and defence

n.a.	1.5	2.4	3.7	—
Spend much more	1.4	1.9	3.0	2.4
Spend more	2.9	6.3	9.9	9.1
Spend the same as now	12.7	40.5	34.7	24.9
Spend less	30.8	32.5	27.9	30.8
Spend much less	49.1	14.5	17.8	31.8
Can't choose	1.4	2.0	3.0	0.9

(f) Old age pensions

n.a.	1.2	1.3	3.2	0.1
Spend much more	15.3	28.0	11.7	25.2
Spend more	38.0	52.1	33.5	55.2
Spend the same as now	41.4	16.9	38.7	16.0
Spend less	1.6	0.4	7.0	1.9
Spend much less	0.6	0.3	2.1	0.5
Can't choose	1.9	1.1	3.8	1.1

(g) Unemployment benefits

n.a.	1.2	2.2	3.2	0.1
Spend much more	9.1	7.5	6.7	15.1
Spend more	26.3	27.3	18.7	37.1
Spend the same as now	48.2	44.5	47.5	30.5
Spend less	10.8	12.9	14.1	9.2
Spend much less	2.3	3.6	5.6	5.9
Can't choose	2.1	2.1	4.4	2.0

(h) Culture and the arts

n.a.	1.5	1.8	3.6	0.2
Spend much more	4.4	2.0	2.2	9.5
Spend more	16.3	9.9	10.0	34.9
Spend the same as now	45.4	39.7	40.1	40.5
Spend less	20.6	27.8	20.2	9.3
Spend much less	7.5	13.6	15.7	4.1
Can't choose	4.3	5.2	8.1	1.5

were more significant differences between countries on these specific programmes than on their perceptions of the more general role of government.

- Respondents in West Germany were strongly in favour of more spending on the environment: 59.2 per cent of respondents wanted to spend much more. There was much less enthusiasm in Britain and the USA.
- Spending on health services was more popular in Britain, Italy, and West Germany.
- There was strong support for spending less on defence in West Germany, with 49.1 per cent of respondents expressing a preference for 'much less spending'.
- There was less support for higher unemployment benefits in the USA, with 25.4 per cent of respondents wanting to spend more, compared to 35.4 per cent of respondents in West Germany. Opinion on this issue was also more polarized, with some support in most countries for spending less or much less on unemployment benefit. Within the USA 19.9 per cent of respondents wanted to spend less or much less, in Great Britain 16.5 per cent, and in Germany 13.1 per cent.

As well as these differences, there were some consensus programmes. There was support for better pensions and for more spending on education: there was also an international consensus against more spending on the arts and culture, apart from Italy where 44 per cent wanted to spend more.

The span of attitudes is completed by the survey results on the level of personal interest in politics (see Table 10.4). These attitudes are not supported or underpinned by high levels of interest in the political process. In no country did a majority see themselves as being very or fairly interested in politics. 'Somewhat' was the most common reaction, and 20–30 per cent were not very interested or not interested at all.

Policy-makers have to try to square the circle between these mainly generous public attitudes and economic realities. Governments have had to accept a growing consensus among the international élite in favour of deregulation and reductions in public expenditure. They have adopted a number of approaches involving different combinations of structural reform and of direct government action to reduce spending-levels. They have sought different routes towards adjusting the demand and supply of public goods towards economic constraints. The United

Public Demands and Economic Constraints 213

TABLE 10.4. *Comparative public interest in politics 1990–1991* (%)

Question: How interested would you say you personally are in politics?

	West Germany	Ireland	Great Britain	USA	Italy
n.a.	0.5	0.2	1.0	3.0	—
Very interested	13.4	8.1	9.1	12.1	3.5
Fairly interested	24.0	25.6	30.2	27.1	27.7
Somewhat interested	41.1	27.9	25.9	33.5	16.8
Not very interested	15.7	21.8	24.3	16.4	32.2
Not at all interested	5.3	16.2	7.9	6.3	19.9
Can't choose	—	0.3	1.5	1.6	—

Kingdom and West Germany can be taken as two contrasting approaches towards reducing spending-levels and adjusting public attitudes to new economic constraints.

2. The Contrasting Record: The United Kingdom, West Germany, and the European Community

The UK approach has stressed the detailed structural reform of programmes rather than overall adjustment of the size of the public sector. The long-term background has been one of rapid growth in total public expenditure at 3 per cent per annum in real terms over the period 1961–81. Over that period much of the growth was in spending on social security.

- From 1981 to 1990 public expenditure rose by 1 per cent a year and the composition shifted further towards transfer payments. A steady rise in spending on social security was compatible with slower overall growth in the total as a result of big reductions in spending on housing and on industrial subsidies.
- From 1990 to 1993 the growth of public expenditure returned to 3 per cent per annum. Most of the increase was in spending on goods and services, although political concern was mainly about social security.
- The main policy response has been in terms of attention to the supply-side problems. In the 1980s the stress was on increasing

throughput and reducing unit costs in health services and education. Now the stress is on longer-run changes of incentives and
management systems while defining standards through a citizen's
charter. These policies include the hiving-off of direct public
functions to Next Steps agencies, the development of internal
markets in health services, and devolution of budgets to schools in
education.

• Privatization has also been widely used, but mainly to deal with
the funding problems of the public sector and the productivity
problems of the post-1945 nationalized industries. These policies
have been successful in bringing about a marked rise in the productivity of the former nationalized industries such as energy, steel,
and telecommunications. However, privatization had a much less
clear role in the core social services.[10] There has been strong professional opposition to any role for the private sector. The government is convinced about the gains from internal markets but it has
yet to convince many in the provider élites, especially in education
and health services.

The Conservative government's policies did little before 1992 to
alter the demand for public goods. In fact, improvements on the supply
side were threatening to make overall control of spending more, rather
than less, difficult. Public goods were seen increasingly as cheap and
desirable. It is easy to control the demand for public goods which are
unpopular and stigmatized, but it is much more difficult when they are
seen as highly praiseworthy, as with places in youth training and higher
education. In the long term, the shift towards higher-quality outputs
made by decentralized producers within internal markets may further
increase pressure on funding. Thus measures designed to help short-
term financing pressures may lead to more difficult problems of public
choice in the longer term.

The United Kingdom has seen little change in the demand-side dynamic for higher spending. Economists have always argued that there
might be an inherent bias towards higher public spending because
benefits are concentrated on recipients, while costs are diffused over the
whole range of taxpayers: but recent experience has suggested there
were a number of other reasons explaining how the political economy
works to promote expenditure.

• Public projects are seen as the personal property of local MPs and
any closure or change is seen as a major set-back to re-election

chances. The level of interest in specific projects by parliamentarians is very strong and possibly more crucial as an obstacle to change than the general collectivism of opinion surveys.

- There is a strong force of sentiment in favour of public expenditure. There is still a deep emotional assumption that public-spending projects are a good way of helping deprivation and that more public expenditure equates broadly with more civilization.

- Decisions about public-spending projects are usually made on returns calculated *ex ante*. There is little review of what has happened *ex post*: yet often when there is, the returns are much lower than expected.

- There are strong forces from producer discontent. Enoch Powell spoke of the never-ending chorus of denigration rising from within the British National Health Service.[11] A similar culture of negativism is to be found in the world of education.

- The public services suffer from a resource mirage. The amount of secure resources which go into them is large—yet there is little sense of local control and achievement.

In effect public spending is an addiction which feeds on itself. There is little correlation between the amount of money spent and the level of satisfaction with the service, and large increases in public expenditure can in fact generate even stronger demands for more spending.

From 1992 the UK government introduced a new system for constraining the total demand. This was based on a control total for non-cyclical public spending, so that any increases in specific programmes had to be financed through reductions in others. The hope was also that, as unemployment fell, induced reductions in public expenditure would not be taken up through new discretionary programmes.

The UK government has had a much clearer long-term strategy for reforming the supply side of the public sector than for changing the way in which it is financed. The most specific target here has been that of reducing average tax-rates for higher incomes. This has involved a shift towards indirect taxation. The net effect of the changes has been:

(1) Increased taxation in proportionate terms on households with lower incomes. The proportion of net income taken in tax from households at the second from lowest quintile was 36.6 per cent in 1990 compared to 33.4 per cent from the top quintile. For non-retired households, the difference was from 38.5 to 33 per cent.

(2) Relatively low taxation on capital-intensive businesses. Reductions in income and capital-gains taxation have raised the post-tax income and capital returns to quoted companies. They may also have contributed to increases in the UK stock market over the past three years. Such businesses benefit also from depreciation provisions, which are much more generous for physical than for human capital.

(3) A high level of taxation on labour-intensive businesses, many of which are small. These have to pay social security, tax, and income taxation: VAT at 17.5 per cent is levied on sales. Once a small business is established and becomes eligible for tax at the 40 per cent rate, it is now paying £57.5 in taxation for every £117.5 in value added. This disincentive probably contributes to continued absence of a UK *Mittelstand* with small businesses growing rarely into medium size.

The UK government strategy has had considerable success in improving the efficiency of the public sector and some, although more mixed, success in improving quality. In effect, it has reduced the supply price of many public-sector outputs in relative terms. Public-sector outputs have become more acceptable to consumers. There has been a combination best seen in British higher education of higher entry, lower unit costs, but higher total expenditure in this instance. Total spending on higher education has risen by a third in real terms over the past five years. Thus the problems of financing a higher volume of output, even though at lower prices, have been the unexpected results of the policy success of the 1980s. The supply-side success has contributed to new demand and funding problems in the 1990s.

The West German approach has been very different, with a stress on long-term action to contain social spending and preference for simple measures at the programme level rather than for structural reform. West German perspectives changed with reunification, which raised public expenditure and led to new concern with employment prospects. For Germany, health and social-security funding led to a direct link between social costs and employment competitiveness. Any increase in spending on health care would raise employer contributions and reduce capacity of firms to create new jobs. The employment outlook was seen as likely to threaten social cohesion and prepare the way for the rise of political extremism. By 1992 a new programme of direct, even brutal, measures emerged to contain growth of health and social spending.

This programme was supported by a strong consensus between the two main political parties of Social and Christian Democrats. Within health services it involves an immediate introduction of budgets for drug-prescribing, with the sanction that doctors' incomes would be reduced if these budgets were exceeded. This measure brought about an 11 per cent reduction in pharmaceutical spending in 1993–4. The reforms also covered new concerns for reducing costs and over-capacity in hospital beds. There will also be a positive list for approved pharmaceuticals. In the longer term, there would be reductions in social-security and pension increases. The immediate effects concentrated in the health sector surprised supporters of the policy and showed how simple measures could have far-reaching impact.

However, there were few signs in other EU member states of willingness to face up to change. The special public-finance problems of Europe can be defined in the following terms:

- The main public demand is from intense minorities of producer groups such as farmers and doctors. The supplier industries also represent an important background influence.
- The most typical European form of public expenditure is the subsidy or soft investment loan for infrastructure. These have serious long-term effects in distorting patterns of output and encouraging protectionism.
- The wider European public opinion is deeply addicted to public expenditure and state action.
- EC budgetary policies can be taken as one important indicator of élite attitudes, given the very low parliamentary and public input into budgetary planning. Current plans are for doubling of EC budgetary spending in real terms over the next few years.

The policy agenda can be summed up as follows:

1. It is necessary to begin the search for substantial long-term reductions in the ratio of public expenditure to GDP. There is no one golden number, but any reduction in the state role and in the tax burden on lower-income groups must mean a substantial reduction from the current EC average level of around 52 per cent. The room for manœuvre is limited, given the claims of an ageing population and the dependence of a third or more of households on the public sector for their basic income; but an initial target might be to reduce the ratio of public expenditure to GDP to the range 40–45 per cent.

2. There needs to be a much more realistic assessment of the equity implications of the current distribution of the costs of public expenditure. There seems to be a common illusion that public-expenditure projects are paid for by the rich for the benefit of the poor, but most of the European increase has been on middle-class public goods and infrastructure projects financed out of consumption taxes on lower-income groups. For labour-market and for equity reasons, the highest European priority must be to reduce the tax disincentive and the tax burden on households with low incomes.

3. Europe can gain from past experience with the use of new supply-side incentives, privatization, pluralism, and internal markets. The actual evidence from UK and US experience is generally positive about the impact of such policies. Such new approaches can increase managerial drive, make more flexible use of staff time, and deal more effectively with the problems of scale and remoteness from customers which have affected the old-style public sector.[11] In the short term, budgetary controls can help with the most pressing problems, but these do not deal with the longer-term quality problems, which can only be addressed by increasing incentives and choice. Health services in Germany and education in France are only two examples where falling service quality is likely unless there are new and fundamental initiatives. Yet in general, even élite opinion is highly negative on such supply-side changes.

4. The current structure of public finance in Europe is a very serious disincentive to the development of labour-intensive small business. Most incentives are to mobile capital-intensive industry, yet it is local labour-intensive business which employs younger and unqualified workers.

Average unemployment in the European Community is now well over 10 per cent and there is every prospect of it rising further. Change in public finance is essential if this grim prospect is to be avoided. At one extreme there was the example of Sweden, with a budget deficit of 13 per cent of GDP and a national debt likely to pass 100 per cent of GDP in 1995. In Sweden, debt levels threatened financial stability as well as employment prospects. At the other extreme was New Zealand, where ten years of deregulation and reductions in public spending had led to growth and budget balance. European governments had reacted to economic constraints only in relation to extreme financial crisis. How far would they face up to adjustment in relation to the less obvious and longer-term crisis of employment? Outside the United Kingdom and West Germany, the outlook was not very positive. Public aspirations were obstinately high, while economic constraints became more ominous. After 100 years of fiscal illusion, we are all Italians now.

NOTES

1. N. Bosanquet, *After the New Right* (London: Heinemann, 1993).
2. A. Jomini, *The Art of War* (London: Greenhill, 1962).
3. R. H. Tawney, *Equality* (London: Unwin, 1964).
4. H. Laski, W. I. Jennings, and W. Robson, *A Century of Municipal Progress* (London: Allen & Unwin, 1935).
5. J. K. Galbraith, *The Affluent Society* (Harmondsworth: Pelican, 1962).
6. J. O'Connor, *The Fiscal Crisis of the State* (New York: St Martin's Press, 1973).
7. J. M. Buchanan, 'La scienza delle financeria: The Italian Tradition in Fiscal Theory', in *Fiscal Theory and Political Economy* (Chapel Hill, NC: University of North Carolina Press, 1960).
8. R. Bacon and W. Eltis, *Britain's Economic Problem: Too few Producers* (London: Macmillan, 1976).
9. Beatrice Majnoni D'Intignano, *La Protection sociale* (Paris: Le Livre de Poche, 1993).
10. N. Bosanquet, 'Is Privatisation Inevitable?', in J. Le Grand and R. Robinson (eds.), *Privatisation and the Welfare State* (London: Allen & Unwin, 1984).
11. E. Powell, *A New Look at Medicine and Politics* (London: Pitman, 1966).

11

The Fluctuating Rationale of Monetary Union

JAMES FORDER AND PETER OPPENHEIMER

In advancing the cause of European unification over recent decades, the relevant European élites—meaning by this, politicians and officials, together with their friends in business, professional, and academic circles—have displayed a nice blend of idealism and opportunism. Idealism was reflected in the vision of the founding fathers that the European Community would above all be a means of maintaining the peace in Europe after two world wars; and in the determination of a variety of European leaders to keep the European enterprise moving forward in the face of sometimes sharp differences of opinion among its members. Opportunism has been seen in the search for fruitful lines of development by those most committed to European integration (for example, alternation between creation or consolidation of European institutions and widening of membership; or between attempts at harmonization and emphasis on 'mutual recognition' in the preparation of the Single European Act (1985) following the *Cassis de Dijon* judgment) and also in a willingness to seek accommodation for key national interests and priorities whenever this has appeared unavoidable. The best-known example of the latter is, of course, the Common Agricultural Policy— even though it has not functioned altogether as French interests had envisaged. The major item currently on the agenda of further steps in European integration is the implementation of monetary union, scheduled by the Maastricht Treaty of 1991 for either 1997 or 1999. Our purposes here are to argue, first, that the conditions for monetary union incorporated in the Maastricht Treaty are seriously at variance with the interests of the European peoples, in that they give excessive priority to the maintenance of price stability at the possible expense of employment and growth. Secondly, we argue that these conditions represent another major instance of capitulation to a sectional viewpoint. In this instance the viewpoint is that of Germany, and especially of the

Bundesbank, without whose full support monetary union in Europe was judged to be impossible.

The next section spells out the argument that the conditions of the Maastricht Treaty are indeed deeply anti-inflationary, to an extent that is unwarranted and detrimental. Section 2 examines the interplay of political and economic interests which led to this outcome, emphasizing the radical shift in European monetary priorities in the course of the 1980s. Section 3 shows how successive reports from the European Commission contributed to the process, and Section 4 states our conclusions.

1. The Anti-Inflationism of the Maastricht Treaty

The Maastricht Treaty covers moves towards political union, a common foreign policy for EU members, and social affairs, but its main focus is on the conditions and timetable for monetary union. In this connection it contains a number of provisions pointing to a new emphasis on anti-inflation strategy in the European Union. The Treaty of Rome is amended to include a new statement on the activities of its members. Article 3.3a now says: 'These activities of the Member States of the Community shall entail compliance with the following guiding principles: stable prices, sound public finances and monetary conditions and a sustainable balance of payments.' There is no mention of employment or growth as possible objectives of policy. Turning to the specifics of monetary union, Article 105 states: 'The primary objective of the European System of Central Banks [and therefore of the future European Central Bank] shall be to maintain price stability.' These provisions bind the members of the European Community even if they are not part of the European Monetary Union. All member countries except the United Kingdom are also committed to joining such a monetary union, but their being permitted to do so depends on meeting certain specific conditions labelled 'convergence criteria'. These criteria, stated in Article 190j of the treaty and elucidated in a protocol, are together, as it happens, neither necessary nor sufficient for maintenance of a monetary union; but they are plainly designed to push both monetary and fiscal policies of member states in a deflationary direction.

The first criterion, self-confessedly concerned with inflation, prescribes that states must have annual inflation-rates no greater than 1.5 percentage points above the average of the three lowest-inflation countries. This condition may be insufficient for preserving monetary union: 1.5

percentage points constitute a very substantial gap in inflation-rates if the low-inflation countries average, say, 2 or 2.5 per cent per annum. The real issue is whether the creation of a monetary union quickly brings divergent cost-levels and inflation-rates into complete alignment before competitiveness in high-inflating countries is damaged.

The second and third criteria are concerned with government borrowing. They lay down that public-sector budget deficits must not exceed 3 per cent of gross domestic product and the outstanding volume of government debt must not exceed 60 per cent of GDP. These criteria are ostensibly designed to ensure 'sound public finances'. Their underlying purpose is brought out in the Commission's report on the economics of monetary union, which states: 'The essential requirement for budgetary policy is sustainability of the public debt without recourse to monetary financing.'[1] Monetary financing of a budget deficit is usually understood as the inflationary creation of cash by a government unable to raise sufficient money in taxes and borrowing to cover its expenditures. Such an inflationary policy might be forced on a government if the outstanding value of its debt is so great that interest payments impose an excessive burden on public finances. By the same token, a present deficit could be a pointer to future problems on this front, since the present deficit is the amount by which the outstanding debt volume grows.

None the less, the respective numbers of 3 per cent and 60 per cent are arbitrary and have no general justification. What is a sound or reasonable level of government borrowing depends on a country's rate of growth, on its private sector savings and investment behaviour, and indeed (in principle) on that of all other countries in the international economic system. The larger the net volume of financial assets which a country's private sector wishes to acquire, the larger is the amount which its government may prudently borrow. Under-borrowing by governments imparts a deflationary impetus to the economy, signified by downward pressure on interest-rates, prices, and economic activity in varying combinations. Moreover, it is a mistake—although one often made in connection with the Maastricht Treaty—to suppose that any financing of the government by the central bank is inflationary. Some monetary financing of a budget deficit is nearly always appropriate in a growing economy. Even with perfectly stable prices, economic expansion calls for an increase in the economy's stock of money, to be procured for the most part by a mixture of private borrowing and public borrowing from the country's banking system.

The fourth criterion is that participants must have adhered to the 'normal' arrangements of the European exchange-rate mechanism for two years before joining the monetary union. It remains to be seen what interpretation will be put on the word 'normal' in the light of the general move to 15 per cent bands of fluctuation in 1993. In principle, this criterion is neutral in its fiscal and monetary impact, since it puts curbs on currency appreciation as well as depreciation. In other words, this rule merely reinforces whatever net deflationary or inflationary tendency emerges from the previous criteria.

Finally, long-term interest-rates on government debt of each participating country must not exceed the average of those of the three lowest-inflation countries by more than 2 percentage points. The significance of this is that long-term interest-rates reflect, albeit imperfectly, a market forecast of future inflation. The assumption is that free movement of capital causes real rates of return to be equalized, leaving differences between nominal rates to reflect differences in expected rates of inflation. Like the first criterion concerning differences in observed inflation-rates, this condition on interest-rates might be thought to allow excessive latitude from the standpoint of entry to monetary union. The penalty in terms of loss of competitiveness if expectations of inflation diverging by as much as 2 per cent were to be realized would be paid by any country rash enough to join the monetary union without recognizing that inflation performance and expectations must be brought much more closely into line than is suggested by an interest-rate discrepancy of this magnitude.

In addition to these criteria, those who wish to join a monetary union are required, in advance, to make their own central banks 'independent' of the governments. Since these banks are in any case scheduled to be superseded by the Eurofed, and since the benefit of central-bank independence is conventionally held to be the guarantee of low inflation, this provision is presumably meant to encourage a further affirmation of the European governments' anti-inflation commitment, rather than to be a development of lasting significance in its own right. Could such an emphasis on inflation control ever be warranted? If the question were whether the single-minded pursuit of low inflation could be necessary under certain circumstances, for a certain period, then the answer is that it certainly could be and arguably, for much of the 1970s and 1980s, actually was. However, the Maastricht Treaty seeks to build institutions which would make such a policy an invariable feature of the European economy. It is this that we believe to be contrary to the interests of the peoples of Europe.

There are, of course, well-known theoretical arguments to the effect that price stability is the only goal which can be reliably achieved by macro-economic, or at least by monetary, policy and therefore the only goal to which the actions of central monetary institutions ought to be directed. This view is expressed in the context of European monetary union by Neumann.[2] The perceived relevance of this theoretical reasoning, however, derives essentially from a period (the 1970s and 1980s) in which West European countries' annual inflation-rates were close to, and sometimes in, double figures. This theory, as it happens, makes a number of extreme and implausible assumptions about the structure of the economy, the nature of wage-bargaining, and the computational capabilities of economic agents. There is, for example, precious little evidence of the rapid clearing of the labour market in the absence of government action, and plenty against it. A more judicious account of the macro-economic consequences of government action would recognize that overly aggressive anti-inflation policy may do long-lasting damage to growth and employment. In any case, it is grotesque to claim that the same theory remains of undiminished relevance after several years in which inflation has been below 3 per cent—let alone in a hypothetical future where inflation could be below 1.5 per cent. If recent levels of unemployment had been associated with greater social or ethnic unrest, political parties in many European countries would already have altered their priorities and would have found the one-sided commitments of Maastricht unacceptable.

It must be reiterated that the Maastricht Treaty aims not at a general target of seeking to return to low inflation-rates whenever the economy deviates from that basically desirable goal, but rather at a continuous achievement of inflation in the very narrow range of 0–2 per cent per year. Inflation at such low levels is subject to random disturbances of small magnitude, yet sufficient to result in a missed target. It cannot be right to have policy dominated by such possibilities. Historically, the price stability which prevailed in Britain and elsewhere in the centuries before 1914 did not involve price levels being constant from year to year. They typically rose in the upswing and fell in the downswing of the business cycle. Occasionally, a trend in one direction persisted for a decade or more, as in the Great Depression of the 1880s and 1890s. The fact that falls in the price level were less of a rarity than they have since become largely reflects the greater share of primary commodities in world output before 1914. Primary commodity prices continue to fluctuate widely in both directions in our own day;

but that is no reason to expect or require money wages to fluctuate similarly.

It might be thought that, because of the train of events since the signing of the Maastricht Treaty—notably the effective suspension *sine die* of the European Monetary System in August 1993, combined with the increasing likelihood that few if any of the proposed participants in the monetary union will meet the convergence criteria at the dates specified—all fears about the anti-inflationism of the treaty can be laid aside. Such optimism would be unfounded. A succession of political leaders have reaffirmed the importance of achieving monetary union by the deadlines set. The convergence criteria may be amended to permit it. This would be an admission that the goal of low inflation has so far proved unattainable, but not that rigid adherence to the goal itself is undesirable. The lasting danger in the Maastricht Treaty does not lie in the convergence criteria: it lies in the constitution of policy after monetary union. The importance of the convergence criteria is only that they make the intended nature of that policy unmistakable.

2. The Aims of the European Monetary System

The first attempt by the European Community to achieve monetary union came with the report of the Werner Committee in 1970. It was an ambitious document, which envisaged the achievement of effective monetary union by 1980 with a large measure of macro-economic policy responsibility being transferred to the Community. The economic problems of the 1970s ensured that nothing came of this plan. Discussion of European monetary arrangements was revived by Roy Jenkins as Commission President in 1978, together with Chancellor Schmidt and President Giscard d'Estaing. This initiative ultimately led to the creation of the European Monetary System, which began functioning in 1979.

While there were those who saw in the EMS a means of ultimately achieving monetary union, what made agreement on its establishment possible was the perception of immediate political interests prevailing at the time—most importantly the combination of French and German interests. The French reason for supporting the creation of the EMS was the defence of the Common Agricultural Policy. The French perceived themselves as being substantial beneficiaries of the CAP and in the late 1970s the CAP appeared to be under threat from floating exchange-rates. The fundamental problem was the difficulty of administering a system which supposedly required uniform prices throughout Europe. Uniform prices meant prices fixed in European Units of Account (a currency basket and forerunner of the Common European Currency, the ECU). If national currency exchange-rates should vary, this implied a corresponding movement in national prices of agricultural products—upwards in a devaluing country and downwards in a revaluing one. While this was economically logical as a means of restoring food prices to the common levels intended, the French and West German governments in 1969 and subsequently found the logic politically unacceptable. In order to allow national food prices to go their own way while still preserving common prices in trade between EC members, EC governments adopted a system of border taxes and subsidies (called Monetary Compensatory Amounts or MCAs) for trade in agricultural products.

Since the European Community was supposed to be in the business of removing border controls, this made a mockery of the claim that the CAP was the great achievement of European integration—an idea the French were keen to promote—and played into the hands of those who would have liked to scrap or drastically reform the policy. The problem was intensified by the advent of floating exchange-rates after 1972–3, which required agricultural prices and MCAs to be continuously recalculated, in principle moment by moment. The first step towards a solution, from the French point of view, was a system like the EMS designed to limit exchange-rate fluctuations and so prepare the ground for eventual abolition of MCAs and return to genuinely uniform food prices across the Community.

A more important consideration than the fate of the CAP, in relation to the later history of monetary integration, is the view adopted by the West German government and the Bundesbank. The Social Democratic government in West Germany had been in conflict over economic policy with the Bundesbank throughout the 1970s. The facts are documented by Goodman.[3] They include the Bundesbank's efforts to bring about the resignation of Finance Minister Schiller; the 'New Assignment' of 1974 when the Bank broke with precedent in unilaterally setting monetary policy, rather than consulting with government and unions; at least two attempts by Schmidt as Finance Minister and later Chancellor to secure a relaxation of policy, with which the Bundesbank refused to comply; and the conflict over the 1978 Bonn Summit when the

Bundesbank was reluctantly forced to follow an expansionary policy to which Schmidt had committed West Germany.[4]

By 1978 Schmidt's thinking was dominated by the problem of the weak dollar. The problem was that when the dollar was weak, the Deutschmark tended to appreciate not only against the dollar but also against the other European currencies. Pressures in this direction had been apparent even in the pegged-rate system of Bretton Woods during the 1960s. In 1978 it meant that the DM was strengthening against the currencies of all its major trading partners. In the simplest terms, currency appreciation can be thought of as having two effects. On the one hand, the internal price level (or the rate of inflation) is lowered. This is because internationally traded goods (especially imports) become cheaper as the currency appreciates. Hence the Bundesbank saw no reason for concern at the weakness of the dollar. On the other hand, a strengthening currency also makes exporting and import-competing industries less competitive internationally, because wages in the traded-goods industries do not respond quickly or smoothly to the movement of the exchange-rate. This effect is likely to squeeze profits and increase unemployment. Given the substantial size and political clout of the West German export sector, Schmidt's concern at the weakness of the dollar is easily understandable.

The point of interest here is that, as with all the conflicts between government and Bundesbank in West Germany in the 1970s, the policy which Schmidt was seeking to pursue in setting up the EMS was one where the rate of inflation in Germany could be expected to be higher than it otherwise would have been. Far from seeing the EMS as a way of lowering inflation, or even of maintaining inflation at a low level, Schmidt's objective was to follow a policy which entailed some probability of Germany's inflation rising. The attitude of the Bundesbank was a corresponding hostility to Schmidt's plans. Its attitude to fixed exchange-rate systems in general can be gleaned from Bundesbank President Otmar Emminger's account of the consequences for Germany of membership of the Bretton Woods system.[5] He found that the Bundesbank's efforts to play by the Bretton Woods rules resulted in a higher rate of inflation than was either desirable or would have occurred without that system. Hence floating exchange-rates were to be preferred. It is clear from this contrast of objectives—Schmidt's and the Bundesbank's—that 1979 was a low point for the influence of the Bundesbank on German and European policy. In 1979 European élites were in touch with their peoples at least so far as the EMS was concerned: the CAP was to be rescued and the German export and manufacturing sector protected against the zeal of the Bundesbank. Over the next ten years, however, perceptions were to change completely.

The aspect of the development of the EMS that is of particular interest is how the Bundesbank came to acquire leadership over the system and how the objectives of the Bundesbank came to dominate future institutional design. It is a remarkable turn-round. Initially the Bundesbank resisted participating in the EMS for fear that it would, like Bretton Woods, force it to adopt a higher rate of inflation. Now, only a few years later, the EMS is widely seen as a device specifically intended to reduce inflation; and this, moreover, not by constraining the Bundesbank, as Schmidt had intended, but, on the contrary, by forcing other countries to follow the Bundesbank's policy. The current view was neatly captured by *The Economist* in 1985: 'If Sterling does join, the biggest change will be the transfer of responsibility for Britain's monetary policy from the Bank of England to Germany's Bundesbank which, as the central bank keenest on sound money, sets the pace for others to follow. This would be a blessing: Tory governments may like appointing City gents as governors of the Bank, but Mr Karl Otto Poehl would do a better job.'

How the Bundesbank gained ascendancy over the EMS is largely the story of how policy priorities changed after the second oil shock of 1979, with the control of inflation becoming permanent. There are several aspects to this. Most important, the appointment of Paul Volcker to the Chairmanship of the US Federal Reserve System provided world-wide leadership in inflation control. Shortly after, the policy 'revolutions' of Thatcher and Reagan focused attention on the importance of market mechanisms and hence of clear, undistorted price signals.

Theoretical perceptions also changed, with the ascendancy first of the monetarism associated with Milton Friedman, and subsequently of the credibility theory embodied in the new classical economics. Each of these suggested that inflation control should be the primary or only goal of macro-economic policy. The popularization of monetarism is discussed at length by Parsons.[6] A similar story could be told of the growth of credibility theory, its adaptation for public consumption, and its influence on governmental thinking. Credibility theory was originated in general terms by Kydland and Prescott, and was rather rashly applied to the EMS by Giavazzi and Pagano.[7] The theory argues that the costs of reducing inflation and of maintaining low inflation depend on the extent to which the government is believed to be committed to that goal. Since the government's willingness to pursue the goal in turn depends on the costs (including opportunities forgone), there will be benefits to policy if the government can successfully persuade the private sector that it is committed to reducing inflation whatever the cost. But, by the same token, it will be doubly difficult to bring inflation below a level which the public judges the government will in fact be willing to tolerate (whatever its previous declarations) if that appears politically expedient.

Giavazzi and Pagano suggested that the EMS gave governments a useful opportunity to commit themselves to low inflation by announcing an exchange-rate link with the DM, which was assumed to be a low-inflation currency. This argument clearly captured an important aspect of the attitudes of some of the governments to the EMS in its later stages. The British and French governments both sought to influence inflation expectations by committing themselves to ambitious exchange-rate targets. Whatever credibility was thereby gained, however, clearly did not include credibility of the exchange-rate targets themselves, since both governments were forced to abandon them in 1992–3.

Perhaps the single most important event in the rise of the Bundesbank was the reversal of French policy in 1983. President Mitterrand was elected in 1981 on a commitment to expand the French economy, preferably co-ordinating with other countries, but if necessary on its own. The policy quickly proved to be a disaster. Rising inflation and a deteriorating balance of payments triggered a serious disagreement within the government and forced a U-turn in 1983.[8] Before this U-turn we can say that, for practical purposes, the French had been ignoring the EMS as a constraint on policy actions, being willing to devalue within the system as and when their economic strategy required. The policy reversal was presented to French public opinion as necessary to demonstrate France's commitment to the European Community.

On the basis of this account, the EMS should be seen not as a technical system for reducing inflation, but rather as providing a political lever to secure acceptance for a shift of policy which would otherwise have been difficult to sell. A pointer to the effectiveness of the political lever is the fact that the whole policy became known as *franc fort*. In other words, the policy was (and is) presented as a strategy for 'looking the Deutschmark in the face' whereas its substance was disinflation and the acceptance of associated costs in terms of lost output and employment.[9] With this in mind it is easy to see how the EMS came to be regarded—in France and elsewhere—as a means for reducing inflation. The Italian case has some similarities to the French. The level of public commitment to European integration and to monetary integration was comparatively high,[10] while Italian disinflation after the second oil shock was severely hampered by the presence of wage indexation. It seems that public commitment to European integration was used, via the EMS, to secure acceptance of the need to abolish wage indexation.

There were thus three factors which combined to enhance the role of the Bundesbank in European policy-making: the emphasis placed on inflation control in the wake of the oil shock, the growth of the 'credibility view' of how that was to be achieved, and the working example of the French approach to disinflation. In particular, the credibility view put the Bundesbank at the centre of the EMS. The whole benefit of EMS membership was now supposed to be that it committed less spontaneously virtuous countries to following the Bundesbank's policy, which itself was guaranteed to deliver low inflation. Far from controlling the Bundesbank, the EMS became a licence for the Bundesbank to follow its own inclinations. Not only does the credibility model absolve the Bundesbank from any responsibility to co-operate internationally; in addition, the Bank's role as leader of policy in the supposed (credibility-enhancing) interests of the whole EC gives it an excellent excuse for rejecting any attempts by German domestic lobbies to influence its activities.

We can begin to see how the enhanced role of the Bundesbank led to the construction of the Maastricht Treaty. The Bundesbank is committed to the pursuit of price stability and has been a highly effective propagandist to that end. For their part, the governments negotiating the Maastricht Agreement may have thought it important to indulge in the supposed credibility-enhancing exercise of committing themselves to a low-inflation monetary union and the imposition of stringent anti-inflation convergence criteria. In theory, the act of signing such a treaty could make the achievement of low inflation easier and less costly, to the benefit of all the economies (and governments) concerned.

The other trend in European integration which is relevant here is the enhanced efforts of the European Commission to popularize the process, sometimes almost seeking to appeal over the heads of governments directly to electorates. The report by Emerson et al.[11] is just such an attempt to sell the goal of the internal market—persuading businessmen that measures tending to intensify competition and squeeze profits demanded their urgent support. A later volume by Emerson et al.[12]

seeks to convince the European public that monetary union is in its interest. The striking fact about the two reports, as the next section shows, is how inconsistent they are with each other. The report on monetary union sets aside all economic goals of integration other than the control of inflation. It is a thinly disguised effort to win the support of the Bundesbank—essential for the purpose in hand, because without the Bundesbank's approval, monetary union would be impossible.

3. Economic Integration, Policy, and Performance

Part of the political impetus behind the Treaty of Maastricht stemmed from the Single European Act of 1985 and the 1992 programme for 'completing the internal market'. It was argued, or felt, that the preservation of separate national currencies among the European members, with the associated possibility of periodic exchange-rate changes, constituted a barrier to intra-community trade (comprising both transactions costs of currency exchange and exchange-rate risk) exactly comparable to those barriers being removed under the 1992 programme. European monetary union was therefore seen as a necessary complement to implementation of the Single European Act, a view encapsulated in the title of the European Commission's own volume on the costs and benefits of economic and monetary union *One Market, One Money*. This line of argument was supported by a survey of business opinion which found that 'opinions on the prospects for the business climate become very much more positive when a single currency complements the single market'.[13] It would necessarily do so since businessmen can respond to such a survey only on *ceteris paribus* assumptions. Asking Italian businessmen about their support for monetary union on the condition that it will involve a substantial increase in taxation, or German businessmen on the condition that it will mean increased immigration of foreigners to their area, one would be unlikely to get the same answer.

In their foreword to *One Market, One Money*, the then Commission President Jacques Delors and Vice-President Henning Christopherson describe it as 'although methodologically quite different, in some respects a sequel to' the Commission's earlier study on the impact of completing the internal market.[14] What is striking, however, is not the difference in methodology between the two volumes so much as the substantial measure of inconsistency between their economic contents. The key difference concerns the scope and impact of macro-economic policy. In the 1988 volume the size of medium-term gains in real national product (as well as other aspects) depends heavily on the orientation of national monetary and fiscal policies. The approach is broadly Keynesian in spirit: government actions influence economic performance in numerous ways, and there is no sharp dichotomy between 'real' and monetary aspects. In strong contrast, the main thrust of the EMU volume is to stress the limitations and constraints which fall upon member countries' financial policies in the context of monetary union. 'In the context of' does not mean merely 'as a consequence of'. Regardless of the actual exchange-rate regime, the limited scope for exchange-rate movements to affect any non-monetary variable at all is emphasized. This, in other words, is a broadly monetarist document: governments can do little to affect the economic performance of the market system apart from providing an appropriate legal framework including a sound currency; and the classical dichotomy between 'real' and monetary variables is a key working hypothesis.

This contrast between these two supposedly complementary studies may be clarified by a somewhat more detailed description of their arguments. The earlier study, after describing the main types of intra-Community trade barriers remaining (differences in technical regulations, frontier controls, government procurement biases, and restrictions on the supply of services, chiefly in finance and transport), argues that their removal and associated enhancement of competition will reduce costs, raise enterprise efficiency, improve resource allocation, and stimulate innovation. The report states, however, that 'it is for macro-economic policy to determine how to dispose of the potential economic gains made available by the micro-economic measures taken in order to complete the internal market'.[15] Policy-makers have a certain amount of choice regarding employment levels and growth-rates, depending on how they interpret their obligation to respect 'the major macro-economic equilibrium constraints . . . notably as regards price stability, balance of payments and budget balances'.

The presentation is not confined to generalities. Most of the report is devoted to various statistical estimations of the possible gains involved, including numerous case-studies of individual industries and services. In pulling these estimates together, a key distinction is made between effects accruing respectively 'with a passive macro-economic policy' and 'with a more active macro-economic policy'. In the former case the study foresees a real GDP gain of 4.5 per cent after five to six years, as well as a 6 per cent decline in the Community's price level (relative to what would otherwise have occurred) and a 2 million (nearly 2 per cent) increase in numbers employed. At the same time there are significant improvements in both budget balance and current balances of payments. This leads the authors of the study to conclude that 'it would be legitimate to consider adjusting medium-term macro-economic strategy onto a somewhat more expansionary trajectory'.[16] The summary of findings then continues:

The extent of this adjustment would depend upon which constraint (inflation, budget or balance of payments deficit) was considered binding . . . In the middle of the range, for example, lies a case in which the GDP level after a medium-term period might be 2.5 per cent higher, in addition to the 4.5 per cent gain suggested under the passive macro-economic policy, thus totalling 7 per cent. In this case, inflation would still have been held well below the course initially projected in the absence of the internal market programme, the budget balance would also be improved, while the balance of payments might be worsened by a moderate amount.[17]

The EMU study *One Market, One Money* does, of course, seek in various ways to present itself as a logical follow-on from the earlier *The Economics of 1992*. In particular, it emphasizes in chapter 3 the economic benefits of eliminating normal exchange-rate variability and uncertainty among member states (as would occur with full rigidity of national exchange-rates) as well as transactions costs of money-changing (as would occur when national currencies are replaced by the ECU). In addition, an ECU which becomes a major global transactions vehicle might generate further gains—discussed in chapter 7 of the report—in the form of reduced needs for external currency reserves, increased international business for European banks, and seigniorage on foreign holdings of ECU banknotes. To be sure, some gains in these categories are already accruing to individual currencies, especially the Deutschmark and sterling, and the magnitude of net additional gains from a single currency remains a matter of speculation.

Beyond these relatively uncontroversial items, however, the study goes on to claim price stability and its consequences for efficient resource allocation and growth as a further benefit of EMU. It is emphasized that a European central bank with independent policy-making authority and an overriding and therefore credible commitment to price stability as its sole objective 'appear to be necessary conditions for a consistent . . . anti-inflationary policy'.[18]

Whether this is an additional benefit is questionable. In principle, national price stability must be considered within reach of any individual central bank willing and able to pursue a policy of the type described. If some central banks do not do so, this is presumably because they are working to other, politically preferred objectives. To deny them or their legitimate political masters pursuit of these other objectives is then a cost and not a benefit of monetary union. This objection would fail only if the transitional or other costs (in terms of forgone output etc.) of achieving price stability for the more inflation-prone countries were sufficiently lowered by the very fact of participation in the monetary union, as credibility theorists envisage. We are not, however, aware of any evidence—as opposed to theoretical argumentation—that any extra 'credibility' which may arise from central-bank independence in fact reduces the cost of lowering inflation or keeping it low. Indeed, the suspicion that there is little or no such evidence is reinforced by the development of the Commission's argument.

Having asserted that an independent central bank is necessary for monetary stability, they go on to argue in the next chapter that fiscal policy as well as monetary policy must be geared towards low inflation. This has two implications. First it reinforces and perpetuates the disinflationary impetus inherent in the Maastricht convergence criteria. Secondly, it is here that *One Market, One Money* is most clearly inconsistent with *The Economics of 1992*. Whereas in *The Economics of 1992*, Emerson *et al.* wrote of the additional measurable gains in gross national product that could come from 'a more active macro-economic policy', in *One Market, One Money* the discussion is all about the constraints that must be put on policy to maintain low inflation. There is no indication that any benefit can come from active macro-policy. The authors of *One Market, One Money* distinguish three requirements for fiscal policy: autonomy for national policy-makers, discipline, and co-ordination. Most of the discussion concerns discipline, consideration of the others adding little of substance.

In part the discussion of discipline reproduces the attitudes that led to the convergence criteria discussed earlier: fiscal conservatism is required to ensure that debt positions will never become unsustainable thereby generating either a formal default or (inflationary) monetary financing. But that is not all. *One Market, One Money* makes illustrative calculations of the requirements for sustainability of government debt, based on assumed real interest-rates of 4 per cent or 5 per cent.

Since the historical norm for real interest-rates has been nearer 2.5 or 3 per cent, this assumption makes any debt position seem less sustainable than it is. To the same general effect the authors of *One Market, One Money* commit themselves to the alarming fallacy that the prospect of increased government outlays on pensions for an ageing population two or three decades ahead requires a tighter fiscal policy in the present.[19]

In reality there is no simple relationship between a government's current fiscal stance (or its future fiscal needs) and the sustainability of its fiscal position. This was well recognized by the authors of *The Economics of 1992*. If expansionary fiscal policy can sometimes stimulate the economy, then it can raise tax revenues and thereby improve the sustainability of any given quantity of public debt. There is no presumption, for example, that a requirement for higher tax revenues to pay pensions tomorrow necessitates a contraction of government borrowing today. If such a contraction leads—as it may—to economic downturn, unemployment, and lower investment, then the ability of the government to meet future obligations is reduced, not increased.

It is difficult to suppose that the economists of the Commission have lost touch with these economic realities. The plausible explanation is that the exaggerated horror of some actors on the European political scene at the prospect of government policies sometimes (and, we would say, justifiably) being such as to lift the rate of inflation was allowed to dominate the Maastricht negotiation. The Commission in *One Market, One Money* is engaged in the delicate task of persuading the peoples of Europe that such domination is in order.

4. Conclusion

Could one say that the inconsistencies of the Commission and its recent blinkered anti-inflationism account for the European public's suspicion of monetary union? That would probably be going too far. None the less, we suggest that the Commission has acted against the interests of the people. It has espoused economic theory which was never previously part of the philosophy underlying the Treaty of Rome and which threatens serious damage to the European economy and ultimately to the project of European integration itself. It is in the nature of any political process that there will not be absolute consistency among the arguments advanced in pursuit of a long-term policy objective. The European Commission and others committed to the progress of European integration naturally adapt the specific policies they promote to the circumstances of the time. In so far as this represents the ongoing search for consensus, it is part of the normal process of democratic politics. When, however, agreements reached are to be embedded in international treaties, the search for consensus involves two risks. The first is that a scale of priorities appropriate only in specific circumstances becomes constitutionally incorporated as an unalterable feature of an integrated Europe. The second risk is that undue influence on the shape of institutions is exercised by those who are most obstinate in clinging to a one-sided or sectional view but whose consent is essential to the process of integration.

The attempt to move towards EMU in the 1990s illustrates both these risks in a glaring way. The Maastricht Treaty was drawn up after a decade and a half, during which curbing inflation had been the principal, indeed almost the sole, objective of European macro-economic policy. There is no need to argue that unemployment should have the same near-exclusive priority in the 1990s. We suggest merely that when inflation is in the neighbourhood of 2.5 per cent and unemployment around 10 per cent policy cannot afford to ignore the latter. Even monetary policy ought not to be conducted without some regard to its direct employment implications.

In the meantime, however, the Bundesbank—as the one institution which feels it has no responsibility for employment—had been allowed, indeed encouraged, to name its conditions for the pursuit of monetary union, and so has led the European Community to the one-sided anti-inflationism of the Maastricht Treaty. The Commission for its part, anxious to promote further centralization of power by any means available, has played a leading role in appeasing the Bundesbank and has thereby done its European constituents a fourfold disservice. It has equated the goals of monetary integration and price stability. It has pretended that the case for EMU on this basis is consistent with its earlier case for the 1992 programme. It claims that monetary union is indispensable to the concept of an integrated Europe. Lastly, even in the face of 22 million jobless, it has endorsed the refusal of monetary authorities to acknowledge any responsibility for output and employment levels. In these circumstances the onus should be on the élites of both Frankfurt and Brussels to show that they have not lost touch with what the peoples of Europe really want.

NOTES

1. M. Emerson, D. Gros, A. Italianer, J. Pisani-Ferry, and H. Reichenbach, *One Market, One Money* (Oxford: Oxford University Press, 1992), 27.
2. M. Neumann, 'Central Bank Independence as a Prerequisite of Price Stability', *European Economy*, special edition no. 1: *The Economics of EMU* (Brussels: Commission of the European Communities, 1991).
3. For a different interpretation, see J. Forder, 'Central Bank Independence: A Conceptual and Empirical Study', D. Phil. thesis, Oxford University, 1995, on which the following discussion draws extensively.
4. A detailed account of this episode, with emphasis on the disagreements among German policy-makers, is given by R. Putnam and R. Henning, 'The Bonn Summit of 1978', in R. Cooper *et al.*, *Can Nations Agree?* (Washington: Brookings Institution, 1989).
5. O. Emminger, *The DM in the Conflict between Internal and External Equilibrium 1948–1975*, Princeton Essays in International Finance no. 122 (Princeton: Princeton University Press, 1977).
6. W. Parsons, *The Power of the Financial Press* (London: Elgar, 1989).
7. F. Kydland and E. Prescott, 'Rules rather than Discretion: The Inconsistency of Optimal Plans', *Journal of Political Economy*, 85 (1977), 473–90.
8. H. Machin and V. Wright (eds.), *Economic Policy and Policy-making under the Mitterrand Presidency* (London: Pinter, 1985).
9. The allusion is to the precisely comparable disinflation imposed by the UK government in the mid-1920s to enable the pound sterling 'to look the dollar in the face'.
10. See W. Buiter, G. Corsetti, and V. Roubini, 'Excessive Deficits: Sense and Nonsense in the Treaty of Maastricht', *Economic Policy*, 16 (1993), 57–101.
11. M. Emerson, M. Aujean, M. Catinat, P. Goybet, and A. Jacquemin, *The Economics of 1992* (Oxford: Oxford University Press, 1988).
12. Emerson *et al.*, *One Market, One Money*.
13. Ibid. 10.
14. Emerson *et al.*, *The Economics of 1992*.
15. Ibid. 2.
16. Ibid. 6.
17. Ibid. 6.
18. Emerson *et al.*, *One Market, One Money*, 98.
19. Ibid. 106, 109.

12

Has Government by Committee Lost the Public's Confidence?

WILLIAM WALLACE

Government by committee, government by officials, and the modern state grew up together. Replacement of arbitrary and personal government by law-bound and impersonal government necessarily brought with it collective, shared decision-taking. The *beamte, fonctionnaire*, or civil servant operated first by rule, second through hierarchy, and third through committees. Public confidence in the administrators of the modernizing state stemmed from respect for the quality and neutrality of their administration (in contrast to the patronage and corruption of the old structures they replaced) and from their ultimate answerability to national political authorities.

In nineteenth-century administration most committees were within single ministries: sharing tasks, building consensus, registering and legitimizing decisions. Moves towards parliamentary democracy made for collective government, with ministers jointly responsible and therefore taking joint decisions around the cabinet (or council of ministers) table, supported by official committees to prepare their meetings and ensure that decisions were implemented. As government became more complex, so interministerial committees became more necessary and more widespread: to co-ordinate activities, to agree priorities, to resolve disputes. Over the past half-century, as the complexities of economic and social interaction have spread more and more across national boundaries, government activities have been forced to follow them. The European order within which we are living was constructed by intergovernmental committees, and is maintained by intergovernmental committees.

Strategic decisions, of course, have been taken by those who are politically responsible—ministers at the head of departments of state, heads of government and councils of ministers determining the 'national interest', ministerial representatives of national governments in striking

major intergovernmental bargains and approving treaties and international agreements. But even there much—most—of the work had
necessarily to be prepared for them by official working groups, ham-
mering out the details and shaping the terms for agreement. The construction of the post-1945 international order was the product of wartime
official working groups, of diplomats, domestic officials, and wartime
temporary officials, setting in place a network of consultative organs
serviced by international secretariats for meetings to be attended most
often by official representatives of the member governments. The conduct of the war itself depended upon a succession of councils and
joint boards through which the Allies—sovereign states pooling their
resources—co-ordinated supplies and concerted military plans. Jean
Monnet was amongst the most expert and influential of these wartime
committee men; moving from the Conseil Franco-Britannique of 1939–
40 to the Washington Combined Board, through which American arms
and materials were shared with Britain and the other dependent Allies.
Many of the contacts which were so invaluable in the construction of
West European institutions under American sponsorship in the post-
war years had been established within these wartime committees; their
style also transmitted itself to these emerging institutions.[1]

Limitations of distance, in the early days of air travel, made for
considerable dependence on the secretariats and resident missions for
such 'global' institutions as the IMF, World Bank, and United Nations.
But Europe was small enough for regular direct consultation among
national capitals well before the introduction of jet aircraft. Basle's
convenience as a railway junction had played a significant part in fixing
the seat of the Bank for International Settlements; officials from all the
major European capitals could reach there by surface transport, without
too much discomfort, within twenty-four hours. The first institutions of
post-1945 European co-operation—the Committee on European Economic Co-operation (which evolved into the OEEC), the Council of
Europe—naturally followed the same pattern: establishing small secretariats to service committees of officials coming out from national capitals, reporting to less frequent ministerial councils (and overseen, far
less directly, by discussions within the Council of Europe Parliamentary Assembly).

Looking back on the era of post-war reconstruction, the central role
played by rational administrators working within the permissive limits
of political consensus is impressive. They planned economic modernization, managed industrial and technological innovation, redistributed

national resources, and expanded the welfare state. The prestige of the *fonctionnaire–beamte* was deservedly high; they saw themselves as serving the long-term interests of their states, while their political 'masters' generated public consent and managed immediate crises. In the French Fourth Republic, in which governments and ministers came and went with distressing frequency, the contrast between those who governed 'the French' and those who managed the interests of 'France' was particularly striking. It was hardly surprising that Saint-Simonian ideas of enlightened administration by the technically expert and politically dispassionate gathered support among the élite, as the Fourth Republic staggered from crisis to crisis while the products of the École Nationale d'Administration and the École Polytechnique gradually rebuilt the state and the economy. Nor that the prestige of the Commissariat au Plan, which Jean Monnet headed in the immediate post-war years, should have attracted many in the 1950s to imitate its style and staffing at a supranational level, just as it attracted admirers in Britain to imitate it (in the National Economic Development Council) in the early 1960s.

The High Authority of the European Coal and Steel Community was a self-consciously technocratic organization: professedly non-political, though pursuing wider political objectives—in the long-term interests of the member states and of that 'ever closer union of European peoples' which the Treaty Preamble proclaimed. The structures of the European Economic and Atomic Energy Communities were more cautious in granting supranational authority for technocratic administrators; but were nevertheless imbued with the same spirit, constructed on a similar model, and staffed by the same self-confident and self-conscious élite. It is characteristic of the style and context within which the Communities were designed that officials like Walter Hallstein and Robert Marjolin should have played such prominent roles in the negotiations and the interim committee which followed, to emerge as President and Vice-President of the EEC Commission; and that Jean Monnet should have played such an influential role, overlapping the worlds of private influence, administration, and politics.

1. A Community of Committees: The EC Structure

High politics and hard national interests were at stake in the Messina Conference and the signing of the Rome Treaties. But after the bruising defeat of the intensely political proposals for the European Defence Community there was a natural inclination to stress the economic and technical rather than the political and controversial. 'The line we are following', Paul-Henri Spaak told the Council of Europe Assembly in October 1955, 'aims at making people face up more fully to their responsibilities, asking them not dogmatically to prejudge issues but rather to be willing to draw logical conclusions from certain facts.'[2] Integration was a logical, rational process, once the political context was set; the politicians must make the overall commitment, but could then leave it to the experts to follow the facts to their logical outcome. The Spaak Committee worked through a series of expert groups. The British, sending along an 'expert' official from the Board of Trade, misunderstood the relationship between political commitment and trust in committees of experts to formulate detailed plans, and failed to follow either the development of consensus among the national representatives or the intermingling of expert officialdom and political direction.

Behind this rationalistic rhetoric, governments, of course, bargained hard for national interests as they saw them: working to include agriculture, transport, social benefits, and financial transfers in the treaties to promote or protect different national positions.[3] For national governments, negotiation of the rules and institutions of European integration was a self-conscious compromise between the post-war re-establishment of sovereignty and the advantages which integration offered in promoting national welfare and enhancing national security. It suited them to disguise from their publics how far this trade-off between sovereignty and integration constrained the autonomy of the state. An emphasis on the technical character of those policies which were to be integrated, contrasted with the political character of what remained under national control, was thus of advantage to national politicians as well. Official committees dealing with detailed regulations did not appear a threat to national integrity. Governments could thus hope to benefit from the additional economic growth which economic integration was seen to provide to raise levels of national welfare, without alarming their electorates.[4]

The European Communities were built around a series of committees. The central tension was between the intergovernmental Council of Ministers—and its rapidly developed substructure of intergovernmental committees—and the European Commission, its small staff dependent in its turn on committees of 'experts' for advice and information. The Council of Ministers represented politics, the Commission stood for

administration. But a settled preference for avoiding wider and more
awkward political issues, for disaggregating problems into their functional and technical elements, ran through the structure of Council
committees as much as through the Commission. Reluctance to reopen
the bargains struck in the Treaties was sharpened by the political challenge presented—as the Communities got under way—by President de
Gaulle. Against his grasp of the instinctive and non-rational elements of
politics—nation, state, and national identity—Walter Hallstein as Commission President urged the validity of calm and collective decision-
taking, both by national ministers and by 'technocratic' officials, to
promote shared interests. 'But perhaps it would be best if we abandoned mistaken and somewhat condescending attempts to distinguish
between politicians and "technocrats". The truth surely is that politics,
the art of governing, has subtly changed in recent times, that it has
become more rational, more detailed, more "technical"—in short, more
exact and professional.'[5]

So the processes of European economic integration developed, in
spite of de Gaulle's resistance, through consensus-building among
national administrators working together in expert committees; coming
through the processes of mutual learning and group socialization (the
process which integration theorists called 'engrenage') to agreement on
common policies. This was the central idea of the 'Community Method'
of extensive consultations and shared policy-making: that functional
expertise and disaggregated agendas promoted an 'upgrading of the
common interest' which would lead in turn to increasing commitment
to the pursuit of common European policies. 'One index of the growing habit of joint consultation and coordination' that the Community
institutions were fostering, Walter Hallstein told an American audience
in 1962, 'is the extraordinary number of daily contacts at all levels that
are now taking place between officials and experts of our member
governments, often under the auspices of the EEC Commission and in
its Brussels offices.'[6] Regular meetings on common-market issues and
exploratory discussions about potential new policies were supplemented
by marathon committee sessions to settle the shape and details of new
policy regimes. The Community's Council of Ministers, he proudly
told his hearers, had finally reached agreement on the first measures
of a common agricultural policy in January 1962 after '45 separate
meetings, 7 of them at night; a total of 137 hours of discussion, with
214 hours in subcommittee; 582,000 pages of documents; 3 heart
attacks—the record, is staggering. It is also, I think, quite striking in

its testimony to the whole spirit of our enterprise.'[7] Package deals, hammered out through exhaustive sessions of intergovernmental bargaining under Commission oversight, were followed by collective implementation and managemant through yet more Council and Commission committees.

The growth of the Community's 'comitology' has transformed the workings of national governments, creating what Wolfgang Wessels has accurately described as 'a new system of shared government' at the European level: a structure with many of the characteristics of German co-operative federalism, but without the accompanying federal structures for political accountability and public consent.[8] 'Being based on dialogue' among a widening network of ministers, officials, and—increasingly—representatives of interested groups, the Community system, Émile Noël (the Community's Secretary-General from 1958 to 1987) remarked in 1971,

bears little resemblance to the concept of government in the traditional sense of the word. The Community does not have a single head or a single leader. Decisions are collective and taken only after much confrontation of view points. The Communities have in fact been transformed into a vast convention. They are a meeting place for experts, ambassadors and ministers at hundreds and even thousands of meetings.[9]

In 1968—ten years after the entry into force of the Treaties of Rome—the Commission convened (according to Hallstein) some 1,450 meetings with civil servants and experts from the member states, involving over 16,000 national officials: that is, some six meetings per working day, linking between 2,000 and 3,000 officials from within each government to the Community process. Most of these were middle-ranking officials (under-secretaries, assistant secretaries, and principals, in British parlance), incorporating their participation in Community policy-making into the regular patterns of administrative life. Alongside this, in addition, the Council Secretariat was servicing a growing number of Council committees, some attended only by officials from the Permanent Representations but many also bringing out participants from national capitals.

The impact on Community policy-making of this process was, as had been intended, to downplay broader political issues by splitting decisions up into functional administrative divisions: thus replacing a public clash among national interests, as far as possible, by a private reconciliation of limited differences. 'Doing things in this way', Hallstein added,

frequently makes it possible to reach agreement at the lower civil-servant level
without taking matters to the Council of Ministers. Certainly it considerably
reduces the length of the deliberations in the Council. . . . It is impossible to
exaggerate the significance of [national civil servants'] participation in this
process. After all, national civil servants are, by the very nature of their jobs,
the last persons one would expect to yield even a fraction of national sovereignty, let alone to encourage actively the transfer of national powers and
functions to Brussels. Here their participation in the law-making process works
its own special magic. It brings them into continuous contact with officials of
the Community who, by the nature of their jobs, must view every problem 'in
the round', not from a particular national viewpoint but with a view to the
benefits for the Community as a whole. . . . They become involved, and sooner
or later their attitude to the problems before them becomes more European.[10]

The 1985 figures—before the intensification of activities which followed from the 1992 Programme and the Single European Act—which
Wessels gives for the intensity of this European committee government
indicate how deeply it had penetrated into the normal procedures of
national government. Of the 1,200 'Referate' (departments or divisions—
the basic administrative units of ministries) in the Federal German
Government about half were directly involved in European Community
or other collective European international business—NATO, OECD,
European Political Co-operation (EPC, which engaged not only foreign
ministries but also officials from justice and interior ministries, dealing
with police and intelligence co-operation, border control, etc.). Forty
Referate, distributed across different ministries, were devoted entirely
to EC business; only a quarter of the 1,200 had no significant involvement
with EC and intergovernmental business.

Those who travelled took part in some 537 Commission expert groups
(meeting an average of six times a year), 180 Council working groups,
218 implementation committees, and 18 EPC working groups. Large
numbers of officials also sat in on the seventy sessions of the Council
of Ministers (in its various forms) and the three European Councils and
their associated meetings of foreign and finance ministers—though
ministers had long since rebelled against official cocooning by inventing
'informal' councils and minister-only lunches, at which (in the absence
of officials) the conversation could be open but decisions were rarely
taken. Overall, these were in 1985 around 8,000 Council and Commission meetings which the interpreters serviced: between thirty and thirty-
five per working day. Alongside this EC structure stretched a further
385 NATO committees and working groups, 200 OECD committees,

and 152 Council of Europe committees; with further groups (not counted here) meeting within the framework of the Western European Union, Eurogroup/Independent European Programme Group, and the Bank for International Settlements.[11]

Wessels suggested that the growth of European committee government was reaching a natural plateau, on which a larger and larger proportion of higher national civil servants were caught up in European business, but where the balance between their national and international responsibilities made it difficult for committees to meet more often. Many officials (and ministers) were members of more than one committee, within more than one organization; bilateral consultations took them to each other's capitals in between multilateral meetings, while telephone, fax, and secure telex allowed for daily informal communication when necessary.[12] The interpenetration of governmental administrations was furthered by shared training courses, and even limited exchanges; so that those who swapped information and assumptions over the phone as they prepared their recommendations for their national ministers often knew each other well.[13] Extrapolation of Wessels's figures indicates a network of over 25,000 officials from the twelve EC countries taking part in these processes of consultation, co-ordination, and collective government, with perhaps another 2–3,000 from the less involved EFTA countries.[14]

The European Parliament, intended since its first direct election in 1979 to provide a degree both of democratic legitimacy and of political accountability to this intricate process, has not been immune to the disaggregation of issues into technical detail. The Parliament works through its committees far more than through general debates in the full chamber. MEPs have learned to make their reputations through good committee work, through acting as rapporteurs to specific committee reports, and through the expertise of their questioning of Commission witnesses, more than through broader or more strategic political interventions.[15]

Here is a highly complex and opaque structure of collective government, within which national officials play 'an ambiguous double role . . . on the one hand to push towards positions in conformity with interests known as "national" and on the other to achieve results in a policy network where consensus is normally seen as a major value in itself'.[16] Ministers, and organized lobbies, are also active participants in this multi-level network. Ministers as much as officials play a deeply ambiguous role, bargaining and compromising in closed meetings and then—addressing their domestic audience rather than their European colleagues—portraying their performance to representatives of their national press as stout-hearted defence of the national interest. The result has been that the gap between these two audiences has steadily widened, with national MPs, journalists, and publics assured that national autonomy remains intact even as ministers agree with each other in private about the necessity to accept further mutual incursions. Lobbies, particularly business lobbies, are well organized and well informed—and well accustomed to operating within confidential networks. The losers have been parliaments and parties, with far less developed networks of transnational interaction, and often little awareness of how far the integration of governments and administrations has taken Western Europe away from old assumptions about sovereign nation states. The wider public, partially informed by the partisan interpretations of their national media, enlightened little further by parliaments and parties, which are uninformed themselves, have lost out more.

2. *The Loss of Public Confidence*

Two factors have combined to feed popular suspicion of this structure of government by committee: the declining prestige of officials, administrators, even of the state as such, in a spreading number of European countries; and the realization that European committee government is no longer dealing with technical matters at the edge of political controversy but with highly sensitive issues that come close to the heart of national politics.

Problems of 'overloaded government', of state administrations which take in, manage, and redistribute a rising proportion of the gross national product, have focused attention in one country after another over the past twenty years. Anti-tax and 'anti-system' parties, revolting against the idea of the state as the rational arbiter of the national interest and disinterested manager of the national economy and finances, have blossomed in northern Europe, and found popular support in some south European countries. The dethroning of officialdom has gone furthest in Britain, where the party in government for the past sixteen years has itself taken up the theme; and least far in France, where *enarchs* and *polytechniciens* still hold high prestige (and positions) in business and finance, politics and intellectual life. But one can nevertheless discern a general trend, which is part of the widespread popular disillusionment with élites. The European Community has contributed to this disillusionment, as the ideal of wise Euro-administrators has been muddied by stories of agricultural inefficiency and maladministration, and as demands on the Community administrative network have outstripped their capacity to manage the policies they have agreed.[17]

The intergovernmental negotiations which led to the Maastricht Treaty provide a classic study of the problems—and unsustainability—of committee government on a European scale. Heads of government and national ministers committed themselves to grandiose objectives without explaining the awkward implications to their domestic publics. They then entrusted to experienced officials the task of reconciling common European policies and acceptability to separate national electorates. Working within the assumptions of the established Community process, those officials managed to produce an agreed text, ready for the (largely artificial) drama of the Maastricht European Council and for final signature. Hardly surprisingly, the text which emerged was long, technical, in places ambiguous, and for the ordinary citizen obscure and opaque. 'If someone had told us when we set out that the text we produced was going to be printed and distributed to the public in Community member countries,' one of the most experienced permanent representatives afterwards remarked, 'we would have understood that this had to be an entirely different exercise.' Yet here was a text which touched on currency, borders, policing, defence, taxation, and citizenship: the core functions of the European nation state. The essentially political nature of the exercise, the need to carry national parliaments and publics along with the arguments advanced, *should* have been evident to all; but the established procedures of European committee government were so entrenched, the conspiracy among officials and ministers to say one thing to each other and another to their national publics so close to second nature, that the problem of public consent was taken for granted.

Worse than this, the compromises between incompatible objectives—efficient decision-making, accountability, national autonomy—incorporated in the Maastricht Treaty made the intricacies of Community decision-making even more complex. Michel Vanden Abeele has described the procedures for 'Co-decision' set out in Articles 189*a*–*c* of the Treaty as 'incomprehensible even to specialists . . . a form of decision-making so complicated that no-one will understand exactly who has taken the decision, what it is or to whom it applies': a *reductio ad absurdum* of the 'comitology' of the Community institutions, in

which committees of the European Parliament negotiate with committees of the Council under the watchful eye of the Commission (advised
by its own working groups) and the European Court, which is well
beyond the comprehension even of the active citizen.[18]

The second and third pillars of the Maastricht Treaty institutionalized
another network of intergovernmental committees, which had grown up
largely outside the Communities over the previous twenty years. The
British and French governments, in particular, resisted the elements of
visibility and accountability which the Community framework would
impose on co-operation in foreign and defence policy, policing, and
intelligence. Their preferred model for extended co-operation was to
return to a more explicitly intergovernmental pattern: more discreet,
less open to challenge by outsiders, dominated yet again by official
committees negotiating behind closed doors, developing ways of thinking and shared assumptions of which national parliaments and publics
would remain largely unaware.

3. The Joint Decision Trap

Multi-level government unavoidably operates through bargaining and
compromise, through extensive consultation and the interpenetration of
different agencies. Federal government in the USA exhibits many of
the failings of the Community institutions, though mitigated by the
political visibility of the presidency and the visible accountability of
Congress. Federal government in Germany depends upon conciliation
by committee. The cost, for Germany as for the European Community,
is the evolution of a policy-making process which is slow and resistant
to innovation; in which the sharing of decisions makes the taking of
decisions more time-consuming and more difficult.[19] Government *has*
become more technical, the subject-matter for policy-making more
intricate and complex. Demands for action on issues which rise to
public attention or have been made the focus for successful campaigns
necessarily simplify what needs to be done; the devil is in the detail,
and official committees serve to summon up the devil when they sit
down to translate political imperatives into workable regulations.

Is there a way to close this gap between the disillusioned public and
their collective governors? The answer of the federalists remains that a
leap forward to democratic accountability at the European level, with
proper scrutiny of the mixed legislative and executive activities of the

Council of Ministers and its substructure of committees, is the only reconciliation possible. But in the wake of the Danish and French post-Maastricht referendums, and the surge of opposition within Germany to the idea of a common currency, it is hard to imagine how *any* national government within the European Union (as it has now become) could persuade its voters to accept such a transfer of symbolic loyalties. The answer of the 'Eurosceptics' and nationalists in different member countries is to return essential decisions to national government, or at least to resist the transfer of any further authority. Yet the continuing integration of European economies and societies—and the decreasing viability of national defence and border controls—makes it impossible for national administrations to imagine how to reverse the process. How then otherwise to rebuild public confidence in a system of shared government which publics do not understand, which is unavoidably both highly technical and extremely complex, and which is managed by officials for whom publics have on other grounds less and less respect? That has become the central dilemma for those within the institutions of the European Union and those within national governments alike. Enlargement of the EU to the rich countries of EFTA, and thereafter to the poorer countries of East-Central Europe, can only make that dilemma more acute.

NOTES

1. Jean Monnet, *Mémoires* (Paris: Fayard, 1976), chs. 6 and 7.
2. *Official Report of Debates*, 21 Oct. 1955; cited in Miriam Camps, *Britain and the European Community 1955–1963* (Oxford: Oxford University Press, 1964), 41.
3. This argument is made most strongly by Alan Milward in *The European Rescue of the Nation State* (London: Routledge, 1992), chs. 4 and 5. Milward, however, underplays both the importance of the American role in pushing West European governments together and (in his ch. 6) the extent to which the language and rhetoric in which national political leaders presented their arguments shaped their perceptions of national interest.
4. William Wallace, 'Rescue or Retreat: The Nation State in Western Europe 1945–1993', *Political Studies*, special issue: *The Crisis of the Nation State*, 42 (1994) 52–76, explores these questions further.
5. Walter Hallstein, *Europe in the Making* (London: Allen & Unwin, 1972), 60.
6. Walter Hallstein, *United Europe: Challenge and Opportunity* (Cambridge,

250   *William Wallace*

Mass.: Harvard University Press, 1962), 53, given as the William L. Clayton Lectures at the Fletcher School of Law and Diplomacy, Apr. 1962.

7. Ibid. 55.

8. Wolfgang Wessels, 'Administrative Interaction', in William Wallace (ed.), *The Dynamics of European Integration* (London: Pinter, 1990); see also Wessels, 'The EC Council: The Community's Decisionmaking Center', in Robert O. Keohane and Stanley Hoffmann (eds.), *The New European Community: Decisionmaking and Institutional Change* (Boulder, Colo.: Westview, 1991).

9. Émile Noel, 'The Permanent Representatives' Committee and the Deepening of the Communities', *Government and Opposition*, 6/4 (1971), 424.

10. Hallstein, *Europe in the Making*, 80–1.

11. Wessels, 'Administrative Interaction'.

12. William Wallace, *Britain's Bilateral Relations in Europe* (London: Routledge, 1984).

13. The École Nationale d'Administration has been running courses for mixed groups of young German, British, Dutch, and other officials for some years; the European Institute for Public Administration in Maastricht runs much shorter combined courses for more senior officials. I recall an assistant secretary in the British Treasury remarking in the mid-1980s that his new principal was always wonderfully well informed on what advice the German Finance Ministry were giving their minister before EC ministerial meetings, since he had shared an ENA course with his opposite number. 'There's only one thing which worries me: how much does he tell him in return?'

14. Figures collected by Jeff Stacey, a graduate student at Oxford, on Council and Council committee meetings in 1989–90 (from Council records) indicate that a plateau in frequency *had* been reached, though the range of subjects covered continued to spread. Wessels noted some seventy Council of Ministers' meetings in 1985, meeting in sixteen different 'functional' groupings: transport, agriculture, fisheries, research, education, and so on. Stacey traced ninety in 1990, meeting in nineteen different formats, including consumer protection, telecommunications, and health. Each of these Councils required its own network of preparatory official working groups and implementing committees, paralleled by EC groups to advise on the formulation of proposals for the agenda.

15. This point was made by Michel Vanden Abeele in his paper to the First Europaeum Conference in Sept. 1993.

16. Wessels, 'Administrative Interaction', 235.

17. Peter Ludlow, 'The European Commission', in Keohane and Hoffmann (eds.) *The New European Community*. 'There has always been a bias within the Commission in favour of policy formulation as opposed to policy execution. . . . The problems of weak management culture are . . . hugely

compounded by the difficulties which stem from under-management.' Hans-Dietrich Genscher warned German enthusiasts for European integration as early as 1982 that the accumulation of agricultural surpluses and agricultural scandals threatened popular commitment to the entire project.
18. In his paper to the Europaeum Conference, Sept. 1993.
19. Fritz W. Scharpf, 'The Joint Decision Trap: Lessons from German Federalism and from European Integration', *Public Administration*, 66/3 (1988), 239–78.

Conclusion

Has European Unification by Stealth a Future?

JACK HAYWARD

From its inception, the post-war movement to achieve European integration was characterized by its reliance upon the exertion of behind-the-scenes influence by a few self-conscious agents of change. Personified by Jean Monnet, who was accustomed to the manipulation of politicians whose expectancy of high office in any government was likely to be short-lived and of bureaucrats more inclined to inertia than innovation, there has subsequently been an endeavour to institutionalize this role in the President of the Commission. While it might be necessary from time to time to adopt a high-profile stance to precipitate a crucial change, this would have been preceded by prolonged and unobtrusive preparations, so that what may appear to the public as a bold initiative has been anything but improvised. Without the assistance of a major cataclysm that can mobilize mass support for spectacular change, reliance has been placed upon those occupying key positions to use their power to make incremental changes discreetly.[1] Rather than engaging in the slow and difficult task of persuading the general public of the need for changes before making them, there has been a proclivity on the part of the few well-informed insiders to place before the many ill-informed outsiders a *fait accompli*. Have the principal agents of European integration been right in believing that this was the most effective way to achieve their purpose?

Whatever the answer to this question may be today, to start the integrative process half a century ago required proceeding surreptitiously and indirectly, rather than openly to the accompaniment of resounding public declarations. Although eloquent exhortations in favour of European unity were made, notably by Winston Churchill, it is significant that his own country refused to take the lead or even respond to the lead offered by others. In a Europe quickly rent by the Cold War, in which the choice was not so much between Left and Right but between East and West, the process of European integration seemed to be a secondary aspect of this decisive global confrontation. It required far-sighted ingenuity to utilize this situation to set in train an apparently more limited programme of action but one destined to outlive the clash between a Russian-led totalitarian communism and an American-led democratic capitalism. It was therefore the Christian democratic and social democratic politicians of the defeated nations of continental Western Europe who rallied to a programme of piecemeal collaboration in the construction of a community of interest for joint peace and prosperity. To do so meant relying upon the negotiating skills of technocrats and the political skills of statesmen to achieve the compromise between national interests and between sectional interests that would convince a sceptical public that it made practical sense to work with former enemies.

Although the élites knew where they were leading their peoples, they felt it would be wiser in future not to arouse their fears. The failure to achieve a European Defence Community in the mid-1950s was a warning that was heeded, and the leaders returned to the terrain of economic co-operation in which mutually profitable trade could be promoted by trade-offs achieved by confidential back-room bargaining. This involved associating the interest-group élites—of business and farmers more than labour—in the process of achieving a consensus that could be presented as in the self-evident public interest and therefore entitled to general support. What was sought was not enthusiastic public involvement in the steps by which the content of the common European interest was defined. All that was required was public support and acquiescence after the event. Assisted by positive association with the prosperity of the quarter of a century preceding the Oil Shock of 1973 and negative association with the cohesion needed to face the military threat from the East, the progress from the 1951 Paris Treaty establishing the European Coal and Steel Community to the 1957 Rome Treaty launching the European Economic Community bypassed the failure to achieve a defence community. In the 1960s the process of European integration even survived the advent of General de Gaulle as French President, although his reassertion of the claims of national sovereignty over the pretensions of the Eurocrats to steer the EEC in a federalist direction did give intergovernmental conflicts of national interest priority over consensus-minded techno-bureaucratic compromises.[2]

Although de Gaulle was an ardent champion of the referendum as a way of mobilizing public support for his own decisions, this technique was not destined to play an important role in the process of European integration until the 1990s, although in 1972 de Gaulle's successor as President, Georges Pompidou, did initiate a referendum *in France* on whether Britain, Denmark, and Ireland should be accepted into the European Community. However, it was the shift of power to the intergovernmental European Council and to meetings of the officials of national governments that was a conspicuous feature of the 1970s, as the damaging effects of the Oil Shock disrupted the 'Thirty Glorious Years' of continuous economic expansion. Rapid economic growth had played an important part in making European co-operation a matter of sharing material benefits rather than beggaring one's neighbour, so that its loss made it much more difficult to achieve reciprocally acceptable compromises. While summitry became a more conspicuous part of European policy-making and the President of the Commission had a relatively marginal role in those proceedings, nevertheless surreptitious integration proceeded inconspicuously. This was so even though British accession tended to inhibit the process, without the wider and long-term vision of a 'European Europe' that had inspired de Gaulle's disruptive tactics. After the brief interlude of the Heath–Pompidou idyll, the Franco-German axis reasserted itself in the shape first of the Giscard–Schmidt duo, followed by the cooler Mitterrand–Kohl link in the 1980s and early 1990s, with Britain on the self-imposed sidelines for much of the time.

However, while Margaret Thatcher—notably in her September 1988 Bruges speech—reiterated her adamant opposition to what she regarded as the Delors Commission's attempt to promote a semi-socialist-inspired interventionism that would simultaneously destroy the political sovereignty and economic competitiveness of the member states, sterling (thanks to her Chancellor of the Exchequer Nigel Lawson) was shadowing the German mark and economic integration through the 1986 Single European Act was proceeding apace. Due in large part to a 1985 White Paper drawn up by the British (Conservative ex-minister) Commissioner Lord Cockfield, the programme for eliminating nearly 300 non-tariff barriers was put into operation, to make a reality of the single market. So, the process of European economic integration continued apace and culminated in the much wider-ranging proposals for a European Union that was achieved in 1993 with the ratification by all the member states of the Maastricht Treaty, although on the way the European Exchange Rate Mechanism suffered a severe set-back in September 1992 with the extrusion of Britain and Italy under the overwhelming pressure of currency speculation.

The difficulties that European progress towards an Economic and Monetary Union by the end of the twentieth century faced were compounded by the resistance that European integration encountered at the same time from the dissipation of public support for the European project. This was especially the case in Denmark and Britain, but also in France, where the September 1992 referendum to ratify the Maastricht Treaty proved a very close-run thing, with a 51 to 49 per cent majority. However, in Denmark the referendum narrowly went the other way and it seemed clear from opinion polls that had a referendum been held in Britain, the result would have been negative. Although the Danish referendum result was reversed and the British Parliament gave its approval after a prolonged period of agonizing and tactical manœuvring that did little to increase the credibility of either the European project or the Conservative Party's support for it, there was a widely shared view that the 1992 impetus towards integration had been halted. Some in Britain even sought to put it into reverse, as opt-outs from potentially popular policies such as the 'Social Charter' were secured and the emphasis was placed upon minority vetoes at the expense of welcoming new members into the European Union.

What some of the founders of the European movement as well as de Gaulle had feared, although for very different reasons—that new members would not share the same goals—seems to have proved correct. Far from feeling an enthusiastic commitment to the ambitious common objectives of a European Union, there has been a loss of community spirit among the élites, whose collusion has hitherto been indispensable to keeping up the momentum of integration. As the stubborn recession exacerbated conflicts that international competition generated and as the problems posed by East-Central Europe switched from a military to a migratory menace, public opinion has been mobilized in defence of national interests rather than in favour of supranational solutions. This condemned the Delors Commission—which lacked the democratic legitimacy to appeal over the heads of the national governments to their peoples—to continue trying to work in the spirit of élite concertation. However, this style of decision-making has been rendered much less effective because of the actions or inactions of sufficient members of the élites which paralyse ambitious initiatives.

To reactivate public support for the European project will require abandoning the strategy of 'unification by stealth'. Jacques Delors was well aware of the problem and, both in terms of seeking collective action to promote a job-creating economic revival as well as providing a public lead in this direction, he did what he could from a weak position. Indispensable institutional reform has been postponed beyond 1996, when what the circumstances require is a European political executive with the democratic authority to deal with problems that élite consensus is decreasingly capable of resolving. Thus far, elections to the European Parliament have failed to arouse public opinion, although the June 1994 election produced greater efforts than hitherto at formulating cross-national manifestos.[3] Nevertheless, it is noteworthy that under Giscardian pressure the French Right's European Election manifesto called for a European President elected by the European Council for a five-year term (and not six months by rotation at present), which would make de Gaulle turn in his grave. To mobilize mass support would probably require the direct election of a European President, such as de Gaulle successfully instituted in France in 1962, but for the present so radical a proposal presupposes acceptance of a federalist Europe that has receded from the forefront of the political agenda. Meanwhile, for those who wish to keep open the road to future advance in this direction, it will be important to prevent European disintegration by demagoguery from gathering momentum and to take the public into their confidence in doing so. That is the only democratic way to prevent the European élites from becoming the prisoners of a backward-looking populism.

The enlargement of the European Union is often presented as antithetical to closer integration—economic and political—both by those who advocate the defence of nation state diversity without increased European unity (especially in Britain and Denmark) and by those who oppose increased heterogeneity as an obstacle to increased integration (such as many in France and Spain). However, it is also arguable that (as the leaders in Germany and the Benelux countries generally believe) the federalist combination of increased integration to achieve common purposes with respect for subsidiarity as a protection for diversity in other matters to permit individuals, localities, regions, and nations to pursue their own purposes provides the best of both worlds. A pluralistic Europe, in which the number of partners and the speed of integration will need to vary, is compatible with an integrated Europe provided the federalizing impetus in decision-making is simultaneously reinforced.

Representative democracy does not presuppose government by the people. This would involve either leading from behind or leaderless drift. Liberal democratic leadership requires persuading most of the public to reject the temptations of inertia, parochialism, and xenophobia. It involves making the prospect of innovation, tolerance, and cosmopolitanism more attractive for those seeking peace, opportunity, and prosperity. Only in this way will popular alienation from the complex processes of EU decision-making be prevented from prompting the return to the tribal pursuit of national egotisms.

NOTES

1. For more sympathetic views of European decision-making, see François Duchêne, *Jean Monnet: The First Statesman of Interdependence* (New York: Norton, 1994) and George Ross, *Jacques Delors and European Integration* (Oxford: Polity Press, 1995).
2. See the contributions, esp. in ch. 2, to Institut Charles de Gaulle, *De Gaulle en son siècle*, v: *L'Europe* (Paris: La Documentation Française–Plon, 1992).
3. See the appendix by Julie Smith, 'The 1994 European Elections: Twelve into One won't Go', to the special issue, 'The Crisis of Representation in Europe', *West European Politics*, 17/3, (July 1995), 203–4.

INDEX

Italic figures refer to tables.

press:
  bias 68, 69–71
  concerns about 67–8
  élites: four types 68
  freedom and its abuse 67, 68, 75–83
  see also censorship
pressure groups, *see* interest groups
proportional representation 119
public attitudes:
  in 1990s 206–13
  see also politics, public interest and trust in
public demands, sources 204–5
public expenditure, public support for 207–12, *210–11*
public office, holding of, opinions and 53–4
public opinion, political expression of 14–19
public opinion polls, *see* opinion polls
public procurement 132

racism, legislation on 78–9, *79*
rationality theories 38
Reagan, Ronald 228
referendums:
  amending EC/EU by 116–17, 253–4
  distinguished from plebiscites 15–16
  as increasingly popular 160
  on Maastricht 102–4, *104*
  in member states 116
  turn-outs *18*
  virtues and vices of 17
religious tolerance 77
representation:
  ambiguities 143–4
  delegate role *vis-à-vis* trustee model 51
  individualistic assumptions of delegate role 36–46
  ingredients 14
representatives, and their responses to their publics 34–6
'retrospective voting' 45
right-wing extremism as increasing? 151–3
Riker, William 17–18
Rocard, Michel 94, 95, 98
Rokkan, Stein 167, 181
Roosevelt, Franklin 92
Rose, Richard 88–9, 90
Rousseau, Jean-Jacques 11, 39
Santer, Jacques 113
Sartori, Giovanni 13, 114, 159
Scandinavia, *remiss* system 169
Schmidt, Helmut 225, 226–8, 254
Schumpeter, Joseph 13, 45, 203
Séguin, Philippe 28, 29
self-interest:
  and candidate choice 44–5
  see also interest groups
self-justification 41–2
self-regulation 27
Sen, Amartya 35, 58
Seyd, Patrick 184
Shils, Edward 20
Sieyès, abbé 11
Single European Act 231
Smith, Adam 11
social research, effects 55
socialists, support for 3
societies, pluralist and mass 14
Somalia 57
sovereignty, national 6
Spaak, Paul-Henri 241
Spain 7, 129, 130
Spinelli, Altiero 116
surveys 101, 102, 103, 104, 146
Sweden 153, 169, 218
Switzerland:
  government type 116–17
  political initiatives 15, 16
'symbolic predispositions' 44

'tactical' voting 3
Tawney, Richard H. 203
taxation:
  apportioning 206, *207*
individual attitudes to 43
  television 69–70
Thatcher, Margaret 21, 25, 93, 110, 113, 136, 169, 172
  Bruges speech 110, 254
Tocqueville, Alexis de 12, 203
trade unions 193
transitive choice 40–1
Treaty of Rome 235
  amending 116–19
  and economics 221–3, 235
Truman, Harry S 54
'trustee' theory of democracy defined 34–5
trusteeship:
  arguments against 56–8
  delegate role of representatives 36–46